THE YOUNGEST REVOLUTION

THE YOUNGEST REVOLUTION

A Personal Report on Cuba

by Elizabeth Sutherland

with photographs by Leroy Lucas

 THE DIAL PRESS, INC.
NEW YORK, 1969

For Tessa
and all fifteen-year-old revolutionaries
now and tomorrow

Library of Congress Catalog Card Number: 68-9462

Printed in the United States of America

Design by Thomas Clemens

First printing, 1969

From an old travel poster:

Discover the real Cuba for yourself . . .
you'll love the difference!

Cuban Tourist Commission
Promenade, Rockefeller Plaza
New York, N.Y.

Table of Contents

PART ONE:
The Real Cuba

. . . we don't want to show our visitors only the pretty things of the country, not only those things achieved by the Revolution; we would like them to see also what we haven't achieved yet, the things still to be done; and most of all we would like them to see where the Revolution is making its main effort, what its direction is and the difficulties we have to overcome.

Fidel Castro
July 27, 1967

Six Voices

"In 1961, socialism was a *pachanga,*" Cubans sometimes say, referring to a festive dance in the rumba tradition. "People are more serious now."

Of all the experiences which human beings can undergo, surely none is more mind-blowing than the early days of a social revolution. To have visited Cuba in 1961 and then return six years later, was to feel a change in the air without at first being able to name it. Slowly it became clear that the difference had to do with people above all. The most striking contrast between Socialist Cuba in the year of its birth and in late 1967 seemed to lie less in external realities—the new landscape of schools, hospitals, economic development—than in the mental climate. Not that the two can really be separated.

On May Day of 1961, two weeks after the victory at Playa Girón (where the Bay of Pigs invasion took place), the island had flowered with redness: flags, hats, scarves. Socialism was the newly proclaimed dream. Six years later, communism—the classless society—was a set destination with some if not all of the maps and equipment necessary for the journey. People had been through a lot in the interim: a year when the only plentiful food was Polish mustard, two months without toilet paper, and graver problems. Fidel Castro himself struck a less euphoric note in his speech of July 26, 1967, fourteenth anniversary of the attack on the Moncada garrison which preceded the final insurrection against Fulgencio Batista:

> We no longer meet simply to shout for joy, to celebrate past glories. We meet to offer the homage, affection, and respect that those men who have fallen for the Revolution deserve . . . but we also meet to affirm that there is only one way to respect and love those who gave their lives . . . and that is by working and struggling.

The people did not clap quite so wildly and lengthily now when Fidel Castro spoke, nor interrupt him so often with long outbursts of chanting—although there were striking exceptions to this. At the same time, the speeches of Fidel (nobody in Cuba refers to him as "Castro") lasted not four or five hours as in 1961 but rarely more than two. The reason which everyone gave, and it seemed confirmed by the content of those speeches, was that he no longer had to explain at length certain basic concepts, because these were now widely accepted; he could proceed to new subjects on established premises. The Revolution was less of a novelty, more settled-in.

Anti-Revolutionary activity had been a serious problem in 1961–62, with active fighting going on in several areas and psychological warfare everywhere. The Revolution had trouble, for example, convincing parents to send their children to the new day nurseries and boarding schools because enemy propaganda painted pictures of babes snatched from the hearth forever, of daughters losing their virginity in the absence of parental control. But by 1967, the neighborhood Committees for the Defense of the Revolution (C. D. R.'s) no longer had to serve almost exclusively as vigilantes on individual loyalty; they were organisms performing a wide variety of community services and acting as decision-making bodies in many areas of daily life. As for the nurseries and schools, the state could not fill the demand for places. In these and many other ways, it was clear that internal opposition to socialism had lost most of its punch.

In 1961, no one could have predicted just what form socialism would take in Cuba or exactly how the island would relate
to other nations, except perhaps the United States. Some leaders from the Old Left, like Anibal Escalante, pressed for a
dogmatic, "Stalinist" society oriented to the U.S.S.R. Six years
later, Cuban socialism was not only freewheeling but de-
fiantly so.

On the international front, Cuba had survived a long, hard
American blockade; it had argued with China over rice; it had
challenged the Soviet Union on various occasions—all in all, an
impressive series of confrontations for a tiny island. Internally
and externally, the Revolution was not following any established Socialist pattern unless it seemed suitable for Cuba. (The
price of this independence would be hard work and fewer mistakes, as Fidel's announcement of the Revolutionary Offensive
in March, 1968, made clear. The goals of that program were a
ten-million-ton sugar harvest in 1970, with every Cuban working at top capacity to achieve it, and a stepped-up socialism.)

In the public consciousness, a sweeping shift of orientation
had taken place. Cuba's Communist Party of 1961 regularly
published the Soviet and Chinese positions on a particular issue
in its newspaper. In 1967, the Party paper was more likely to
reprint an editorial from The London *Times* attacking United
States policy in Vietnam, while another newspaper had a regular feature called "The International Press," where sympathetic
or revealing items from the U.S. press predominated. China
seemed very remote to ordinary people; its two-year-old Cultural Revolution didn't exist at all as far as the press and general public were concerned. The Soviet Union seemed a little
more real but often from a negative viewpoint, regardless of its
heavy trade with—and vital support to—the island.

Latin America, the United States, and the war in Vietnam
were always in the public eye and ear as focal points of the
anti-imperialist struggle. Marx and Lenin turned up in
speeches and writings but rarely in the slogans, pictures, or
names of places which create the visual consciousness of the
island. Instead it was "Long live the Colombian Guerrillas,"
"Our homeland is America" (meaning the whole continent),

"Create two, three, many Vietnams," "The duty of every revolutionary is to make the revolution," and especially, "Armed struggle is the road to liberation." This last was, of course, a keynote of the year—of Cuba's intensifying conflict with the Soviet Union and Soviet-oriented Communist parties in Latin America, which Fidel criticized for advocating peaceful coexistence. The Prime Minister's August, 1967, attack on the Communist Party of Venezuela received widespread publicity among the people. Most Cubans probably lacked a deep understanding of the issues involved, but they did sense that Cuba was concentrating on its own hemisphere and determined to pursue its own definitions regardless of pressure from any source.

(This was reconfirmed in 1968. Anibal Escalante, who had led the 1961 sectarian group and been ousted the following year, surfaced later and was again defeated. His "micro-faction" of people from the Central Committee of Cuba's Communist Party were tried and sentenced to prison terms in 1968 for having urged Soviet and Czech representatives to use economic blackmail in order to compel Cuba to change its political and economic line, and to drop its advocacy of armed struggle. Since then, Escalante has been released from prison and is now reported to be working on a rehabilitation farm.)

Intellectuals do not offer the most reliable barometer of popular feeling and thinking, but they sometimes provide shortcuts to understanding the spiritual climate of a country. In a number of long, informal conversations, several of these people discussed the changes they had seen since 1961, the effect of those changes on the popular consciousness, and their personal visions of the future. All of these people had lived for extended periods in non-Socialist countries, including the United States. All had been accustomed to comfort for some years, if not their entire lives; several owned cars, mostly old American models but nonetheless rare—and hard to maintain—in Cuba. All lived in the big city, Havana. Thus for several reasons they were more likely than any other group of people to be critical of the Revolution.

Among them were a young American woman and her Cuban husband. She had come from a very rich family and one of America's most snobbish suburbs; her trail wound from fancy boarding schools to that pad in Greenwich Village to Cuba in 1960, a translation job, and marriage to an economist. She and her husband had a spacious, suburban apartment, a live-in maid, and a car.

"Things are better now than in 1961," she said, in English which had acquired a Spanish kind of preciseness. "For one thing, the economic blockade has made people see that basically they have to make it on their own. Cubans don't really like to analyze, to figure things out, unless it's something pretty—like a philosophical problem. But they are doing it now. The method is entirely trial and error, pragmatic; each project they undertake is an experiment. Of course they overdo things—for instance, the 'Three and One Plan.' They decided that every office or factory worker should spend one week a month in the country doing agricultural work—in rotation. That was fine for a lot of bureaucrats but not for workers in a tool-and-die factory, for example, where you need almost everybody on hand all the time. So it was a mess. And they changed it. The Cuban Revolution still runs on a certain kind of madness—it could only work here, with the Cuban temperament and circumstances. The Cubans are very full of *dignidad;* they will thumb their noses at anybody, including the Soviet Union, if they feel some principle is at stake. It drives the economists crazy. But Cuba will probably get away with it.

"Life is hard here, especially for older people—they don't want to wait ten, twenty years to enjoy things. People in the cities are tired of standing in line for everything. The laundries and dry cleaners—which are better than in the U.S., by the way—take three to four weeks. Little things like paper clips are almost impossible to find. As for food, if you have an aunt or grandmother who can spend a lot of time waiting in line—and many people do—you are all right. That way, you catch items that come in unexpectedly and supplement the regular rations. If you can afford to eat out, or if you are a worker and eat at one of their special dining halls, you are all right too. Food isn't a problem for us because we make over five hundred pesos a month after income tax and we can eat out. Also, foreigners from capitalist countries get a little more rations than the Cubans—Socialist technicians get almost unlimited food. For others, there is just not enough rice and tubers like *malanga* to keep them happy." She neglected to mention that one could wait for hours to get into a restaurant. The endless *colas* had two main sources: unresolved distribution problems arising from nationalization and the fact that many more people could afford eating out than before.

"But things like rent, education, medical and dental care, places for women to leave their children while they work—those are just not problems that you normally think about. Those things are all free, except for the medicines themselves in some cases. Some people still pay the ten per cent rent, but many have already been given title to their homes. Lots of little things have become free too, like sports events. And calls from public telephones—that just happened last week.

"There are still certain kinds of injustice. Too many bureaucrats have found a comfortable niche and they protect it. When something wrong happens, they don't challenge anybody—they don't speak up. They just go along with it, protecting their jobs and homes. There is an opportunism which bothers me a lot. And Havana is the land of gossip, what we call *tiqui-tiqui*. It is easy to ruin a person here—his name is mentioned, somebody lifts an eyebrow, and soon fifty eyebrows are being lifted. The man becomes surrounded by a climate of negativism, without being able to put his finger on the cause. If he can cut his way through to the top leaders with his problem, he will be all right—they are really ethical people and deeply concerned with ideals. But too often he can't."

Her husband, who had been shifting around in his chair, exploded. "Look at the Party—it's a form of security to people. They get in and feel safe, superior. It's better than in some countries because all the members aren't just bureaucrats, they work in factories and keep a sense of where the people are at. The top Party people are sometimes brilliant. But too many yes-men get in easily.

"The key to success of the Cuban Revolution is the *vanguardia:* Fidel, Raúl, Che—well, he's gone—Carlos Rafael Rodríguez. Fidel is a sort of permanent Opposition. He represents the people against any injustice from the state structures. And the people know this. There is a sense of communication. I don't know whether this exists in China, the country is so much bigger. But the Cuban Revolution is the only one worth watching right now except for China—and Cuba is even more interesting than China because the population is more racially mixed.

"Fidel will revolutionize Marxism, and he has time to do it—Lenin and Mao were old when they started. He isn't trapped in dogma. He believes in thinking ideologically but not being trapped *in* an ideology. The result of all this is that we are not married to Marx or Lenin," he said, stressing each syllable. "The only thing we are married to is the Cuban Revolution."

His mood changed suddenly and his voice became more pensive. "When you talk to people, they complain a lot. You could get the impression that eighty per cent are against the Revolution, twenty per cent in favor. Then something happens, like Playa Girón [the Bay of Pigs] or the Missile Crisis, and suddenly the proportion is reversed. Everybody stops complaining and gets himself organized—people don't need to be told what to do.

"But it can also happen in daily life. One night I came home angry about some stupidity of the Party—I was really furious, you know I get very excited. I went to bed. About midnight, the doorbell rang. There stood a young man from the Defense Committee. He asked, 'Does Carla Rodríguez live here?'—that's my eight-year-old daughter. I was surprised and said 'Yes.' Then this youth handed me a package and said, 'This is the polio vaccine for her. You must give it to her tomorrow at'—he mentioned a certain hour—'which is the best time for assimilating it. Keep the vaccine in a refrigerator if you have one, otherwise the coolest place in the house. Thank you. Good night.' I closed the door and that was that.

"In one evening, they distributed vaccine to the entire district, and by the next evening all the children were vaccinated. There was a lot of boasting in different districts—'We made the distribution in three hours' or 'We did it in only two hours.' Anyway, I stopped being angry that night. Other things seemed more important."

The young painter arrived late; he had been cleaning his newly acquired apartment all day with a group of friends. The place had stood empty for two years, after its former tenants left Cuba. "It was filthy," he said. "But now my only problem is furniture. Housing is a real struggle here."

He had recently returned from half a year abroad—"in swinging London," he said with a wry smile, in English. "There is still a gap between classes here," he went on. "Doctors make big salaries and save their money. Then they get a car, usually a Skoda. And they buy things on the black market, like air conditioners—they may have to pay five hundred dollars for one, but they can do it. Yet Cuba is different from other Socialist countries. The Soviet Union was a terribly underdeveloped country, more so than Cuba. But today you have a fantastic increase of consumer goods there—and new attitudes. In 1962, it was a luxury to have a Soviet Volga; now that's *trash* and the thing to have is an Italian Fiat. People are still reacting to Stalin. If Lenin or Trotsky could have built socialism there, things might have been different. But under Stalin, a whole new class of bureaucrats with special privileges evolved. The worker saw them passing in big cars with curtained windows—something he could never dream of attaining. People became alienated from the government. And the youth found symbols for rebellion in the prohibited culture of the West."

The young painter's analysis of the Soviet Union might be disputed by many people, but the belief that Cuba would be different could be heard from all quarters—and with various reasons given. For this Cuban, it was because: "Here, Western culture is not generally prohibited. The young people like the Beatles' music even if they don't understand the words, because they feel the Beatles represent a rejection of many values of the older generation—and that is a strong mood here. But the youth feel identity with the government, they are participating in the Revolution.

"On the whole, people are not alienated. The ideal prevails of having maximum democracy under conditions of semi-war and underdevelopment. Therefore, I think Cuba will have a different set of problems from the Soviet Union in fifteen or twenty years —not a reaction to a Stalin. And I don't think that when there are more consumer goods we will see the same thing that has happened in the Soviet Union."

One Sunday afternoon, a Cuban writer of about forty sat in the living room of a spacious home. "Havana is boring," he sighed. "All the cultural activity is in the countryside. A few years ago you would have had your choice of ten theaters or concerts on a day like today. Now they have pop music in the theaters—fine for dancing, but it doesn't belong in the theater. The Salón de Mayo—that was fine, it was the first time Picasso and other leading abstract artists from Europe were shown in Cuba. But those two hundred thousand people who went in a month—probably ninety per cent went for the musical entertainment. . . . I don't know, maybe that's the way to expose them. Get them in there for the band, but they will at least glance at the paintings.

"There is a cultural crisis here," he said. "It is strange. Cuba has many fine artists in all fields, and increasing recognition. The play, *Night of the Assassins,* will be the first play from Latin America—not just Cuba—ever presented by a major London theater. It has also been presented in Paris, in the original Spanish, and it will be produced there in French—with the Cuban director invited to direct that production. The first exhibit of Cuban paintings opens in London. We have fine dancers, writers. But somehow there is no real movement.

"The closest thing to a movement in Havana is Casa de las ·

Américas"—a cultural center which sponsors many events in Cuba, as well as international competitions, and publishes a magazine. "It has a wonderful spirit, a spirit of do-anything, because the people there have worked together for seven years and because of the director, Haydée Santamaría. She is a remarkable person, absolutely free from prejudice, absolutely. And because she was in the Revolution from the Moncada days, nobody can argue with her about whether something is Revolutionary enough or not. When the Casa planned to have a Happening for July twenty-sixth, somebody said, 'That's not serious enough.' Haydée told this person, 'You're telling *me* about the seriousness of July Twenty-sixth?' " (Haydée Santamaría had not only been jailed and tortured after the Moncada attack; her fiancé and brother had been murdered by Batista's men, who subsequently presented her with the shattered testicles of the first and an eye of the second.) "So they had a Happening," the writer continued, "with the composer of the July Twenty-sixth anthem leading a conga line—it was marvelous! The top people in Cuba are fine—Fidel, Dorticós, Celia Sanchez, Haydée. But unfortunately there are others who make policy, small people afraid of making mistakes.

"People still juggle for position, people still manipulate, there is still much petty jealousy. Most people have to manipulate if they want to go abroad, for example—and this is inevitable as long as everyone can't go. I am afraid that the next cultural generation will be opportunistic.

"There is still a certain hypocrisy which bothers me. In 1961, a poem was rejected for publication: it had 'dirty' words in it, and the poet was asked for something 'nicer,' " he said, emphasizing the word with mild sarcasm. "He offered two poems—which were accepted. One was about a whore and the other about a homosexual—but the dirty *words* weren't in them." He smiled—not bitterly, but with a sort of relish at the absurdity in his tale. "Last year, the first poem was published," he ended. "Things are not as bad as they were for a while."

The Cuban Revolution saw the arts not as isolated fields of endeavor but as part of a society in which the artist was another worker with his particular skills. In that scheme of things, the question of creative freedom should not arise—but of course it did. The sectarianism of 1961 made it a painful issue for a while, though never to the extent of some other Socialist nations. The worst abuse was often not some form of direct censorship but the way in which individuals with petty jealousies or grudges against others, or just ambition, used politics to their own ends.

In January, 1967, a group of Cuban writers—including some of those who set policy—had joined other Latin American writers in issuing a statement on the revolutionary artist: ". . . the most unrestricted creative freedom is the true capital of the revolution to which we aspire . . . we therefore reject no technique, no method, no form or approach to the various areas of reality . . ." A vividly detailed, Joycean novel of homosexual experience, José Lezama Lima's *Paradiso*, was published later in the year. Reportedly, this was thanks to the intervention of Fidel, who overruled opposition with his attitude that "you can't *not* publish Lezama Lima"—an author of long-standing repute. A novel by Edmundo Desnoes, *Memorias del subdesarrollo* (published in the United States as *Inconsolable Memories*), was not only put out in Cuba but also made into a major film—despite some leaders' view of it as "too liberal." The Instituto del Libro, the central publishing house, has put out translations from a variety of non-Communist authors; "the only control exercised is in the size of printing and price of a book," said a staff member. "Books not deemed appropriate for the general educational level come out in small (five thousand copies or so), and therefore higher-priced, editions. But books like the new series to benefit farmers and workers—clear, readable titles like *What is Chemistry?*—are printed in fifty or sixty thousand copies."

Certain more subtle lines were drawn outside the scope of publication. "A friend of mine is never invited to lecture to students around the country or to teach *aficionados*," said the writer, "which is where all the real action is." He was referring to the hundreds of cultural centers which had been established in the cities, towns, and villages of Cuba, with full programs in

23

all the arts, where students preparing to be professional artists as well as *aficionados* (amateurs, devotees) participate. "They would say that he is formed in the wrong way. For example, he would teach about Genêt as a great writer whose roots lie in his homosexuality—not as a man who is good in spite of his 'sickness.' People like us are not banned, we get published and produced. But our generation is out of it." His level voice took on an edge of sadness.

"Ah, but the mini-skirts and all that are a good thing," he said with a bright smile. "They will help break down a lot of old prejudices." His mood had changed; he rattled along cheerfully now. "I feel good here, really good. You know, something absolutely new is being made in Cuba. I don't think Cuba will become like the Soviet Union." He echoed a familiar theme, but with new reasons. "Our nature is tame, we have fertile land, sun almost all the time, our people are not closed in. . . . As for Hungary, Poland, and Czechoslovakia—they never had revolutions, so what has happened there is not surprising.

"The changes that have taken place here are truly incredible to me. And I have changed too—somehow, I have lost my desire for things. I could never live in a capitalist country as a citizen. I could never work for a *boss,*" he uttered the English word with a grimace.

That was apparently enough political talk for him that day. "Would you like to see some of my new writing?" he asked, and hurried off to get it from another room without waiting for an answer.

"In 1961, I was crazy, I think. We were all a little crazy then. There was so much happening—the Revolution changed so many things so fast."

The speaker was an attractive woman in her thirties, who worked as a magazine editor. "I was going through a lot with my father in 1961," she continued. "I fought with him about the Revolution for a long time but I could not convince him, and he left Cuba.

"Things are more settled now. I used to talk a lot then, now I feel quiet. I think we still don't fully understand what happened. People are just more quiet now, perhaps a little saddened—no, anyway, more serious. There is a decline in the spirit of personal acquisition. Cubans always used to share, but they do it more now. When I go to cut sugarcane for fifteen days in the spring, I take along lots of clothes, and others do too, because we know there will be people who need them. As for myself, I always seem to have what I need, and I don't need much.

"Cubans used to be very crazy. I had a friend who was going to commit suicide one evening; the next day I called to see how she was, and she said, "Oh, fine." She had forgotten all about it. There is a little less of that now. Cubans are funny in other ways, they laugh at tragic moments in a movie. But they are good people and they don't have that terrible hatred of foreigners. I think the secret of Cuba's success is that it has no deep roots, no very rigid traditions. The Catholic Church had much influence, but it was never as strong as in other countries. The African roots are deep and go far back, but they are not rigid. So it is not so hard as in other places to build a new society.

"The revolution in Latin America will be so bloody, but here it has been very unbloody. I heard that some leftist foreign journalists were upset because coffee was served to the captured counter-Revolutionaries while they were being questioned at the press conference last week. That was very surprising to Cubans —we separate a man's ideas from his body. We do not tie the hands of prisoners, for instance. I remember in 1961, a counter-Revolutionary was caught in a house very near here. He had guns there and he was shooting—he wounded a militiaman and a young boy. After he was caught the crowd wanted to kill him. We formed a circle around him to keep them back. We told the people that there were laws to deal with such men; to kill him there would have destroyed our own humanity."

She went to the kitchen to make coffee and poured water out of a pot. "There is water only from six to seven in the morning, eleven to noon, and six to seven in the evening, so I put some aside each time." Her motions were neat, thrifty. "You know,

Cubans like to complain a lot, but they always manage. Once we had a big problem here—no deodorant, and in this hot country! Then an old woman told me that the best deodorant was milk of magnesia. So I got it powdered, mixed it with a little water and cologne. It works very well.

"My mother cannot stand it when people here complain about the lack of something—she remembers the war years in Europe, so she tells people, 'You think *you* have a hard time!' Cubans are really somewhat spoiled—they have strong food prejudices, for example. They want meat, they don't like fish— although the *becados* [live-in scholarship students] get it and are becoming used to it. Cubans call green vegetables 'grass.' Once I got very angry with a taxi driver who complained about the lack of food, that there was only rice and beans and no meat. I asked him, 'Why don't you get some fish?'—I mentioned a certain kind which is fairly available. He said, 'Ugh—I wouldn't eat that.' So . . ." She shrugged. "The diet has never been good —they use a lot of fat, even when they cook rice they drop a big lump of lard into it. But Cubans like their bodies and they love to do things which are 'good for the health.' They used to think yogurt was awful; then Fidel said in an interview that it was good for the health. So they began to eat it, and now it is very popular here—of course, they put a great deal of sugar in it.

"Last spring Fidel made a speech in which he said something that almost made me cry—and I do not cry much. He said, 'Cuba will not be a Communist country until all the world is Communist.' " The Prime Minister had been speaking of the lack of cars for private owners and the fact that the Revolution would not be providing such goods for many years. His words meant that Cuba could not sit back and be comfortable as long as others in the world were not; that helping others would have priority over attaining a maximum standard of living in Cuba; that therefore the Revolution would not for a long time be able to provide goods and services "to each according to his needs," as communism specifies. (Fidel's statement was considered by some of the Russians present as a slur on their homeland, which had just imported from Italy an entire factory to manufacture cars for private owners.) "What was important," she continued, "was not what he said, but how the people reacted. They applauded—oh, for five minutes.

"Fidel also surprises us very often by saying in his speeches what people have been thinking, perhaps without realizing it. He talks a lot with the people, listens to what they are saying. He catches what's in the air and then puts it into his speeches. Once, when we were watching the prisoners captured at Playa Girón on television, my mother said, 'They shouldn't shoot them —they should trade them for something we need.' A minute later Fidel said the same thing—and that is what was done. In a recent speech, Fidel talked about the reactionary nature of the Communist Party in many Latin American countries. I turned to my friend and said, 'But this is exactly what we were talking about last week!'

"Cuba is such an exciting place to be now," she said. "Last year I went to Europe for the first time in many years. People thought I would be thrilled. I went to see all the things I wanted to see, but with one or two exceptions they did nothing to me. In London, we met a lot of talented people, but they were so involved with personal problems—some of them were certainly problems, but these people seemed to have nothing else on their minds. People in Cuba also used to be very concerned with personal problems. Of course, we still have them. But we forget them in a crisis—and there will be crises for a long time."

Her husband had arrived a few minutes before and now sat down on the couch, tired. It was after midnight and time for me to leave. The couple offered to drive me home, and we went down to the garage of their building. On the road, the night seemed even softer than usual; a large moon hung in the sky and the city lights gleamed prettily. No one spoke for a long time. Finally the man said in a quiet voice, "In other countries, you feel that what is outside you is less than you are. Here, what is outside you seems bigger." Then he fell silent again.

Otra Cosa

"Havana is the super-developed capital of an underdeveloped country," Fidel Castro often says. "He who visits Cuba and sees only Havana leaves without knowing Cuba. Get out of Havana if you want to know Cuba."

As in most colonies or former colonies, the main city of Cuba long enjoyed a wealth and importance disproportionate to the country as a whole. Today, the Revolution is trying to redress that long-standing imbalance; the nation, after all, depends mainly on its agriculture, while the city—aside from some industry—serves primarily as a center of administration and services. So the city's residents, and also people in the towns, will have to wait for certain things—like more housing—while those long at the bottom catch up. "Get out of Havana" thus means: get out where the economy is, where Revolutionary change is most meaningful, where yesterday and today stand in sharpest contrast.

On the map, Cuba looks something like a long, thin salamander, lying slightly curled rather than straight. Its spinal cord is the Central Highway, which runs almost the entire length of the island. Completed in 1931, the Carretera Central covered about seven hundred and sixty miles before the Revolution; today, it has been extended to leave only a bit of unpaved road at each end. It is mostly two-lane, sometimes wider, and as smooth as a mango.

Leaving Havana province, the land begins to roll in low hills. The province of Pinar del Río has a striking physique, characterized not only by mountains and hills but also by giant configurations of reddish rock and earth which look like lumps arbitrarily dropped on the island rather than anything rising from it. There is beauty as well: the palm trees marching in gray, matchstick formation up the dark mountains, and the *flamboyán* trees with their startling, lavish orange flowers. Several hotels dot this landscape, but their swimming pools and lovely views are not the main reason that foreign visitors go to Pinar del Río. They go to see something called the Plan of San Andrés de Caiguanabo.

San Andrés proper is a town built from scratch, so new that its little park—painted pink and white, with concrete benches—has trees that do not yet give shade. Nobody could want to sit there during the blistering day, and nobody does. The park lies along the main street, the only street; much of San Andrés feels like a nineteenth-century town of the Wild West. It is, in fact, a frontier on the Cuban dream.

Once three large landowners ruled this valley, people say. When one of them wanted a road built to a pleasure spot, he took *campesinos* who were in his debt and paid them twenty cents a day for the job—from which fifteen cents were deducted to pay off their debts. A doctor in town asked sixty pesos to come and see a child sick with typhus; the family could not pay and the child died. Three schools served the entire area.

Today, this region of some thirty miles square has twenty-two schools, a hospital, and mobile medical service. The small farmers who owned land before the Revolution retain it, enriched with Bulgarian tractors, milking cows, fertilizers, and electrification provided by the state. Some incomes have quadrupled (residents say that even pacifiers for babies are free under

29

the San Andrés Plan). But the point of San Andrés is not a mechanistic exchange of goods for loyalty. The point is mostly an idea, represented by children who have come from hovels in the hills to prim boarding schools; by mothers who have brought their younger ones down to the day nurseries so that they can work; by doctors, teachers, and administrators who have left Havana's comfort to serve here. The idea: "Well, to be simple, the idea is to make communism right here," explains the diffident, blue-eyed Party chief in San Andrés, glancing off at the hills as if he would rather be out there in a jeep checking on a fertilizer problem than talking abstractions at his office.

Boarding School No. 1 is one of the more-or-less experimental schools in the area where the children receive free every item of use in daily life, from clothing to medical care to recreational equipment. Inaugurating it at the end of January, 1967, Fidel said, "The children's lives will be organized perfectly; they will receive the best of care . . . they will progressively acquire the best habits that society can give a human being, its best sentiments, its best concepts . . ." It's a little hard to imagine Cubans organizing anything "perfectly" (a cultural fact for which one can be grateful); but, in addition to receiving the paraphernalia of life for free, the students have a modern, attractive, and well-equipped building where the staff seems warm and personal. The atmosphere around the buildings and inside classrooms—though not oppressive—does feel tight. The children line up in formation quietly before meals and classes, and when the flag is raised or lowered. Most of them stare in silence at strangers; the camera of a foreign visitor draws a small crowd but not one question.

Then a young woman teacher speaks fervently about what she has seen happen here: "The children lived in great isolation before. They came from the poorest families, they had absolutely nothing. They didn't even"—she drops her voice modestly—"know how to use a toilet. From nothing, much—it is a tremendous change in just a few months." The students have broken with more than the domestic habits of their parents; they have left behind domination by fear of hunger; mental and emotional horizons closed by illiteracy and prejudice; a whole world in which there could be no dream of brotherhood beyond the next mountain. They are shy, they mumble and falter in the classroom, because everything is so new in this San Andrés world where the purpose of life is not grubbing for a few pesos.

Someday the trees in the pink-and-white park will give shade, and the adults who are children now will sit there. Beyond that, who knows what might happen in a town where the sign posted at its entrance says, "Revolutionary ideas gain strength in our land, faith in human beings grows"?

The same Carretera Central that leads east to San Andrés also runs west from Havana through the island's four other provinces. A four-lane turnpike connects the city with the Central Highway. There is little traffic here normally and even less on a Sunday morning. A ridge in the road, once placed there to slow vehicles down for the tollbooths, makes it necessary to brake—with a sense of frustration, for the booths have stood empty since the Revolution abolished this charge. "I will have to speak to Fidel about that," a man on the bus says. Other passengers laugh. "They will remove the ridge and then everybody will say, 'He did it—he talked with Fidel.' " To the left of the road stands the big housing complex called East Havana. The park is still empty, a few women are hanging out laundry on their terraces, and groups of militiamen sit on the grass smoking, their rifles lying beside them, waiting to drill. On the other side of the road, an abstract metal sculpture emerges surrealistically from high weeds. An entire new town was to have been built there, and the sculpture was to embellish its entrance. "They built the entrance before the town," a guide later explains with a little smile, "but then the town never got built."

The city of Matanzas offers a last glimpse of the sea before the Central Highway tears inland to the next city of size, Santa Clara. There, a statue of Christ stands on the road across from a sprawling new factory imported from Czechoslovakia to manufacture electrical appliances and other items. In the center of town, the façade of the hotel Santa Clara Libre shows bullet holes from a crucial Revolutionary battle. Then the long flat road leads into Camagüey, past hundreds of new, bright-yellow tractors and miles of sugar, tobacco, maize, cattle. Especially cattle, which are rotated from one grazing area to another so that the best cattle will consistently get the most plentiful grass. Cuba modernizes its agriculture, and the beef goes abroad along with other produce to bring back things like Czech factories.

The Revolution also pays one hundred thousand dollars apiece for prize Canadian Holstein bulls to crossbreed with its own Cebu, which is of Indian origin and well-acclimated but not a good meat or milk producer. The goal: to create, after four crossbreedings, a cow with the milk yield of a Holstein and resistant to disease like the Cebu. The whole population is following this experiment, the first major one in tropical husbandry anywhere. Meanwhile, in the provincial capital of Camagüey, women cluster in lines outside stores for scarce food and clothing items. One of them states the obvious: "You cannot buy super-bulls or factories for tomorrow, and also have lots of steak and nylon panties today."

According to Batista's statistics, 95 per cent of the rural population never ate meat and 88 per cent never drank milk. "We have to think of the children," a hotel chambermaid in Camagüey pronounces in a sober but pleased tone. "At my daughter's school, they give them breakfast, lunch, afternoon snack—well-balanced meals with lots of milk. *Cow's* milk. And it's all gratis. We older people just have to sacrifice, you understand?" Fidel Castro put it another way, on another occasion: "We are going to leave underdevelopment behind, and just watch us go. . . . By 1975, nobody will be able to refer to this country as underdeveloped."

The Central Highway runs on through the flatlands, but now in a different province, Oriente: "the *only* province," its people say proudly. Holguín, the first city on the road, looks and feels like many of the small, faded pastel cities of Latin America. But the Sears Roebuck store has been nationalized and shows only Chinese statuettes in its windows; the local hospital (new) is named Lenin and has two thousand beds instead of a pre-Fidel ninety-six; United Fruit no longer owns three hundred and fifty thousand acres of plantation lands. MIG's from a nearby base zoom overhead at night, drilling in anticipation of another Bay of Pigs. "Housing is our biggest problem here," says a local official, "that and the skilled labor shortage. We have built two thousand units and are building a prefab factory but . . ." This man, like most of those who run things in Cuba, prefers to talk about current problems and how to solve them rather than to proselytize.

Leaving Holguín, the Central Highway veers south to Bayamo—where the War of Independence against Spain began, a town that once burned itself down rather than surrender—and east again to the capital of Oriente. Hot, crowded Santiago de Cuba has downtown streets that often look like some place in West Africa or Haiti, then suddenly outlying districts with bright new prefab housing for three thousand workers. In July, 1967, Santiago means carnival above all. For almost a month, two long streets are closed to traffic at night, and their walls are lined with booths selling roast-pork sandwiches and beer. Dozens of bands play simultaneously. People—most of them black, because that is Oriente's main population, some in costume but most not—stroll up and down or dance or just stand watching. Small children and old women blink at the half-naked, sequined girls in the elaborate floor show imported from Havana's biggest nightclub. A tall, thin black man walks by, majestic in a turban and mauve-satin cape with silver words embroidered on it. He looks like an ancient Watusi prince; the words read *Reforma Agraria*.

Midnight passes and the river of people flows on. A man in his thirties steps out from the crowd to chat for a while with an obvious foreigner, who happens to be a reporter from New York. The man satisfies his curiosity and then resumes his rumba with the crowd. "Tell them" he shouts back at the reporter, grinning over his shoulder, "tell them that 'the slaves' were dancing in the street!"

Mountains rise in the area around Santiago: mountains of a crazy steepness, ranges that never seem to end, rugged peaks where the Revolution was born and where a real peace now reigns. Many little dirt roads lead off the Central Highway into these mountains, and the traveler's progress depends on chance. One afternoon in August, several people are silently waiting in a mountain shed where trucks traveling between the town below and the heights above customarily pick up anyone who needs to get somewhere. Except for the shed, there is only one palm tree for shade from the brutal sun. In the distance, an almost perpendicular mountainside has somehow been terraced; *malanga*, the tuber staple of Cuba's diet, grows there. Closer by, yellow butterflies flit across a small field, and the murmur of children's voices rises from a one-room, white schoolhouse. Naked boys shout to each other across the hills. Pigs snuffle in the mud near a shallow river.

One of the people waiting there is a round-faced man named Carlos, about forty and black, from a working-class district of Havana. He has said almost nothing to his companions all day, but now he abruptly breaks the silence. "How I would like to live here in the *campo* [country]," he says, mostly to himself. "Get a little place and bring my family from the city here and just live." He sits motionless, studying the hills and the sky; his voice has a faraway quality. "The people in the city used to think of the *campo* as something apart—something different from their lives—and the people of the *campo* as entirely different from them. Backward. Nobody from the city came here unless it was to do some business or visit his sick mother. Now we all come here." His voice quickens. "We know about the *campo* now. We come to the *campo,* and its life is our life, too. We have got our country back and now we are one people."

It is just possible, though not probable, to go to the easternmost tip of Oriente province on four wheels. Possibility has always been enough for Fidel Castro, who decides in the summer of 1967 that all the foreign visitors in Santiago for the July 26 celebration should get out of their comfortable beds the next morning at 4 A.M. and make the trip. The visitors include OLAS (Organization of Latin American Solidarity) delegates, musicians from the Canción Protesta activities also taking place then, artists with the Salon de Mayo, journalists from many nations. One thousand of these dignitaries get into a fleet of special buses, then trucks and jeeps, to go to a new community of private farmers and state agricultural workers, with housing, schools, clinics, and nurseries in an area that has never before known electricity or running water.

The name of the place: Gran Tierra.

The trip there is one hundred miles long and, except for a flat stretch at the beginning, is by dirt road through wild mountains with few visible inhabitants. It takes twelve hours. Little signs hanging over cliffs or between banana trees say things like "Welcome OLAS" to cheer the travelers on. Just as the dust and jouncing seem to become intolerable, a sign pops up in the wilderness announcing, "There is only one enemy —Imperialism." Somewhere in the middle of nowhere, all the trucks and jeeps pull up at what everyone takes for a moment to be Gran Tierra. It is only a rest stop; by impressive logistics, enough ice cream has been brought up into the wilderness to give one thousand people a pint apiece in a choice of flavors. Washrooms and toilets have also been erected by the roadside, and women stand by holding towels and soap. Then back to the road, the dust, the bouncing.

Gran Tierra has long seemed not a place that really exists, but a figment of Fidel's imagination, when the travelers arrive at last. Ghostlike in their masks of dust, they descend to find a quarter-mile of dining table nestled between mountains, and waiters in white jackets with little black ties. Within half an hour everyone has been assigned a bunk in the new housing units. That night, before dinner, a special program is offered. A local chorus sings, a Revolutionary drama is enacted, and the Modern Orchestra of Oriente plays noisily while its young conductor keeps trying to retrieve sheets of his windblown score.

35

Finally he gives up and walks off the stage in frustration, leaving the band to finish alone. The music rises to a crescendo, climaxes, and a fabulous show of fireworks rockets into the night sky, POW, BAM, POW, as the unguarded sheets of the conductor's score fly in all directions.

A few minutes later comes a speech by one slightly tired Fidel Castro, and a few hours later, at dawn, the caravan starts the twelve-hour return trip to Santiago. The visit has been mostly road but Fidel made his point: the foreign guests left their hotel rooms and learned from up-front a little about what it takes to develop this island.

There is only one road on which to begin the journey from Santiago back to Havana, and that is the Central Highway again. But at the town of Sancti-Spíritus, a little more than halfway back, a turnoff leads south and connects with a secondary route that can be followed all the way to the capital. Along this road lie the Escambray mountains.

Oriente, home turf of the July 26 Movement, never offered a likely base for those who wished to overthrow the Revolution, but the Escambray—the next best mountain stronghold—were the scene of bloody struggle in 1961. That was also the time of the great drive on illiteracy, when one hundred thousand young people went into the countryside with their lanterns and books to teach reading and writing to the *campesinos*. Some of these youths, like Conrado Benítez García, were murdered by the counter-Revolutionaries. Now they are national heroes and the bitter battles have ended.

A twenty-three-year-old Party member recalls these and other events over dinner in the Motel de las Cuevas, a luxurious spread of buildings at the foot of the mountains. There had been a night when he was fighting in the Escambray with two companions; both of them were shot dead by counter-Revolutionary fighters. He picked up their weapons and started climbing through the rough terrain. "Then they shot me in both legs. The legs were broken. So I lay there bleeding, from three to six in the morning. I was wondering who would find me first, the

enemy or friends." He pauses and smiles. "Three machine guns
—that was a heavy load."

"Well, I remember Playa Girón," says another, even younger
Cuban at the table, who clearly wants to get in a word about
his memories of battle too. "I was only a boy of thirteen when
they bombed Havana. But I got a pistol from somewhere and
when the planes came over, I fired at them—bang, bang, bang!
Of course, it was foolish to shoot at a plane with a pistol, and
dangerous, too. But that was the way I felt.

"Ha, but that was nothing," he goes on. "Do you know, they
sent me to Prague at the age of nineteen to be office manager of
the Cuban Consulate?" He begins to giggle. "Now, *that* was a
catastrophe!"

Not far away, past the city of Cienfuegos and the hustle-
bustle of its new industry, is Playa Girón itself: the beach on
the Bay of Pigs. The road there runs flat and straight. At the tail
end of a sunset, the land on both sides seems empty and no
sound can be heard except the scuffle of giant crabs, hundreds
of them, bright red, hastening across the black ribbon of highway. The smell of the air changes and some kind of expectation
fills the atmosphere; finally the road ends at the southern coast
of Cuba.

Like so much else in Cuba, Playa Girón has been turned over
to the youth. A maritime school lies along the shore, its two
thousand students housed in dozens of small, pastel buildings
scattered over several acres. Near the main entrance is a small
museum with a historical display on the area. In its first section,
photographs show the uniquely miserable life of the *carboneros,*
charcoal-makers, before the Revolution. They worked in a large
swamp nearby; no road led there from the outside world, and
for many families it was a thirty-kilometer walk to get a sack of
cornmeal; no doctor lived in the vicinity and anyone with a
serious illness just died. For them the Revolution began when
roads were built—roads that soon took on another significance.

The exhibit quickly shifts to pictures of the pre-invasion
bombing of Havana and other cities in April, 1961; the victims

of those attacks; the mass funeral procession through the streets of Havana. The photos taken during the invasion itself show truckloads of Revolutionary soldiers and militiamen being rushed in over those new roads; the tanks and gunfire, planes, ships, explosions. There are no captions with these photographs, only a quotation of a statement by President Kennedy made the day before the invasion began: "There will not be, under any condition, an intervention in Cuba by United States armed forces." Farther along in the exhibit, a photograph of Adlai Stevenson denying United States involvement at the United Nations carries no text and needs none. The final pictures show the defeat of the invaders, their withdrawal, and groups of captured prisoners with a statistical breakdown of their backgrounds indicating that the great majority were former owners of land or businesses.

Scattered casually around the exhibit hall, on tables and stools, are a number of relics from the invasion. Except for the shell which Fidel himself fired from a tank, they are all captured matériel: a camouflage parachute, helmet, supply case, another helmet. Young boys from the school bring over the items, one at a time, and politely ask an American visiting the exhibit to translate the English label which can be found in each. "Made in U.S.A." "Do not place near heat." "Made in U.S.A." "Made in U.S.A." The students seem merely curious; the American looks shaken. Then the students become more interested in talking about the different courses they take each year, their practice sails, their new swimming pool.

Outside, the school lies in total darkness now. Music from a radio or phonograph in the main building comes over a loudspeaker as the last boys wander out of the dining hall. Suddenly the music sounds familiar. It is the voice of Frank Sinatra, in love as usual.

Across the island from Playa Girón, on the northern coast of Cuba, is another beach of almost equal fame and even greater beauty. Luxurious Playa Varadero serves various purposes. For people leaving the country, it is a final jumping-off point: two flights a day to Miami, five days a week, seventy-five to ninety persons on each flight. Under a U.S.-Cuban agreement from 1966, an American plane shuttles back and forth between the two countries, empty on the hop to Cuba and full on the way back to Florida. Before each flight from the island, a Cuban doctor of the Revolution stands by in case any of the emigrés gets too upset or ill; other Revolutionary Cubans serve them juice and sandwiches. The travelers wait to pass through Emigration and then U.S. Immigration.

Of those who will talk, the majority say that they are leaving to rejoin family members who have already gone. One young woman complains that she could not get her hair done the way she likes and also that she has run out of excuses for not going to cut sugarcane. They have all had a long wait, as much as two years, for Cuban and U.S. clearance and for transportation space; most of the adults lost their jobs as soon as they applied. But then, this is the first revolution to let people leave legally. (As of 1968, every able-bodied person who applied to leave had to work full-time in agricultural production while awaiting departure—or not get clearance to go. "In other words," as one observer said, "the Revolution will not simply maintain people like that; they must help produce what they eat.")

"I encourage them to go," a Cuban who is not departing says later in Havana. "That way, you don't have counter-Revolutionaries around." She was speaking not only of the gunmen who once infested the Escambray or Pinar del Río. Among the buildings erected in Cuba during the early sixties were a number which had to be extensively repaired or abandoned, almost certainly because of sabotage by architects and skilled laborers. Roofs on schools leaked; a theater in Havana never opened because of bad ventilation. Varadero is only one way to lose these problems; other emigrés go to Mexico or Spain. You cannot export revolution but you can export counterrevolution.

There is one last city on the way back to Havana: Matanzas. At six in the morning, the town stirs. A few black figures hurry by the pale houses under a sky which has not yet lightened and several men stand waiting for coffee at an open-air counter. A few minutes later, trucks pass jammed with men and women on their way to work; a rooster crows, the streets lift. The sun begins to show itself, with giant rays filling the sky like a child's painting of a sunrise. On the main street, the words of a large sign become visible. They are a saying of Camilo Cienfuegos, beloved number-two Revolutionary until he died: "Those who struggle, it matters not where, are our brothers." The words are quiet in the early light.

On the other side of town, the road dips into a plain which stretches wide and deep toward the horizon. No color is yet visible here. Thousands of palm trees fill the plain, their gray trunks and dark heads rising up out of white mist: a single, vast, furry, mysterious landscape, tropical Poe, more probable under the sea than on land, soundless. Then, on the car radio, a Miami station comes through very clear with a long commercial. "Jordan's furniture sale, hurry down for your bargains, remember, Jordan's, today only, come on down and buy everything you've always wanted."

An hour later, the car enters Havana and the trip is over.

Havana is a place to get out of, but also a place to come back to. Whether the city seems depressing after the countryside, or exciting, it cannot be ignored. Only 14 per cent of the island's people live there, but they earn nearly half of the nationwide income and they spend most of it in the capital. Much government policy is still made here. Havana also has the greatest degree of contact with the outside world, meaning everybody from revolutionaries and Socialist technicians to French movie makers and Americans with the New Sound in their suitcases. Changes in Cuban mores, styles, and tastes emanate from the capital.

In terms of cultural penetration, no place in Cuba can compete with the capital. The neon-lit neighborhood of Vedado, with its Miami Beach–style hotels and restaurants, visually represents the height of United States influence. It would be impossible to eradicate all that without a massive demolition job. The Cubans could hardly afford to be so wasteful; furthermore, they believe it is possible to choose the best of a culture, discard the worst, and stir well with their own spirit. (When the Revolutionary Offensive was launched in 1968, all Cuban bars and nightclubs closed down; however, liquor could still be consumed with food in restaurants. The reasoning: such places had not only been centers of counter-Revolutionary activity but they also flaunted inequality—one man drinking all evening while another came home from long hours in the fields. This was seen as incompatible with the new push in production and toward a Communist Cuba. Later that year, though, the nightclubs were reopened by popular vote.)

Cuba never seems more surreal than here in Vedado. For one thing, there is the seaside Nacional: a genteel, older hotel of Spanish rather than Florida-modern style. On the lawn behind it can be found an antiaircraft gun, a militiaman on guard, and a sign saying "Military Zone"; the effect is of a missile installation planted between rocking chairs at The Breakers, Atlantic City. Not far from the Nacional is the Pavilión de Cuba, where the local arty set strolls around on opening night of the Salon de Mayo, sipping daiquiris and munching hors d'oeuvres; right beside the open-air galleries, on the lawn of the exhibit itself, are two of those valuable Holstein bulls in neat white stalls.

Soon after that opening, the Pavilión de Cuba is turned over to the people and Joseíto Fernández sings there for several nights running. Joseíto, who composed the original *"Guantanamera"* in 1929, has one of those fantastic faces found among older people all over Cuba. Confronting his audience, he is lean, erect, relaxed, dressed in the *campesino*'s loose-fitting pants and the shirt-jacket called *guayabera,* both garments immaculately white. The light mulatto skin stretched over high cheekbones, the large almond eyes, the Zapata mustache, make him look more like a Mexican Indian than the average Cuban. A fine Panama hat covers his head, and pointed white shoes show under his trousers. On his elongated hands, jeweled rings gleam. At last he begins his famous song, improvising contemporary verses in a light, sailing voice with a faint whine, nodding his head and rocking a bit to the rhythm. It is a very different *"Guantanamera"* from Pete Seeger's: swingy rather than nostalgic, the words bitten off instead of plaintive. The audience shouts remarks to their performer, teasing and affectionate. In a regal gesture, Joséito's arm stretches out inviting the crowd to sing the chorus with him, and his face breaks with a smile of ultimate warmth, delight, love. He looks serious again, emphatic; then the smile flashes once more and the song goes on.

But Joseíto is not where it's at for the kids who hang out in Vedado. Their world is La Rampa, a stretch of avenue running down a soft slope from the Hotel Habana Libre (ex-Hilton) to the lovely seaside drive called Malecón. Here, again, surrealism dominates. Mini-skirts parade by the restaurants, nightspots, and an exhibition of anti-imperialist cartoons. At one of the luxurious movie theaters, built before 1959, a Cuban-produced documentary called *Hanoi Martes 13* is on the screen. "A baby was born in Texas," the text says, and the film cuts to a shot of a cow giving birth—then to baby pictures of LBJ. He grows up, becomes President, and Vietnam is bombed. Mothers weep over dead children, and suddenly there is Ladybird, laughing gaily. The effect is devastating. A few minutes later, a newsreel comes on with interviews in which teen-agers debate the burning issue of mini-skirts and "tight pants."

Out on La Rampa again, there go the *mini-faldas* for real; they are heading toward the coffee shop of the Hotel Capri. The lobby of the Capri, once George Raft's hostelry, is filled with honeymoon couples in from the countryside for a few days of Revolution-paid glamor. Upstairs, the chambermaid has gone; she is now on militia duty, standing guard in the basement of the hotel. There is only one man on Room Service, taking orders by telephone and delivering them too. "Well, everybody is off doing agricultural work or something," he explains with uncalled-for cheeriness. In the hotel nightclub—which is packed, like every other entertainment or eating spot in the area—the last show has begun. Two comedians rap in old Martin-and-Lewis style; a hefty young woman looking Swedish makes out to be a deep-throated French *chanteuse;* a young black couple goes through frenetic modern-dance movements. Then comes the inevitable climax. Four young men dash out onto the stage with electric guitars and blast into an almost perfect imitation of the Rolling Stones' "Satisfaction"—but in Spanish it comes out *"Satisfecho."* Older members of the audience look startled, but the younger spectators wake up and begin to nod with the beat.

At Coppelia, the lines of people waiting to get a table have finally disappeared. Coppelia, a new mecca for the young, has thirty—or is it fifty?—flavors of ice cream served in an exotic variety of sundaes and sodas by waitresses wearing plaid uniforms and little caps. The architecture, however, bears no resemblance to Howard Johnson coyness. Set by itself on a full city block of grass, Coppelia looks like a giant diamond with steel wings; it's a super-modern, glass-enclosed, multi-leveled, indoors-outdoors, plastic-fantastic temple to the Cuban sweet tooth. Across the street from Coppelia, the pizzeria is still serving. There, a Cuban film-maker talks about wanting to try LSD and about the new Ginsberg-Leary magazine he has just seen. A small party is going on that evening, he says, with pot and a chance to hear "Sergeant Pepper's Lonely Hearts Club Band."

La Rampa and its adjacent streets swing until one or two o'clock in the morning, even on weekdays. Then, finally, the area becomes empty and quiet enough for one to notice the long beam of a searchlight sweeping back and forth across the harbor. In the lobby of the Hotel Habana Libre, a symbolic tower of real guns rises behind the circular staircase where ladies in mink stoles paraded not long ago. The lobby is deserted now except for a group of Haitians, speaking in low voices. Among them sits a very slender man in his early thirties, black, with large eyes that seem to burn through the dim light. A girl hands him a five-page declaration, typed on flimsy white copy-paper which rustles in the silent lobby: "In 1916, Yankee imperialism invaded our country and occupied it for twenty years, transforming it into a veritable neo-colony of the United States . . . the last twenty years have seen the bloody, backward and tragicomic regime of Duvalier . . . our Party has paid dearly for its

43

sporadic efforts against this regime, mostly in the towns and mostly in the form of nonviolent struggle . . . these efforts were not useful . . . under the conditions which exist, popular armed struggle is the fundamental, essential, and basic form of struggle to take power and establish a democratic regime . . . armed struggle . . . armed struggle . . . the revolutionaries and the people of Haiti have no other choice . . ."

In an hour, the young man will leave for another country to help make final plans, and from there to still another country for guerrilla training, and from there—home. It is four o'clock in the morning.

The mini-skirts come, the world's revolutionaries go, and most of the ordinary people of Havana stay. If there are Cubans who regret the Revolution, they are likely to turn up here—especially in that small layer of society which once serviced American tourists. There are also people in Havana as intensely loyal to the Revolution as anybody on the island. They seem not only less difficult to find, but impossible to avoid. A visitor can meet both types within a block of each other.

Down in Old Havana, which was the place to go for rum, girls, and good food during an earlier period of this century, there is a restaurant called the Floridita. Inside, red velvet suggests the elegance and popularity of bygone days. "Cradle of the daiquiri," it says in English on the drink stirrers, but the daiquiri machine has broken down today. The place is almost empty in the late afternoon; "Body and Soul" plays on the Muzak. The Floridita has been called Hemingway's place, or one of them, and a bust of the author presides over the bar here. An elderly white waiter talks about him.

"A splendid man, a good man. He came here very often. When he was going on a trip, he would give me the equivalent of what I would have made from him in tips during the time of his absence. He was a good man—he would treat a dark-skinned person as well as a white." The waiter rubs the back of one hand with the index finger of the other, an old gesture from racist days.

"This place was very busy then. It was always full of people talking and having a good time—look, it was once chosen one of the best bars in the world." He points toward a glass case in which a tear sheet from an old *Esquire* is on display. It shows a photo of the Floridita with the caption: ". . . where man's spirit can be elevated by conversation and companionship."

"Now it is *otra cosa*," something else. The waiter shakes his head. "Only Cubans with a certain position come here. The *campesinos*, others, even if they have the money, do not. Probably because of the long tradition here—before, only rich Cubans and foreigners came. It is *otra cosa* now," he repeats, with a shrug, and goes away to sit down alone in the round, darkened dining room beyond the bar.

A block or two from the Floridita, a sort of Revolutionary souvenir shop offers scarves painted with the likeness of Cuban heroes, postcards, flags, banners. Two men are in the shop, chatting with one of the clerks. A young man from the United States enters, and the Cubans begin talking with him. One of them, about thirty years old and black, introduces himself as a painter, but he is clearly not of the middle-class intellectual world. He prefers representational art to abstract, he affirms, but he wants to make a new art, about the Revolution. "Before, art here was under heavy European influence and it was only for the rich," he says. "A *campesino* could not draw because he did not have a pencil. And he did not have a pencil because nobody thought he could be an artist.

"But the son of a rich man could go to Europe, whether he had talent or not. And come back and make a painting. Then somebody would hang it in his living room and all his friends would say 'How wonderful!'

"The only art you could call Cuban was the things they made for tourists," the painter rattles on, as if he has too much to tell. "The little statutes of *negritos* eating watermelon—with big teeth, like this." He makes crunching movements with his teeth, shaping his mouth into a gruesome "happy" grin. Then his face becomes very straight.

"We used to work for Don Fulano on his *latifundio* because

45

we were afraid of him." (Fulano is Cuba's John Doe or So-and-So; the "Don" makes him a master.) "That is finished. We do not work for him anymore. But we also do not work for *sí mismo,* for ourselves. We do not sit back and say, 'All right, we will build our Revolution and *vaya* with the rest of the world. We cannot do this as long as there is suffering anywhere in the world. There are no frontiers between men. *No hay fronteras,"* he repeats.

His companion is a thin and dark mulatto, about forty-five, a factory worker. He was a Communist before the Revolution, he says, and worked as a peddler; it was impossible for him to get a better job because of racial discrimination. "Last year," he relates proudly, "when Fidel spoke here in Havana about Vietnam, I was away cutting sugarcane. I read the speech and went immediately to write a letter to Commandante Fidel Castro Ruz offering my services in Vietnam.

"I was at Playa Girón," he continues. "What a time that was! On the day they bombed Havana, I was here. Boys of eleven and twelve rushed out asking for guns, begging to fight. My daughter, who was thirteen then and a Pioneer, said to me, 'If you die in the trench, I will pick up your gun.' In the trucks going to Playa Girón, all the people were beating on boxes and cans, like drums, and singing. They made music all the way." Both men grin with pleasure; then the worker continues.

"You must understand—we are a most peaceful people. We do not like war. But we must fight if we are attacked. And we will be attacked, as soon as the United States is through in Vietnam," he added, expressing a belief held throughout Cuban society. "But the revolutions which are coming in Latin America and the United States will be very, very bloody. They are seeing this already, with the blacks."

"We love the North American people—truly we do. But they are not always allowed to understand things by their government and they do not have a clear idea of things."

The painter, who has been nodding with him, adds a softening word. "The North Americans read the baseball scores and believe them, then they turn to the front of the paper and believe that too!"

Outside the shop, the streets are filling with people on their way home from work. A coffee vendor, carrying a large thermos bottle in a straw basket, enters the store selling tiny paper cupfuls. The painter buys one for the American. A newspaper vendor passes and the factory worker gives a paper to the American. "We are old," he then says, "what matters is the youth. We remember the Revolution, they do not—yet they must build it. But we old people are ready to die."

"Look," the painter puts in a final word, "we have learned something very important here. It is not what you possess that counts, but the dignity with which you possess it."

Days of Casablanca

Land embraces the Bay of Havana with two short arms, one flat and one rising to a ridge, both bordered on their outlying sides by the Caribbean. On the flat stretch lies Havana, first the old and then—fanning inland—the newer sections of the city. On the other arm, at its tip end of sheer cliff, squats the lonely Morro Castle: Spain's answer to seaborne invaders of other centuries. Some distance back from it, also facing out to sea, a statue of Christ rises against the sky. It is fifty feet tall and dead white. People say that a few minutes after Batista inaugurated the statue with words about "this eternal vigil against atheistic communism," a storm began and lightning struck its head, and then Fidel marched into Havana a week later (the statue's face, sculpted to resemble Batista's wife, does look mangled today).

This giant Christ incongruously dominates the place called Casablanca, whose houses cluster along the waterfront below. Officially part of Havana, Casablanca is connected with the big city by small ferryboats which make a quick crossing to and fro every few minutes. It is also possible, though circuitous, to drive there by way of tunnel and superhighway. But in the early fall of my visit, Casablanca seemed more a separate village than part of a big city. This was mainly because of its strong identity as a port and shipyard; the little town had a trademark in the Soviet freighter or tanker which always floated in its offshore waters. Casablanca was also an old settlement, whose people often still lived in the same houses where they had been born; a town once known mainly for its whores, pimps, and beggars; a town which had experienced many of the benefits of the Revolution but still contained some of the shabbiest housing in urban Cuba. It was a town to be trusted if you wanted to find out how some of the ordinary Cuban people lived—both the good things and the bad.

I went there the first time almost by accident: with some photographer friends. Cruising down the main street, their Cadillac (government-provided) almost filled the roadway. We stopped in front of a run-down building and a crowd of children gathered around the car immediately; they crawled on the hood, peered inside at the plush lining and gleaming ashtrays, asking questions about everything. They were so lively and friendly that when one of them said, "And when will you come back?" it seemed natural to answer "Very soon." I noticed that the number of the building was 61, but no street name could be seen.

The next time, I made the trip by five-cent boat ride from Havana. The ferry landed at a small dock where townspeople gathered, sometimes in the few cafés clustered there, sometimes just leaning against a wall to watch the passengers coming and going. There was a weatherworn Coca Cola sign painted on a pink wall and a radio played "Never on Sunday." Railroad tracks ran parallel to the shore; on a hillside above sat a small park, dominated by one large tree. A narrow, paved street led into the town from there; it was lined with houses, small shops, and cafés. Most of the buildings were large and solid stone, others were dilapidated frame structures. Some turned out to be tropical tenements—*solares*—like the house numbered 61.

Four battered steps led up from the street into a one-story wooden complex of rooms built around an inner dirt courtyard. It was a rambling spread of dwellings, musty and dark, with one

49

very small window per room or none at all. Bits of laundry hung near the walls neatly. At first there seemed to be no one at home, but after a minute or two people were popping out of their rooms or coming in from the street. Mothers introduced all their children and went home to bring back pictures of relatives. A nine-year-old girl asked for a cigarette, and then said, "Why don't you have a camera to take my picture?" She backed up to demonstrate a sassy, sexy pose. Nobody told her not to be naughty; they were too busy asking questions. "Where did you get the fabric of your dress?" "Do you have any *chicle?*" "Is it hot like this in the United States?" "Do you like Cuba?"

"Yes," I answered. "I was here twice since the Revolution and now I have come back, so you see that I must like it." Some of the children stared; the mothers grinned. "How fine that an American likes Cuba!"

"Do you know the Monkees?" asked a pale, thin boy of fifteen. "I like them."

"But it's terribly hot," one of the mothers interjected before I could answer. "My God, what heat!"

The conversation rambled on in its desultory way and the crowd began to thin. I glanced around the courtyard and asked a few questions. The people at No. 61 lived in one room apiece, with electricity but no running water. The first family on the left was white and the first on the right, the González family, was black except for the mulatto stepfather and youngest child. Next to the black family lived a young mulatto couple with one baby. By and large, the society of No. 61 seemed more often black or mulatto than white, and definitely poor rather than middle class. Women and children prevailed; although it was after working hours, no men came in sight. Most people kept their doors open and the place had a friendly aspect. But it also had the particular oppressiveness of urban slum life.

"This *solar* is terrible," said the white woman of the first home on the left. "But we will get a better place soon. My sister has already moved from here to the new houses in East Havana. Her husband is a fisherman and they were the first ones to go."

"Will you move there too?" I asked her.

"I don't know where we will move," she answered, "I don't even know when."

"Neither where nor when," echoed the pregnant González mother. She seemed pleased with the phrase.

When it was time for me to go, the young mulatto woman who lived next to the González home, and who had unusual orange hair, asked if she could come with me to the ferry. She went back into her room for a minute to finish bathing her baby, a brown child with golden curls, in a small tub of water sitting on the dirt floor. When we were ready to go, the young white boy who liked the Monkees asked if he could come too. His name was René and he lived in another part of town. A high school student, he had a pale, agreeable face with waving brown hair which tended to fall over his forehead; from time to time he pushed it back carefully. His eyes held a quizzical look and he seemed a little apart from the others, more sophisticated. He stood very straight, almost formally.

On the way, we passed a pharmacy where people stood waiting in line. "A *cola,* for cotton," he volunteered the information. I could see him glance to catch my reaction.

"Yes," I replied, wondering about his attitude. When I had spoken of liking Cuba an hour earlier at No. 61, I noticed that René had said nothing and just looked at me in his composed, faintly quizzical way. Now he seemed to be almost challenging me to acknowledge that there were difficulties in Cuban life.

"Will you come back and visit my house?" he then asked.

"Yes," I said. There were no foreigners living in Casablanca except one Russian woman, I had been told; an American visitor might be an interesting curiosity for his family. "On Saturday. I'll come to the *solar* and we can go from there."

When I returned to Casablanca on Saturday, the González mother and her fifteen-year-old daughter seemed to be the only people at home at No. 61. Fina, the daughter, saw me coming from the small window of their room and shouted to her mother, "The American is here!" Then she dashed out with a wide smile; it was a fine welcome. She led me into the room where she, her mother and father, and three other children lived —a room so filled by two double beds that there was space for little more except a picture of the Virgin and the elementary school diploma of the elder son. Shortly afterward, René arrived on his bicycle; Fina and I sat down with him on crates in the courtyard just outside her door.

Everybody else, they said, was down the street getting their ration books for food and clothing, or helping to give the books out. Then, pointing to my shoes, Fina asked how much they cost. She went on to ask the price of every item of clothing in the United States and after each figure she told the price of the same item in Cuba. René listened attentively, sometimes adding a word of his own.

Then Fina pointed to the sandals on her feet. "They are unrationed and they cost only three pesos twenty-five centavos," she said. (The Cuban peso officially exchanged with the dollar at one to one.) "But the quality is terrible. Look—and I bought them only three days ago." The straps on top were intact but the soles, which looked like cardboard, were almost shredded. "You can get good ones made, but they cost thirty pesos."

"Huh, even fifty pesos," said Fina's mother, who had come out into the courtyard. "That's impossible for people like us. My husband makes ninety pesos a month." It was the minimum wage.

The father—a big, gruff-looking shipyard worker—emerged from their room a minute later. "Aghh, they treat us like pigs here!" he exploded and stomped off into the street without a word of explanation.

Apparently he had overheard the conversation, but it was hard to be sure; in any case, no one seemed startled by his outburst except me. Fina merely glanced at him and went on talking. "I also got a dress," she began.

"A very *simple* dress," her mother interjected.

"It cost eight pesos," said Fina, and went to bring out a yellow cotton print. She walked with her head high, short hair flying back in disarrayed points, large eyes—a fine African princess. She returned, holding up the dress in front of her. "We get only one dress a year," she explained. The people at No. 61 seemed a lot less disinterested in "things" than the Havana intellectuals.

"But you also get twenty-one meters of fabric and seven meters of good fabric," René added, in a precise voice. It began to be clear that he wanted me to know life in Cuba was hard but at the same time he disliked exaggeration.

While we talked, people were constantly coming and going at No. 61. A meterman entered the courtyard to take a reading and left again. Out on the street, children began to pass in their *colegio* uniforms; it was 4 P.M. and primary school had let out. A small boy came by and asked René if he could borrow the bicycle. "If it were mine, I would lend it to you," René answered in a tone of fatherly reason, "but it is my brother's and I don't have his permission, you understand?"

"We just got a letter from my oldest son," Fina's mother announced to me with pride. "He is doing agricultural work on the Isle of Pines. He will be there for two years." Then she went back into the room to feed her baby son and the four-year-old daughter.

"Would you like to work on the Isle of Pines too?" I asked Fina.

"Yes," she answered in a low voice. "But they won't let me." She nodded toward the room and then shrugged.

"Do you have a boyfriend here?"

"No—not yet," she smiled shyly and fell silent.

"You said you would like to meet my family," René put in; "we should go now, if you like. My house is quite far, on the edge of town." As it turned out, his house was even farther than he said.

The three of us—René, Fina, and myself—headed out on the main street, which ran parallel to the shore. There was so little motor traffic that we could stroll down the middle of the street, moving over only once to let a jeep get by. Acquaintances of Fina and René passed and murmured greetings; human voices made the only noise in the town. There was a feeling of procession about the walk, and also a sense that this place belonged to people more than anything else.

"That's my school." Fina pointed to a building at the side of the street. "I go at night."

"Why at night?" I asked.

Fina hesitated. "She has to stay home during the day to help her mother, who is pregnant," René answered for her. "Her father is away at work during the day and the mother needs help at this time with the other children, especially the baby boy and the girl of four."

"Why doesn't your mother put the girl in a *círculo infantil*?" I asked. The child-care centers, which formerly charged according to income, had become free in January, 1967.

"My mother says she prefers to have the child at home." Again Fina shrugged. She would not complain openly about her mother's tight rein—her old-fashioned habit of keeping daughters close to home—but she was obviously chafing under it. Then she changed the subject. "My father works very hard. He was named an exemplary worker at the shipyard," she said proudly. "So we all got a holiday at the INIT places. It was wonderful—the whole family, and we ate so much!" INIT is the tourism institute which, among many functions, administers resort hotels and restaurants for Cubans on holiday and for foreign visitors.

"My father is very Revolutionary," René put in. Then he stopped walking at that moment. "Look, it's a long way to my house still, let us take the bus."

As we headed toward the stop, Fina met a friend and paused to talk. From another direction, a tomboyish girl bounced out into the street and greeted René. It was Rita, age fifteen, René's girl friend. "She is being punished because she doesn't come home on time," he explained. "She is not allowed out of the house for a week. But she manages." He smiled in a worldly-wise manner.

Rita's father, he said, worked on a steamship line and brought her back gifts from abroad—records and clothes. The family had applied to leave Cuba. "You can't get clothing here," Rita added in a fierce tone, fingering her blouse. "Or food. It's very bad. Babies have to eat the same food as adults."

Her last statement was untrue, and René looked as though he was about to correct her. But before he had a chance, Rita tossed her head and said, "Anyway, I don't like Casablanca. The people here gamble. They can't save money—even if they make it, they just spend it," she sniffed. I wondered whether she would have said this in the presence of Fina, who came from one of the poorest families.

No one spoke for a moment and then René pointed down the road. "This is the road to East Havana, where I go to school. I am starting my first year of secondary school in a few days. I would like to study languages, I think. That's the kind of thing I like. Some students are more interested in politics than others —I, for example, read the newspapers only for sports or to find a good movie. Others read about politics. My father would like me to be more interested but I just am not. Nobody forces you to be political in school—it's just that some are more interested than others."

An elderly black woman also waiting for the bus pounced on him unexpectedly. "They make you be political with *force*," she shouted. "With force! I know many of the students and—"

René turned to her. "Now look, *abuela*," he began, addressing her as grandmother the way all women over fifty are addressed in Cuba. Both of his arms were thrust backward and down, as if in despair at such ignorance. "You know you don't know many students. Now, I am a student and I am saying that—" One arm came forward and up, in a gesture of sweet reason. But the old lady had already lost interest; she had seen a neighbor with a package across the street and wanted to know what was in it—perhaps some scarce item had come in at the store. She bustled across the road without another word.

René shrugged and smiled. "Let's go to see Susana for a minute," he suggested. "This bus isn't coming anyway." The trip to his house no longer called for haste, it seemed; it had become more of a wandering than a journey. Fina rejoined us and we headed toward a small but solid-looking house at the roadside.

Susana, Rita's blond girl friend, was sitting at the sewing

machine making a bag to match a dress. She had a *Seventeen* magazine prettiness and wore a crucifix on a gold chain around her neck. Her father was an *oficinista*, an office worker, in a factory; the house had a tile floor, good wooden furniture, a china closet, and a painting of Jesus on the wall. Susana and Rita began to chatter while Fina fell silent in her chair and looked uncomfortable. This house was very fine compared to hers, these two white girls seemed to be from another world.

René, Susana, and Rita talked about school for a while. The two girls had no special interests, they said. All three liked movies: "French, Italian, Japanese, Spanish, and the Franco-Italian productions—there are many coproductions," René reeled off. "But not Russian movies. They sent a lot of war films here and we don't like them."

They also disliked the *guajiro* music—the old songs of rural Cuba, in the tradition of Joseíto Fernández and others. "It's hicky," Rita said, "we like the modern music."

They discussed the different combos which they liked, and then got up to leave. It was still a long way to René's house, but it seemed as if we might finally be going there. Walking on the shoulder of a road which now led through a semi-rural area, I stumbled and almost fell. "Watch out," shouted a passing driver with a very Cuban sense of humor, "you'll break the road!" Fina repeated his last words to herself and laughed lightly; it was such a bad joke that it seemed funny.

René's house stood in a small row of concrete prefabs, painted white and pink; behind them lay an empty field and, in the distance, a large new hospital. "I don't feel good about asking you into my house, we have no furniture," René said as we drew near. "Our old house was destroyed by a hurricane. We had no other place to go for a year and then we were given this place. But we didn't bring our furniture here because it was in bad condition after the storm."

As we walked in, René's mother hurried out of a room with "Excuse the way I look—I have been cleaning." She invited me to take the best chair; Fina sat down primly in another. There were three other chairs and a small table in the room; nothing else. "We haven't been able to buy new furniture yet," said the mother. "It's expensive." René's father worked late at the Casablanca shipyard and had not yet come home, but his grandfather was there: an old man with an intelligent look, who sat in silence smiling from time to time. René's brother, Roberto, was also in the house. Two years younger than René, he had a round, open face; he seemed much more sturdy and lighthearted than his brother.

I looked around for a place to put out my cigarette. "We don't even have an ashtray," sighed the mother. Roberto quickly improvised one out of an empty cigarette pack and handed it over with a pleased expression.

"Do you work at a job as well as taking care of the house?" I asked her.

"Oh, no, I'm too old to work—I am forty-two. Anyway, there is no work for old people . . ." René eyed his mother but said nothing; there was, in fact, a labor shortage in Cuba at that time. "Will you eat with us?" she asked me then. "I can offer only eggs and rice—it's terrible. And Roberto eats so much, I can't fill him up. But René forgets to eat and also he smokes so he has no appetite. Will you eat with us?" she repeated.

"No, thank you. I have to go soon."

But René's mother was determined to offer the traditional hospitality. She went into the kitchen, and the smell of oil, the sound of frying, filled the room. René called out to her, asking where the *libreta* was; he wanted to show it to the visitor. Then he went into one of the bedrooms and came back out with the ration book for food and a second *libreta* for clothing. He sat down and began to explain each page, item by item.*

"Here is the ration for meat—three-quarters of a pound per week per person." (It was less in the countryside, where people can supplement the ration with purchases on the free market.)

---

* In January, 1969, sugar was added to the list of rationed items, with each Havana resident getting six pounds a month and those elsewhere a little more. The reason: some 200,000 tons were being wasted in various ways, which represented a loss of $15 million in foreign exchange.

"And here is the rice, we get three pounds a month per person. And the beans, fish, chicken. Eggs and some kinds of fish are not rationed. Then condensed milk and regular milk and coffee. This is for oil and this is for lard—we don't get much of either, but if they both come in, it's all right. Sometimes both come in and sometimes neither. This last page is for the Christmas rations—they are very good and—"

"Roberto," his mother interrupted from the kitchen, "where did you put your bicycle?"

"Oh, mother," exclaimed René, "I'm trying to explain the *libreta* to her."

"Listen to the way he talks to me, isn't it awful?" she moaned somewhat mechanically.

René looked tolerant and resumed his explanation. "Now, here are the clothes. . . . We get three pairs of shoes a year, not including tennis shoes and sandals. So here they put the quantity and here the date you actually bought them. *Ay!* Somebody has made an erasure, that invalidates the whole book!"

The room stirred with agitation but René's mother called from the kitchen. "Don't worry, the erasure was made by the *libreta* people themselves." She came out into the living room at that moment, bringing two little dishes of fried, sliced bananas for Fina and myself. Fina said nothing during the entire visit but she did not seem uncomfortable, only shy.

When we had finished eating, René suggested that we go to see the garden. Outside, he lit a cigarette. "My mother says I smoke too much," he murmured. Then he turned to the garden. "We grow beans—black and white—bananas, tomatoes, melon, and squash. There is very little of each but it is enough for our family."

"Do you like agricultural work?" I asked.

René made a face but Roberto said eagerly, "I like it very much. We, René and I, worked this summer under the new *Escuela al Campo* program—school combined with working in the countryside. I like agricultural work, I want to be a lab technician and also a biology teacher. There is a special program to train students for both at once. That is what I want to do. Do you know," he went on, his eyes very bright, "do you know that Cuba grows strawberries and asparagus now? The women in the Plan of Banao do it. Imagine, *asparagus* in Cuba! The strawberries go to make ice cream. . . ."

Roberto looked ready for a long talk about agricultural development but a car had stopped in front of the house and we went back to see who had arrived. It was the meat man, coming for his cup of coffee.

"He delivers the meat and—you know, we give him coffee," René explained with his worldly smile. It paid to stay in the good graces of the meat man.

"Do you have to give it to him every day?" I asked. "Your ration—?"

"No, the neighbors share it. We take turns."

The meat man, a lean, grizzled type, came up to the door of the house and René's mother brought the cup from the kitchen. René introduced me and the man began talking at once.

"It's terrible, life is very hard. You don't know, you're probably staying in a big hotel."

"She knows, I showed her the *libreta,*" René protested. "She knows now."

"Don't you think things will get better?" I asked the man.

"Huh," he grunted, "when?"

"Oh—in two or three years."

"Hah—by then there won't be anybody left here, and those of us who are will be too weak to eat!" he snapped.

It was a common type of joke, but I did not realize this at the time and answered him seriously. "Well, don't you think that perhaps other countries have things you lack now, but then you may have more of certain things which are lacking in other countries?"

"Such as?" he challenged with a hard, inimical look.

"Justice," I snapped back, too impatient with this disagreeable man to think of a less didactic answer. But no one considered it a cliche; they were gathered around, listening intently to see how the argument would turn out.

"And in what way is that lacking in other countries?" he asked. But he had lost momentum by now and turned to go.

After he had left, René spoke to me quietly. "You know, it is more fair with rations. Nobody can get a lot just because they have money. And everybody gets a little," he added. "Until we have plenty, it is more fair that way."

René looked happier than I had ever seen him. Perhaps he felt that he had made me see with my own eyes the kind of problems that the people faced, and he was readier now to show his enthusiasm for the Revolution. Perhaps the meat man's rude manner or irrationality had been too much for him. Whatever the reason, I thought, René will complain and criticize but he is not going to leave. Rita and others may fly to Miami; he is going to stay on this island, in his way.

"Our youngest son is in the hospital," Fina's mother announced as I arrived the following weekend. "He came down with diphtheria a few days ago and we took him to the hospital right away."

The news did not seem surprising, given the living conditions at No. 61. The mother, however, seemed less worried now than awed. "They are feeding him in the arm," she said. "Six pints already—imagine, six pints!"

"Six pints," repeated the father, smiling for the first time since I had met him.

A young man entered the room and then a nurse, both of them stooping to pass through the low door. They had come to inoculate the four-year-old girl against diphtheria, they explained; the other children had already been vaccinated. Everyone crowded around to see the list they carried of people in the neighborhood to be inoculated. The four-year-old had been crying ever since she saw the nurse's white uniform. "Coward, it is like a pin prick," the father tried to calm her, but the child knew better and it took two adults to hold her down.

"You can come with us to East Havana," Fina said to her when it was over and the child was still crying.

Fina, René, and I had planned to go there that day to visit the sister of the family that had already moved out of the *solar*. But I arrived at No. 61 more than an hour late, and René had come and gone. We decided to look for him at his house—Fina, her nine-year-old sister named Lupita, the smallest girl, and myself. He wasn't there, or at Rita's house or at Susana's house and finally we trailed the half-mile back into town. On the way, Fina asked different people if they had seen René. Nobody knew where he was but they did have other information to offer: Rita was still being punished, René's parents had had a quarrel and his mother had gone to stay at the grandfather's house, bananas and yucca (a tuber vegetable) were in stock at the store.

Fina stopped once to buy ice-sticks for the children from a woman who apparently kept a supply in her home. This person and many others along the way inquired after Fina's younger brother who had diphtheria. "He's better, thank you." "Yes, he's getting well." As we approached downtown, Fina mused aloud; "Casablanca is *triste*," she began. Not only were many of its houses old and shabby but there was also no movie, no *cafetería* or pizzeria, no place to go. "—But the people are very good about helping each other. Not all, but many. Two years ago, a man died and his wife had no money to bury him. We went around and people contributed—we collected over a hundred pesos. Now funerals are free. But people still help each other like that."

In the heart of town everybody was walking around with his two bananas and two pieces of yucca. Near the ferry landing, René suddenly appeared. "I didn't think you were coming," he said to me; "it was so late." He seemed reluctant to go now to East Havana. "I have no money," he whispered to Fina, "and I must pay the bus and treat to ice cream." Under pressure, he agreed to overlook his male obligation.

We walked to the little park where the bus stopped, the children silent and solemn-looking. When it came, nine-year-old Lupita held out her arm to help me get on board; she repeated the gesture when we got off at East Havana. Then we waited a few minutes for the bus to move on so that we could cross the street. For some reason, it did not pull away immediately. Looking up at the large, stolid vehicle with exasperation, the four-year-old muttered *"Dále ya":* in free translation, "So move already." It moved.

East Havana, the large housing development started before

the Revolution for the upper classes, now housed several thousand not-so-rich tenants in a combination of very high and low apartment buildings. It had spacious, landscaped grounds of trees and shrubs, its own playgrounds, stores, restaurants, schools. Saturday afternoon there looked in many ways like the same day in an American suburb: people were milling in and out of the supermarket, the clothing and shoe stores, the barbershop; kids howled for a ride on the mechanical horse in front of the special barbershop for children. There were differences, too. The clothing store had only two pairs of men's trousers for sale, no automobiles lay in gleaming rows in a parking lot and, at the back of the supermarket, a huge pile of green bananas lay unattended. "They know people won't steal them," René explained, when I pointed it out.

The family we were to visit lived on the sixteenth floor in an apartment full of furniture and knicknacks. It was hard to imagine that they had ever lived at No. 61 as the wife led us out onto the terrace of her apartment, where a pleasant breeze from the sea was blowing. "When some of the people first moved here," she said, "they didn't know how to take proper care of the things. Some sold the fixtures from the bathroom and the kitchen. They were poor and just didn't know. But things got very bad, so there was a meeting and people talked about the problem—about how everyone had been given these apartments by the Revolution, but they themselves were responsible for them. There was more than one meeting about it! But gradually the attitude changed. We don't have that problem any more."

Inside, she showed us around the apartment. It had a living room and two bedrooms, a bath and kitchen. Her cousin and his wife lived in one of the bedrooms; in the other was a large double bed and a double-decker for the children. The kitchen stove was not in use. "It's electric and that costs too much, so we use this oil stove." The old-fashioned burner looked out of place. "Would you like coffee?" she asked, and we stayed a little longer.

We had promised Fina's sister some ice cream, and now headed for the store where it could be bought, unrationed.

Then, sitting in a row upon a stone bench with two pints of caramel to work on, we watched the world go by. René pointed out his school. Girls and boys walked past our bench often, and many of them greeted René. "They are from my school," he said offhandedly, but he looked pleased to be so widely known. Fina was talking about shoes again. "They stopped selling them for a while," she said, "because some people were getting three pairs at once. They know somebody working in the store and they talk to that friend and, you know. . . . So they stopped the sale. And I hadn't bought mine yet," she ended in a rueful tone. The nine-year-old Lupita nodded sagely. She had not spoken all day but she often smiled: a broad, brilliant grin.

As a light rain began to fall, we headed for the bus stop to go home and I handed a dark-blue nylon poncho to Lupita for protection. Without a word she put on the flowing garment, pulled the hood up over her head, waved her arms like wings, and flew off. *"Fantomas, Fantomas,"* she whooped, *Fantomas* being a currently popular movie figure, a parody combination of Dr. No and Batman. The four-year-old, catching her mood, snatched the cigarette which René was smoking and began puffing on it, then passed it to Lupita as the girl zoomed by. *"Fantomas, Fantomas,"* she hollered in delight, a black space-child whirling through her own universe.

Standing on the curb, a boy was beating out a strong Afro rhythm with a stone against the lamppost, ba-da-*bam,* ba-da-*bam.* René looked at the boy and smiled lightheartedly; "Cubans make music with *anything.*" Fina managed to get the cigarette away from Lupita just as the bus for Casablanca pulled up in the twilight. On board, the child rollicked around in her seat for a while and then quieted. *"Fantomas, Fantomas,"* Lupita muttered to herself all the way home.

On my last visit to Casablanca, there was big news at No. 61.

"We are moving!" Fina's mother said the minute I arrived at her doorway. "Really, we are moving—they told us this morning. Tomorrow we will find out where our new house is." She had just returned from the hospital, where the boy was doing well.

"How did it happen?" I asked.

"That girl did it—the fifteen-year-old, of the Local Government. We have heard about moving for a long time, but she did it."

"That girl" was one of three persons from Casablanca who had been elected by the townspeople a week earlier under a new, nationwide system to break through bureaucracy and stimulate popular involvement in government. Across the country, the Local Government delegates ranged from young to old, but fifteen was exceptionally youthful. On the other hand, the job to be done—working with the community to resolve all types of neighborhood problems from a broken streetlamp to creating a park—would call for a lot of energy. I was curious to meet the girl, so Fina and Lupita took me down to the office where she was still at work, well after seven o'clock in the evening.

It was the same office where they processed the ration books. The girl came outside onto a balcony and leaned over it to talk. She was slim and white, obviously more educated than many residents of Casablanca, but not middle class in manner like Rita or Susana. When we were introduced, she made it clear that she had no time for chatting. She smiled in a perfunctory way and accepted my congratulations with a quick nod. Then she launched into a little speech. "Conditions have always been inadequate here in Casablanca. There are many problems. But we have a real plan for Casablanca now. Everybody will move out of the bad houses. We are also going to improve the health conditions. We are going to make a pizzeria and a *cafetería* and . . ." I looked at her straight shoulders, the clipped brown hair, her pointed chin, and just nodded. When she had finished her statement, she was gone again—back to work.

That was it. Then the young mulatto woman with orange hair, who lived next to the González family, came up the street at that moment and invited me to visit. We walked back to No. 61 while she murmured an apology about her home, which contained nothing but a bed and some crates. "But we're moving," she said as we got to the doorway.

"Would you like to go to East Havana?" I asked.

"No. They only have double-decker beds and I like one big bed." She smiled saucily and glanced at her husband.

"That's not what I saw there . . ." I murmured.

The husband had been trying to get a word in. "Look, the house is furnished free. We pay only the rent. It is deducted from my paycheck under the Urban Reform Law—ten per cent of my salary, the ᵔame that we pay now. That is nine pesos a month. In a few years"—the law says in 1970—"the house will belong to us and we will pay no more rent. Of course, there is also the electricity, that—"

"I hope we get a refrigerator," his wife interrupted, and walked over to the small table radio to turn up the volume of a popular song that was playing.

Now eighteen years old, she had finished seventh grade and married at fourteen. Her husband, who repaired fishing boats, had an angularized face with a big smile swooping across the deep weather lines; he had finished fifth grade, was now twenty-six years old. Both of them had been born in Casablanca, she at No. 61 itself. "Tell me," I asked them, "has Casablanca changed much over the years?"

"There used to be one club here for whites and one for blacks," the husband said. "There was a lot of discrimination—"

His wife interrupted again. "I like to *pasear*"—go out, bop around—"in a mini-skirt," she said, and began to act herself out to the music, swinging through Havana, making eyes.

The husband laughed helplessly. "She is a child. But she is very integrated in the Revolution. She—"

"I belong to the Federation of Cuban Women, the militia, the Committee for the Defense of the Revolution *and* I am a member of the Communist Youth League," Rosario announced.

"She is very integrated in the Revolution," the man repeated.

"But I don't like to work," she grinned. In fact, she had no regular job.

65

"We'll have more children when I get a raise," the husband put in, "which will be soon." They had one baby then.

"No, we won't. I don't want more," Rosario said emphatically. "I like to *pasear*." Then she leaned over and whispered to me, her eyes serious. "But I'm afraid I may be pregnant again."

I had to leave them to pay a final, courtesy call on René's mother. In the courtyard, René appeared with his brother Roberto. "Have you heard?" he rushed up to ask me, "have you heard, the people are moving to new houses? It is another work of the Revolution," he said with a personal kind of proudness. "And they will all be living in the same place, they will still be together."

Roberto was still talking excitedly as we all headed up the hillside to the house of René's grandfather. The parents' quarrel had not yet ended and the mother was still staying there. Everyone went along for the visit: the fifteen-year-olds—René, Rita, and Susana—together with Fina, Lupita, and Roberto. The house was a hideaway, high on the ridge, invisible behind banana trees. Only three wooden steps could be seen. "I call it the *campamento*," Fina said as we arrived. "I like it here."

We climbed the rickety steps, pushed past the thick leaves and into the front room of the tiny shack. I handed René's mother a box of Russian chocolates with an apology for the fact that they were probably tumbled out of place by now. "Thank you," she said, "it is the thought not the contents which . . ." Rita began to sing a current hit in a mocking voice and danced a few steps in front of the grandfather, who was sitting on the bed. "*Abuelo* doesn't like that music, he likes tangos," she teased.

"We have a gift for you," René said to me; "I hope you like it." He reached into his pockets and took out a pair of wooden ashtrays, wrapped in tissue paper. They had small pictures and the word "Cuba" painted on them. "You see," he said with precision, "one has a scene of the beach and the other of the mountains. That way, you have both landscapes of the country." Then, sounding younger than usual, he asked, "Do you like them? Do you really?"

When it was time to leave finally, René's mother decided to walk with us down to the ferry. We set out on a road which ran along the ridge, with a broad view of Havana Bay. On the other side of the water, above the city, the end of a sunset streaked the wide sky and wisps of smoke from the oil refinery mingled with a low bank of cloud. Havana's lights were already shining: distinct on the long, curved waterfront, becoming blurred as the city deepened inland. The small ferryboat was speeding across the bay toward the lights. Still closer to us, a Soviet freighter lay white and motionless off Casablanca. Immediately below, on the docks, army men in olive green were nailing down the roofs of certain buildings with boards; a hurricane warning was out and no one yet knew whether it would strike Cuba or veer off toward Mexico. "I like hurricanes," Fina said, "they evacuate us and take us to the Marina. Last time, we had a wonderful meal with barbecued pork, rice, beer, everything!"

Fina was in high spirits. She had many friends along this street, all of them black, and she called out to each noisily as we passed their homes. Most of them came out on their porches and stood there talking a few minutes, silhouetted against the yellow glow of house lights. A few came down to walk part of the way to the ferry. Soon there were a dozen people, young and not so young, black and brown and white, parading along for no particular reason except that it was a beautiful evening and someone had to take the ferry to Havana.

The sound of a drum being pounded in a steady, Afro-Cuban rhythm rose from one of the houses below as the last bit of color disappeared from the sky. We walked along in the darkness, everyone talking or singing a love song or arguing or joking except René's mother. She plodded down the road in silence, looking worried. René spoke to her and they whispered together for a while. Then he put one hand on her shoulder. *"Mira, mi hija,"* he said. "Look, my daughter, everything will be resolved." She smiled wanly.

It was the final procession through Casablanca. Soon René and Roberto would be back in school and have little time for hanging out, Fina and Lupita would be moving to a new home in another part of the city, Rita and perhaps Susana would have left the country; Casablanca would be having its face lifted. René's mother and father would make up—or perhaps not; Rosario might be pregnant—or not. Everything was changing but some things did not change so quickly, and I thought perhaps that is what living a revolution means.

We reached the dock and the boat puttered in. A young woman whom I had never seen before paid for me at the turnstile without my realizing it until we were on the water. She refused repayment with a look of dismay. When the ferry reached the city, she gave a quick smile and hurried off in the night. The waterfront was silent then except for the clicking of her high heels on the street and the flat sound of water lapping against the dock, boats, shore.

The City

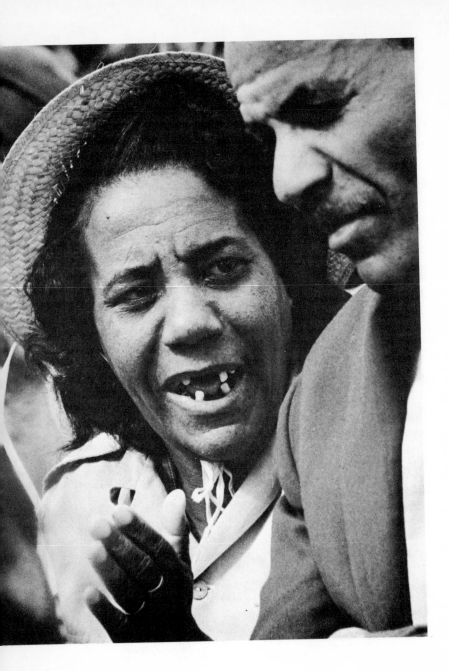

PART TWO:
The New Man and Old Ideas

The most difficult task was not exactly the overthrowing of Batista. . . . The most difficult task is the one we are engaged in today: the task of building a new country on the basis of an underdeveloped economy; the task of creating a new consciousness, a New Man, on the basis of ideas that prevailed in our society for centuries . . .

The attack on Moncada can be said to have been the first attack on one of the many fortresses to be taken. . . . Among them were the Moncada of illiteracy . . . the Moncada of ignorance, the Moncada of inexperience, the Moncada of underdevelopment . . . the Moncada of a shortage of resources in all fields. And our people have not hesitated to storm these fortresses. But another and more difficult Moncada was left to be taken—that was the Moncada of old ideas. And that Moncada of old selfish feelings, of old ways of thinking and looking at things and solving problems, has still not been completely taken . . .

Fidel Castro
July 26, 1967

. . . in moments of extreme danger, it is easy to activate moral incentives; to maintain their effectiveness, it is necessary to develop a consciousness in which values acquire new categories. Society as a whole must become a huge school.

Che Guevara
Man and Socialism in Cuba, 1965

So we needed a doctrine for transforming Man, and it was easy to find. What I didn't want was a false doctrine; I would not accept, before or after, a false doctrine. For in my own case—and I speak very personally, *compañero*—for me, being a Communist isn't belonging to a party. For me, being a Communist is having an attitude toward life.

Haydée Santamaría
July 13, 1967

The formation of the New Man . . . cannot be reduced to a slogan. Che viewed it as the result of an integral, multi-faceted formation in constant critical relationship with the society which this man will both forge and be forged by. Such men will be as varied and complex as the society of the future, but absolutely equal in their duties and in their prerogatives as human and social beings.

The building of that society, of the conditions which generate these men, is our historic task. . . . In that struggle, we Revolutionary students bear the obligation to be eternal nonconformists, eternal rebels against all mediocrity, all vice, everything undesirable hanging over from the past. The new society is not possible without a profound and uninterrupted ideological revolution. . . . We must engage in a constant and conscientious battle against the past, without, in the process, falling into an improvised or shallow concept of what the future should be. It should be constantly more beautiful, constantly more universal, constantly nobler and more humane.

Declaration of Cuban Students
July 26, 1968

Cuba is a land of youth. That observation has become a cliché; but the emphasis given to the schooling and activities of children and young people, the prevalence of persons under thirty in jobs of great responsibility, the predominance of men and women under forty-five in top leadership positions—all this confirms the truth of the cliché. Everywhere on the island, youth seems to be on the move: a hundred and fifty thousand volunteers go off to plant coffee seedlings in the Escambray mountains in one year; forty thousand sign up for two-year stints of agricultural work; twenty thousand young men head for special training schools in housing construction. Somebody, probably Fidel, decides that chess is good for the mental development of youth, so twenty thousand tables are set up in a Havana plaza and five-year-olds come to play too. Nobody is too young to be mobilized for anything.

All this activity has a larger purpose than advancing education or production in itself; Cuba's youth must be seen as a key to the whole Revolution. "To talk about age as well as class is very Marxist," Fidel has said. The generation struggle has been and continues to be a moving force in Cuba's history.

A sharp awareness of that struggle prevailed in the original

July 26 Movement, led by Fidel and others in his age group—
"the generation of '53"—who were not merely disgusted with
the tyranny and corruption of Batista's regime but also saw their
elders as hopelessly compromised by past actions or inaction
under Batista. Twenty years before, another group of young
people had helped to overthrow another tyranny—the Machado
regime—in the same spirit. Then, in the 1961 Literacy Campaign, youth again led the way. Of the more than one hundred
thousand teachers who participated in that drive, the vast majority were teen-agers. All secondary and pre-university (grades
ten to twelve) schools closed down in April so that students
could do their thing from spring on through the summer.

The Revolution in general has become their thing. And if
revolution means turning the social structure upside down, it also has to mean turning old ideas on their heads and creating a
new consciousness. In taking that Moncada of "old ideas," as
Fidel said, "there is a vanguard . . . made up of our youth."

It was not pure chance that made fifteen-year-old René of
Casablanca, and others like Rita or Fina of the same age, less
committed to the Revolution than twelve-year-old Roberto.
René was already nine when Cuba set its Socialist course; his
younger brother was just starting school. Their ideologically
formative years fell into very different periods. (Of course the
two also had personality differences, and René, as the elder son,
had a responsibility in the household which made him more
sensitive to material needs. Furthermore, the girl who had been
elected to Local Government, and who was the same age as
René, demonstrated that generational differences were not absolute.) René and his contemporaries were largely shaped by the
Cuba of the past, while Roberto was a child of the present—and
almost of the future.

What it means to be a child of the past has been described by
various Cuban writers, among them Edmundo Desnoes in an
essay called "The World on its Feet," from the collection en-
titled Punto de Vista (Havana, 1967):

. . . We know with more than enough words and statistics . . .
about what economic exploitation . . . dependency, foreign occupa-

tion, underdevelopment, represent in the history of our island—but very little about . . . psychological exploitation, about the spiritual penetration, dependency, underdevelopment, and foreign occupation of our minds . . .

. . . The personality of the man of the Third World has been as distorted as the economy of his lands. And although all this is obvious, although Marxist texts talk about structure and super-structure, it is an area of study which remains little explored, dark, and depressingly static. The most moving expression of our world is Frantz Fanon's *The Wretched of the Earth*, but Fanon did not live through a new social reality . . . we inevitably know more than Marx and Fanon about these problems. . . . We know that it is not enough to transform the production relations; that in ideology, customs, in the superstructure, we can go on being bourgeois and reactionary—and, in our case, colonized, underdeveloped.

I have been, and in many ways still am, colonized by Western literature, by North American and European culture. I tend to think and feel sometimes in accordance with French intellectual concep-tions or North American attitudes. I still feel torn between an image of Man as a creature with only his pleasures and his anguish and his daily life, and the intuition that man can be different, that he can transcend, that the New Man is possible . . .

Desnoes has suggested here one of the crucial questions for any Socialist revolution, a crucial question in Cuba today, and a question affecting the youth in particular. How can ways of thinking and behaving, rooted in old economic relationships between people, become altered to harmonize with the new re-lationships? How can you change something as basic as Man's old attitude toward work (a way to make money for himself and family); toward his fellowman (a competitor); toward his gov-ernment (an alien force)? How, in the case of Third World countries, can you overcome huge economic problems at the fastest speed possible without falling back on old incentives of material self-interest? How, in the case of Cuba, can you change men's attitudes toward women, women's attitudes toward them-selves, white attitudes toward black, and black attitudes toward blackness? How, in short, do you change what is commonly called "human nature"? And finally, can people who are them-

selves products of the old system direct the creation of a new consciousness?

Before the Revolution, Cuba was a colony: poor and under-developed—that euphemism for colonized, exploited—though less so than some other countries of this hemisphere. It was a society of Haves bossing Have-Nots, with a somewhat larger petty bourgeoisie than other parts of Latin America; a society of white supremacists and male supremacists. The majority of people scraped out an existence while a city-based minority held hands with Uncle Sam to their mutual benefit. That minority, the ruling class, created a subclass of rulers who sat in offices and thought of "the people" as document numbers (and nuisances). The exploitation of Man by Man determined the nature of life and the reification of Man determined its quality.

Of the many old ideas embedded in that pre-Revolutionary scene, those which in 1967 seemed hardest and most vital to solve fell into three areas of human relationship: class, race, and sex. Outside those broad categories lay many prejudices which were primarily by-products of, rather than rooted directly in, the past structure of Cuba's society. For example, patients released or escaped from the Havana Psychiatric Hospital sometimes returned voluntarily—while others cut short their visits home—because of the outside world's attitude toward locos, *"crazy people." (The hospital itself, once a classic Snake Pit, now had almost country-club facilities and comfort; it was inevitably easier for the Revolution to accomplish this than to change an attitude rooted in long-standing ignorance.) Cuban food prejudices offered another example of habits which time and a certain amount of effort should alter. But old ideas in the areas of class, race, and sex relations—these seemed to present the Revolution with its most difficult and long-range challenges.*

They are major issues, involving all the institutions of the nation and sometimes its foreign affairs as well. Without examining the entire society, we can look at some aspects of those old ideas in Cuba, some of the attempts made to uproot them, and the role of youth—particularly within the educational system—in creating a new consciousness.

"Doctors and the Like"

Cuba is no longer a society of Haves oppressing Have-Nots. The country is run in the interests of "the people," meaning the agricultural and industrial workers who form the vast majority of its population. By 1967, 70 per cent of its agricultural production, all of its heavy industry, foreign trade, education, and culture were state-owned. Some 30 per cent of the land remained in the hands of individuals* as did at least fifty-five thousand businesses, the vast majority of them small retail or service enterprises. (With rare exceptions, like shoe-shiners and seamstresses working at home, these enterprises were all nationalized in March, 1968, as part of the Revolutionary Offensive.) Wide-scale exploitation had ceased; profiteering, speculation, and privilege had not.

The existence of what might be called Haves and Have-Mores was affirmed by many Cubans, including the Prime Minister. In a 1967 speech, Fidel told about his conversation with a farmer who wanted a plot of land to plant rice. He had said to the man,

---

* These small private owners kept their profits but since they sold mostly to the state and received aid from the state, the setup was about as "private" as much farming in the United States.

. . . with this small amount of land, you can only produce for yourself and a few wealthy people who might come along to purchase rice." And the farmer answered, "That's true! That's true! Do you know what it means to get as much as two hundred and fifty pesos for a sack of rice?" And I said, "Two hundred and fifty pesos? Tell me, who are these people who pay two hundred and fifty pesos for a sack of rice?" And the farmer explained—obviously in a rather unfair way—"Doctors and the like."

Fidel went on to state that of course there are many Revolutionary doctors, "but for that farmer the title 'Doctor' meant a rich man . . . there are still a lot of wealthy members of the bourgeoisie in this country."

Even more widespread seemed to be the petty bourgeoisie, mainly composed of *oficinistas* and other bureaucrats. They too created a problem much discussed by Fidel:

When I want to have an idea of whether someone is a Revolutionary or not . . . the rule I use is whether or not that man has an idea of . . . what it takes to produce a hundred thousand pesos worth of milk, of meat, of grapes, of sugar. . . . How much sweat, how many acres of land, how many hours . . .? And if one of those bureaucrats who could carry out his work with twenty people invents jobs, invents posts, so that eighty more are working without producing anything except papers . . . that man, the bureaucrat, that antisocial person, that enemy of the Revolution does not waste only a hundred thousand pesos in unnecessary salaries. . . . There is something worse than wasting money and that is wasting intelligence and energy, wasting human beings. . . . *That* is a bureaucrat . . . and there is still bureaucracy . . . there is still much petty bourgeois spirit . . .

The continued existence of bourgeois or petty bourgeois privilege, attitudes, and conduct came as no great surprise in such a very young revolution. Privilege was to be seen in the glaring contrast between the spacious suburban homes of the bourgeoisie (including the intellectuals) and the huts of the countryside. Wages for many workers and farmers ran lower than those of many professionals and bureaucrats, mainly for reasons dating back to a wage freeze which the country could not yet afford to redress.

Old ideas of status accompanied these realities. People in Havana particularly complained about bureaucrats wielding the superiority of their titles, secretaries, and intercoms; about the snotty "professionalism" of some doctors toward some patients, especially those who wanted an explanation of an illness instead of just a prescription; about the whole petty bourgeois mentality with its selfishness and opportunism. When a Havana sociologist could not make studies among people in the *campo* because "the mosquitoes are terrible" and "how do you talk to those people anyway?" his attitude reflected the long-standing attitude of superiority and apartness which some city people, usually over-40, still maintained toward those of the *campo*. The class struggle was often paralleled by the old city-country relationship.

There were other attitudes and practices which seemed inappropriate to a Socialist country. Some of the fancier restaurants and nightclubs in the Vedado section of Havana would not admit a man without tie and jacket or a woman in pants—unless they were in uniform—in 1967. Waiters wore black tie everywhere (including at Gran Tierra). At big receptions, almost all men who were not officials or in the military would come wearing tie, jacket, and city shoes, no matter how hot it might be. A less visible but more important example was medical education, which still took the clinical (doctor and individual patient) rather than public-health approach.

These phenomena cannot be labelled as remnants of old ideas about class relationships and left at that. The petty bourgeois values were also rooted in underdevelopment and colonization, and certain Afro-Spanish cultural traditions. *Machismo*—that complex package of masculinity definitions which places great importance on keeping up appearances—made it woman-ish and therefore unthinkable for a male office worker with any stature to dial his own telephone calls. Sandals were hicky but also homosexual ("If only Fidel would put on a pair and talk about how good they are for the health, how they save leather," said one Cuban, "then—freedom from Athlete's Foot at last!"). Consciously or unconsciously, many Cuban men were still trying to be Spanish gentlemen. The "gentleman" may have reflected a class notion but the "Spanish" echoed a cultural inferiority complex typical of colonized peoples. Cuba also had hangovers from a tradition of servility that the American film-maker Saul Landau has called "Cuba as Caterer to the West": the waiter in black tie, who over so many years took orders from American tourists for anything from a steak to a woman. The class struggle was thus accompanied by a need to decolonize Cuba's values and cultural identity.

While the class struggle continued, the Revolution intended to move ahead with the development of a New Man. This under-taking proceeded from the key assumption that, as the Party newspaper put it, "it is impossible mechanically to separate the building of socialism and communism . . . they should, in one sense, be built at the same time. A fundamental implication of this is the education of the New Man, the Communist man, beginning now."

The Revolution saw selfishness as one of the toughest "old ideas" to be uprooted so that the New Man could emerge. Fidel Castro said in 1967, "It was impossible to advocate the concept of human brotherhood when the cardinal condition for survival was that of getting things away from others . . ." To put it another way: under the old economic setup, life was a rat race and Man an object trying to sell himself—his work—in order to survive. If he succeeded, it was at the expense of others. Talk of brotherhood could have reality only on an individual or paro-chial level. But the New Man—the twenty-first-century man or woman—would be a person, for whom work is a function of one's interdependence with all beings in a society where wealth is created and shared communally. "Man truly achieves his full human condition," Che said, "when he produces without being compelled by the physical necessity of selling himself as a commodity." The goal might therefore be called not simply the wiping out of selfishness but the creation of *a new definition of egoism—a new sense of self.* (The influence of Che Guevara in developing Cuba's ideology of the New Man took on even greater importance after his death in October, 1967. Never more alive than now in the hearts and minds of the Cuban people, Che has become a symbol of the humanism to which the Revolution aspires.)

The problem of selfishness was aggravated in 1967 by the fact that "conditions for survival" had not yet reached an ideal state. As long as scarcity remained, work would have a coercive aspect. As long as the state could not meet all needs, people would be tempted to place individual self-interest above the social interest. Cuba's leaders recognized this.

But no "realism" would make Cuba resort to capitalist stimuli to solve the scarcity problem. Its leaders had rejected material in favor of nonmaterial incentives. The Vanguard Movement was aiming to replace stimuli used in the past—particularly overtime pay—with such new ones as greater participation by the workers in problem-solving. The Revolution had giant economic problems to solve and many past mistakes to overcome. It had to perform a constant juggling act between trying to meet the serious material needs of the people and creating a new consciousness free of mercantile values. Cuba was searching out its own answers to these problems; it seemed clear that she would not choose the way of the Soviet Union and Eastern Europe. (Fidel Castro spelled out this position in his commentary on the 1968 Soviet invasion of Czechoslovakia. He condemned that action as a violation of international law and national sovereignty but justified it as a political necessity caused by Czechoslovakia's increasing alliances with the American camp. Some observers felt that he should have said "a pox on both your houses" but failed to go that far because of the Soviet Union's past and present help to Cuba; a viable relationship had to be maintained. The message came through clear enough, anyway, in Fidel's sharp analysis of how a would-be Socialist nation went wrong.)

Closely related to selfishness and greed was the syndrome of old ideas represented by the word *burocratismo:* leadership's fear of, or lack of faith in, the people; the people's lack of faith in themselves; self-perpetuating structures; red tape. In a society where Man was an enemy and an object to Man, it followed that human beings would be administered like enemies—objects —by those in power. These ancient problems were aggravated in a country emerging from colonization.

For centuries, the "mother country" had taught the colony one basic lesson: *you* can't do it, and don't try. The assumption of responsibility, the impulse to ask "Why?" and to act on the answer when desirable, had been thwarted. Real administrative responsibility, making the wheels go round, remained the province of non-Cubans. The little guys, local people, maneuvered in accordance with a loyalty system whose main techniques were cultivating the right big shot, not sticking your neck out, bringing in friends or preferably relatives, passing the buck. Know-how and performance counted for little; initiative could be dangerous. Playing office power-politics the right way was everything.

Then, overnight, people were asked to make decisions about the lives, goods, and services of others. Bell Telephone had left; communications—among a hundred things—was the Revolution's worry now. The Americans and most of the Cubans who knew about such things soon left: a staggering lack of trained personnel emerged. And the gap had to be filled by people nurtured on that old, anti-merit system. Confronted by a problem to solve or a decision to make, they chose to go by some rule, invent some new form, ask for more personnel, or maybe just put the whole thing in "Pending" forever—anything but risk a mistake which might mean loss of a job. The monster grew as nationalization increased.

Another reason for the mushrooming of bureaucracy was the struggle to do away with *guerrillerismo* (sometimes called *porsimismo*), a hangover of do-it-yourself-ism from the fight against Batista. In trying to adjust anarchistic habits of the insurrection to the need for tightly organized, Socialist production, bottlenecks and unnecessary delays were created. The goal of orderliness sometimes produced only more confusion.

All these factors had created a climate that often made it

hard to tell which way to jump. A minor government official sent out to a provincial area in the early sixties came across a school where half a dozen classes were being held simultaneously in one unpartitioned building. He went to the nearest city and spoke to the Party people about the situation; they sympathized, "but what can we do?" The official led the way to a nearby sugar refinery, where the man in charge—impressed by the caliber of his visitors—picked up the telephone and learned from his chief carpenter that there was a supply of board lying around which could probably be spared. Back at the school, a volunteer crew gathered and over the weekend put up walls to separate the classes. Everybody had a feast afterward, but back in Havana the official—who was supposed to have spent his time in another area—faced accusations of being undisciplined. Perhaps he had been, technically. But perhaps his on-the-spot decision about the greater importance of the school job had been wiser than the thinking in a Havana office. Perhaps the boss just felt envious and nervous about his own position. Certainly, nobody should have had to come all the way from the capital to solve the problem; it could have been done locally if the spirit had prevailed.

The "I-don't-want-to-get-involved" problem was intensified by the Latin American tradition of *caudillismo,* a type of Big Bossism in which the head of state is a giant father figure toward whom everyone feels, at best, awe and, at worst, fear. Nothing moves without his saying so; the people do not think for themselves on major issues or, if they do, they don't admit to it. "My mother is head of the C. D. R. in her neighborhood," said a Havana resident, "but it would never occur to her to think she has 'power.' " There was a Cuban slogan which turned up in many signs, often with a picture of Fidel on a mountaintop: *"Comandante en Jefe, Ordene!"*—"Commander-in-Chief, give your orders!" The slogan supposedly dated back to the October (Missile) Crisis, when it might have been appropriate. In more recent times, it seemed the only truly un-Revolutionary motto on the island.

In working to uproot *burocratismo,* the Revolution has used various approaches. The main way to get rid of any undesirable idea is by changing the material reality which breeds it; at the same time, a new consciousness must be cultivated to replace the old. On one level, then, Cuba has tried to solve the problem of *burocratismo* by straight elimination of petty bourgeois strongholds. In the early 1960's, the Revolution appointed Commissions to Fight Bureaucracy and moved nearly ten thousand functionaries to other work. But then many of the bosses simply replaced those people with new functionaries. Also, the Commissions themselves became bureaucratic. A new attempt at "rationalization" began in early 1967; this time, over twenty thousand jobs were abolished outright. The staff of the Ministry of Education, for example, was reduced from about twelve hundred and fifty to two hundred and fifty. Most of those who left went into agriculture.

A striking example of efforts to create a consciousness against *burocratismo* was a feature film produced in 1966 by the Cuban Film Institute (ICAIC) and directed by Tomás Gutiérrez Alea. *Death of a Bureaucrat* begins with the funeral of a model worker; the man is buried with his *carnet* in the tomb, making it impossible for his widow to collect her pension. A nephew tries unsuccessfully to get the pension without it. In desperation, he removes the casket from the grave at night and finally gets the precious card—but now he has a new problem. He was almost caught body-snatching and had to race the coffin home in a wheelbarrow; how to get it buried again? The bureaucrat of the film's title, whom the nephew then goes to see, refuses to issue a burial permit; according to his records, the body has been buried.

Advised to get an exhumation order so that the body can be officially out of the grave and then officially reburied, the nephew sets out on a round of office visits with endless lines to wait through and functionaries who leave on the dot of five just as his turn comes. While he waits, pretty girls pass wearing banners proclaiming the Campaign Against Bureaucracy (which is not the film's only touch of irony). He finally gets his document in order and returns to the bureaucrat, who orders an immediate exhumation of the body: this is what the piece of paper says to do. The newphew explains that the body has already been exhumed; he wants to *bury* it.

The bureaucrat proclaims that impossible. The nephew, still holding the new burial wreath, attacks him while flowers and papers fly. The bureaucrat lies dead; the nephew is led away in a straitjacket, and the film ends with the pomp of the bureaucrat's burial.

More sardonic than this main plot, however, is a secondary relationship in the film between the nephew and an acquaintance who advises him on how to deal with the system. This man designs Revolutionary posters during the day and at night takes his blond secretary from fancy nightclub to big car to luxurious house to bed. The bureaucrat, by contrast, seems rather shabby and himself almost a victim of the system whose real monsters might be men like the opportunistic poster designer.

In the fall of 1967, the Revolution took an important and basic step toward eliminating the mentality of *burocratismo*. After several years of experiment, it set up the national system called Poder Local—literally, Local Power, more often translated Local Government. Its aim was a sort of participatory democracy for administrative matters; its guiding spirit, as proclaimed in the press, was expressed by Lenin: "It is not enough to trust the 'representatives' of the people in certain organisms. It is necessary to build a direct democracy from the bottom, with the initiative of the masses themselves, through their effective participation in all activities of the state."

Under the new system, over twenty-three thousand Local Government delegates—among them, the girl in Casablanca— were nominated and elected at some eight thousand public assemblies in September, 1967 (the election process continued into 1968). It would have been literally impossible during that month for a Cuban not to know the date, time, and place of the Local Government Assembly in his geographic area or work center, so intensively were the meetings publicized. Those elected acquired the power and a budget to construct and maintain parks, playgrounds, social centers, restaurants, barber-shops. They would also be responsible for all free community services such as street-cleaning and, except in Havana, for all commercial establishments, handicraft production (bricks, hardware, furniture, etc.), and bread production. The delegates would not administer those activities directly but serve as co-ordinators and troubleshooters in the interest of their communities.

Cubans used to joke that there was a time when "you had to get authorization from Havana before you could have a pile of dog shit removed from the sidewalk in some town three hundred miles away." Now Local Government could get it cleaned up. If a schoolroom needed walls, the Local Government delegate was expected to scrounge that board and nag those volunteers into doing the job instead of just complaining about shortages while waiting for the man from Havana. Every six months, Local Government had to give an accounting of itself to an assembly of the people.

The delegates were responsible upward to chairmen at the municipal, regional, and provincial levels, and finally to a national coordinator. They were to work with existing organizations, particularly Committees for the Defense of the Revolution: neighborhood groups that already had some experience in local decision-making (the tax on beer sold in the more expensive restaurants, which goes toward providing free schoolbooks, was levied by popular agreement reached in meetings of those groups, for example).

At the neighborhood assemblies to elect delegates, the public participated actively and critically in some locations. In others, candidates were nominated and elected with enthusiasm but little real discussion, despite frequent exhortations from the chairmen that "this is *your* meeting" and "only *you* can make Local Government work." To what extent the delegates represented the Party's choices was hard to say, but in any case, those elected often seemed to have the genuine support of the people.

Potentially the most significant fact about the new Local Government system was that 61 per cent of the delegates elected had less than a sixth-grade education. That figure meant that the ordinary *Fulanos,* not the bourgeoisie or petty bourgeoisie, predominated—and in a society where constant politicization could make their power more than nominal. Local Government thus offered a political parallel to placing guns in the hands of the people, as the Revolution had done in its first years.

The Tribunal Popular was another, not as new, grass-roots institution: a neighborhood court empowered to conduct trials and hand down verdicts on many types of misdemeanors and felonies, especially cases of disputes between individuals. They were organized by town or city zone, with the bench drawn from residents of the area. A democratic style could also be found in the way that people became members of the Communist Party in 1967: through nomination by their fellow workers, not through being tapped by those already members. And it was good to see that this revolution has learned some things from others: nothing in Cuba can be named after a living person, nor can the image of a living personage be displayed in public places.

In general, Cuba's struggle against *burocratismo* seemed to be following the lines spelled out by Che Guevara in *Man and Socialism in Cuba:*

We are seeking something new that will allow a perfect identification between the government and the community as a whole, adapted to the special conditions of the building of socialism and avoiding to the utmost the commonplaces of bourgeois democracy (such as legislative houses, for example). . . . Some experiments have been carried out with the aim of gradually creating the institutionalization of the Revolution, but without too much hurry. We have been greatly restrained by the fear that any formal aspect might make us lose sight of the ultimate and most important Revolutionary aspiration: to see man freed from alienation.

*   *   *

When Che wrote in that same article that "society as a whole must become a huge school," he meant a total educational process which included some of the tools already mentioned here as well as Party discussions and activity; rewards and honors for Revolutionary conduct; speeches by leaders, the press, propaganda (a non-pejorative word among the Cuban people); actions designed to counteract a specific form of selfishness, such as the new oath taken by all medical school graduates that they would not go into private practice. He also meant the schools themselves and student activity. The education of youth was the Revolution's long-range hope for uprooting the old ideas associated with former class relationships and creating a new consciousness.

In the early sixties, the Revolution had reduced illiteracy to 3.9 per cent (the world's lowest rate), an achievement later verified by a United Nations team of investigators. This was only its first step in setting out to educate every citizen to his maximum ability. During 1966–67, over two million out of Cuba's eight million people were studying formally under a wide variety of programs. There were schools of agriculture, fishing, industrial technology, artisanship, languages ("The School of Easy Living"), sports; schools for workers who had become literate and wanted to go on with full-time study at government expense; schools for the Improvement of Women (sic); two provincial universities and the University of Havana, where attendance had plummeted after 1959 but then climbed back to more than its pre-Revolutionary level. Almost half a milllion adults were studying at night, many of them waging the "Battle for the Sixth Grade," a follow-up to the 1961 Literacy Campaign. But facts or figures have limited value in Cuba; statistics are not that reliable and the Revolution's style is fluidity.

"The Cubans never sat down and devised a ten-year educational plan," said a staff member of the Ministry of Education. "There was a drastic need for teachers. Most countries would have said, 'Look, we can't start massive education until we have the teachers for it and that will take X years; then we'll start.' In Cuba, many of the teachers today are students who just started teaching after a few years. It's that basic idea of the Revolution: push people into doing things they supposedly can't do." (And, he might have said, use every modern technique that helps. In 1968, many Cuban schools began to use television in the classroom—another answer to the teacher shortage.)

As a result, there was not much of an age gap between pupil and teacher in Cuba, and nobody seemed surprised that many *profesores* didn't have their degrees yet or that the head of the Philosophy Department at the University of Havana was in his early twenties. "Study" never meant pure book-learning. Students of industrial technology went out and worked in sugar refineries; students of political science and law helped to organize the Local Government structure; journalism students alternated two weeks of study with two weeks of actual work in a medium.

The combination of study with work began early in life, when primary school students entered the new *Escuela al Campo* program. For forty-five days in the summertime, they went out of the classroom and into the countryside. Between sessions of picking potatoes, planting coffee seedlings, or whatever, they continued to do regular academic work. The program applied in the secondary schools also.

Students in other programs—including advanced ones—all performed a required stint, usually forty-five days a year, of unpaid agricultural labor in the *campo*. "The combination of such work and study wasn't easy to establish," said the Ministry man, "given the old idea of school—especially higher education—as an ivory tower for the privileged." The activity of the youth in the fields had a double purpose. In a country with a labor shortage, their contribution increased production—thus helping to eliminate that scarcity which sustained old ideas. On another level, the work in itself was a way of learning to think along new, Socialist lines. The student-worker would hopefully realize that food was not goods to be bought in a store with money, but the product of someone's calloused hands and aching back. Old ideas of class status and city-country status would thus be broken down. Old ideas about work would change, and this in turn would alter old attitudes of Man toward Man. Work would become a calling, and people would labor in a context of broad, social relationship rather than in isolation or the small, closed world of immediate colleagues. Then, perhaps, human beings would achieve *compañerismo*: a word meaning not merely one-to-one unselfishness but true contact, authentic involvement with mankind.

The model held up to youth for their activity in the field (and the factory and the classroom) was that of the guerrilla fighter. Units of young agricultural workers were called brigades and columns; their progress in the *campo* was followed by the press with the same intensity as if they had been guerrillas in Guatemala or Venezuela. This gung-ho approach to underdevelopment could seem a little forced or ponderous ("Charge!"—the weeds?) but not unsuitable to Cuba's economic situation. It was a matter of life and death for the people. The guerrilla model personified the spirit of combat, of the disciplined fighter. It also embodied the spirit of initiative, of improvisation, as suggested in the newspaper article about agriculture headlined "Against Conformity and Routine: The Guerrilla Spirit."

The chief guerrilla and therefore chief teacher of the Cuban Revolution was, of course, Fidel Castro. Much has been said about Fidel as the person who basically determines Cuba's domestic and foreign policies, but it would not be a distortion to say that Fidel—like the late Malcolm X—is above all an educator of his people and constant self-educator. When he spoke in public, the scene often resembled a huge and very relaxed classroom. People ate, women nursed babies, members of the audience fainted from the heat at regular intervals and were rushed off in stretchers. Up on the platform, Fidel was educating. During a speech to inaugurate a new dam on the Isle of Pines, he mentioned that there were not yet great numbers of youth working in that area. Someone in the audience called out a few words and he replied, "No, ordering people to come here is not a good idea. The important thing is that people come on their own feet and their own initiative."

A concern with morality, especially honesty, often dominated his teachings. It seemed to be a concern based on responsibility to, and faith in, the people—not on the more common need for vice to pay tribute to virtue. In his speech at the closing of the OLAS conference, he criticized the idea that social revolution in Latin America could be accomplished without struggle—not simply on the grounds that it was unrealistic, but also because it meant *"deceiving the people."* At Gran Tierra, he talked about how outside pressures had stimulated enthusiasm in the people: "It is possible that if we had not been faced with the imperialist blockade, we would not be doing all that we are doing today. It is possible that if we had not had all those difficulties, we would not have achieved the pace of work enjoyed by the Cuban Revolution today. And that is the truth." Cuba had to face the truth; dishonesty with self would serve no purpose.

Fidel's style had great variety: he could be a superb ham actor, quoting from American press fantasies about Cuba with mock amazement; a walking encyclopedia of economic facts; an imploring mother, his voice cracking slightly; a unique world leader reading aloud the entire, lengthy text of a violent attack on himself and Cuban policy by the Venezuelan Communist Party. Indignant, funny, or serious, he was the teacher whose class you never cut or fell asleep in.

It was not only in his speeches but also in his daily confrontations with people that Fidel sought to break down old ideas about the role of the masses and to bring people into politics. In the *campo* once, he was confronted by a fifteen-year-old girl who talked to him about a certain production problem on the farm where she was working. "You," she said, using the familiar form *tu,* "you have to come here and do something." "Well, I'll come as soon as I can." "No," the girl told him, "you must come right away. And you can't just stay a short time, the way you sometimes do. You must really talk to people here because it's a big problem—understand?" He smiled, delighted: this was the kind of Cuban he wanted, not yes-men, he had frequently stated.

Fidel the Educator waged a constant struggle against old ideas about class and city-country relations. It was he who instigated the trip for foreign visitors to the wilds of Gran Tierra; it was he who had the entire, first class of doctors to graduate since the Revolution climb to the top of the highest mountain in Cuba with him to receive their diplomas, as a reminder that doctors belonged out with the people rather than in air-conditioned offices. Like the best teachers, Fidel also educated himself constantly—on every subject from cattle and new medical cures to methods for making a good lemon ice cream and bagels. The man's appetite for new techniques of potential benefit to his people seemed insatiable.

Fidel set an example for Cuban education but it was the masses of young teachers who performed the day-to-day task of shaping consciousness. And no one played a more important role in developing the New Man than the primary school teachers of the near future: those preparing to instruct the generation born since socialism was established.

In September, 1967, about 17,800 of these young people were enrolled in a five-year, three-stage training program. It began with a year at Minas del Frío in the Sierra Maestra mountains of Oriente. The students then spent two years at Topes de Collantes, in the Escambray, and two final years at the Makarenko Institute at Tarará near the city of Havana. This sequence of locales took them from a rugged mountain fastness down to urban comfort in a very deliberate educational process. Students boarded at all three schools, both because it was impossible to construct such institutions in every corner of Cuba and because it proved easier to replace old ideas with new ones in the absence of parental influence.

Minas del Frío was, first of all, a place to get to. Only trucks and jeeps could traverse the twelve kilometers of steep-angled road, creeping through wild ravines, in and out of riverbeds. The school itself seemed like an apparition amid this wildness: a little city scooped out of the mountains, with dozens of concrete dormitories and open-air classrooms sprawled across several slopes and, lying in a sort of valley, administration buildings, dining halls, storehouses. Because of continuing construction, bulldozers stood here and there; the earth was red and bare. Around and below the school, flowers and palm trees grew lush; mountains dropped away toward a vast plain stretching into the horizon. The air had an invigorating coolness. It was a beautiful spot, but why put a school here?

"There are two reasons," said the young, black sub-director of the school, looking as though he really enjoyed talking about this; "one is that at the time of the triumph of the Revolution, most teachers were used to living in the city and they liked the comfort of the city. They didn't understand the *campo*, which forms the main part of life in Cuba. We want to enable teachers to go anywhere, to teach under the most difficult circumstances. They have to learn to climb mountains and live in the way of the *campo*.

"Then, this zone has a Revolutionary history. It was the area of many battles led by Fidel and Che. The hospital and the radio station of the Rebel Army was very near here, also an abandoned mine tunnel they used as a shelter. Just a few yards from this office is the *bohio* which served as Che's command hut and a school for recruits. All this history creates a good ideological atmosphere for training teachers. They relive some of the feats of the Rebel Army—climbing mountains, withstanding cold and rain. They learn to be part of the Revolution right in the middle of Revolutionary history."

In 1960, the first people came to study in what had been the scene of guerrilla warfare only a few months before. They were taught under a tree with tablet and pencil. Slowly, better facilities were built. By 1967, Minas had fifty-seven hundred students. Three-quarters were girls; most came from *campesino* families, almost half from Oriente. (In the summer of 1968, Education Minister Jose Llanusa announced that from then on only students from Oriente would be admitted; other provinces would have their own schools.) They ranged in age from thirteen to fifteen, with some as young as eleven; the only requirements for entry were successful completion of the sixth grade and their own desire to come. The teachers were all former pupils; the oldest of them was twenty-four. "I myself first came here as a pupil, in 1962," the sub-director said.

The school year ran from January to September. The following January, the students went on to Topes de Collantes; during the three months between, they worked forty-five days and had forty-five days of vacation. While at Minas, they could not leave the premises except in the case of serious illness or family problems. "Their families come to visit them here—about five hundred people every weekend. On Mother's Day, *¡ay!*, about two thousand came." On weekends they were free from Saturday noon to Sunday noon—to write letters or take photos, to have group parties for everyone who had had a birthday that week. Sports were not obligatory. "We do prohibit smoking—if we didn't, when the students went home their parents would say that they had acquired the bad habit here. But family opposition to their children coming to Minas isn't a problem—if you have eight or nine children, having one come here is a godsend.

"Our main problem is vocation. Formerly, many students came for the glamor of being in the Sierra Maestra. Then they found out it was hard work, and quit. Today, the biggest problem is developing a sense of vocation—although that's not just a problem *here*—because how do you instill a sense of vocation in an eleven-year-old? Some ten per cent drop out in their first year. But they can be moved by history, they can respect the martyrs. When somebody says, 'Go to the mountains to teach,' they go. It is like saying, 'The Moncada must be assaulted,' and it was.

"By the time they finish at Tarará they really know what it is to be a teacher. They have climbed the Pico Turquino at least once and they are ready to go to work where they are needed— not just where they want to. So if they are needed on top of Pico Turquino, they will go there. And if they are needed in Venezuela, they will go there." The sub-director smiled, not because it was a joke (it wasn't) but with pleasure at the thought of revolutionary victories in Latin America which would call for help from Cuban personnel trained in many fields, including education.

"I don't think we will have a problem with the new generation because of the fact that it has no actual memory of the struggle against the dictatorship. The only difference between then and now lies in what you prepare to struggle against—victory over Batista or something bigger. The only difference lies in the job to be done, the role you can play. Now the role to be played is to dominate nature and to become technicians."

Living conditions for the students at Minas del Frío were styled to suit the school's purpose. The dormitories—one-story, concrete, plain but pleasant—were named after Revolutionary heroes like Conrado Benítez García, the young literacy teacher killed in the Escambray. Their decor might be called Guerrilla Modern. A small sitting area just inside the entrance contained chairs and a couch covered by folded, overlapping towels of different colors, laid side by side to form accordion pleats. Beyond that was a large, open space where hammocks hung at night; at the back stood a separate area with showers and Turkish toilets. The walls were lined with shelves and cubbyholes for personal possessions and blankets. Hammocks, folded with absolute precision like the towels, hung over the shelves as curtains during the day. The total effect of these improvisations was another image of the Cuban ability to make do—to please the eye with what's at hand.

Minas gave classes in Cuban history, biology, math, and Spanish, from eight in the morning until noon, two-thirty to about five-thirty or six, and sometimes again at night until ten. A classroom was several palm trunks holding up a roof of thatched palm leaves, plus some rough wooden benches and tables, a small blackboard. (As of January, 1969, classes would be held in new buildings. The students would sleep in bunks instead of hammocks. A host of electric and water plants, repair shops, and other new construction had also been recently completed.) The morning began with all the students standing up in their open, airy classrooms to recite, "Good morning, teacher. With more study and discipline, we shall reach the peak of advancement"—the peak being a symbolic reference to Pico Turquino. Then they sat down: about twenty-five to a class, about 60 per cent black (as might be expected in Oriente), the girls in pants and boots, everyone taking history during this first hour.

The same instruction method was used throughout the

school: a student read one or two sentences from a basic text; then the teacher lectured, amplifying on that passage and asking the class occasional questions; the student read again, and so forth. The pupils took notes quietly, some of them looking bored but most of them very attentive. The subject in all the history classes that day was Jesús Menéndez, a black, Communist union organizer of the thirties who was assassinated. He had been born poor, one teacher emphasized, and cut sugarcane to support his family.

"In 1932, he became a union organizer," she went on, "but he was not just interested in economics, he organized libraries and trips for the workers." The class scribbled away. "Menéndez was a threat to the creole bourgeoisie and to the imperialist interests," she said. "In capitalism, there are workers and bourgeoisie. But in Cuba there was an even worse enemy than the bourgeoisie—there was imperialism . . ."

The voice of a teacher in another class was shrill—a common characteristic among the staff at Minas, probably because the open classrooms stood close together and each teacher was trying to be heard clearly. This teacher announced at the beginning that if the students did well on a test the next day, they would finish history on Monday. Then she told the Menéndez story, driving home certain points about the bourgeoisie and particularly the "governors" (Presidents) of Cuba from 1902 to 1958. "Did they concern themselves with the need for hospitals?" "No," answered the class forcefully. "Did they concern themselves about the lack of schooling?" "No!" At the end of class, she asked: "We're having a test—when?" The class answered, "Tomorrow." "And if you do well, what?" The reply came promptly: "Class ends Monday." The teacher looked very pleased and put up a "five," the highest mark, for that day's work in history by that group. And so it went in several other classes, until the story of Jesús Menéndez seemed to echo across the hills.

The arithmetic, Spanish, and biology teachers used this same mechanical method (but the grammar concerned revolution instead of Dick and Jane). *"¿No hay dudas?"*—"Any questions?" —was the usual windup to any explanation, and there were rarely questions. "Unfortunately, we haven't got away from the memoristic style yet," the Ministry of Education official had said. "It was the style of education in Cuba before the Revolution—of course, it's the style of most schools in most countries. We have just about won the quantitative struggle in education; the struggle now will be qualitative."

Between three and four thousand of the students belonged to the Minas del Frío branch of the Unión de Juventud Comunista (UJC), the Communist Youth League. The UJC dates back to 1962, when it took over from the Association of Rebel Youth, founded in 1960. Members range in age from fourteen to twenty-seven (younger Cubans can be *pioneros,* pioneers). A person is invited to join by decision of existing members. He then becomes an *aspirante,* with a voice but no vote—an aspirant to becoming a *militante,* a full member who does vote. The Communist Youth are boosters and example-setters, the Jaycees of the Revolution, yet usually they also seem to include the brightest and most appealing young people in a given group. The Propaganda Secretary of the UJC at Minas was like that: a quick, pretty, mulatto girl of sixteen. One night, sitting with a group of her fellow students around a table, she almost bounced in her chair with eagerness to answer questions.

I had asked the small group their ideas about this "New Man" to whom Fidel often referred. The girl, her eyes sparkling, said, "The New Man will have a world conscience. He will have the same feeling for a Guatemalan or someone of another nationality as for a Cuban. He will be the international man." A boy of fourteen added, "The New Man will not be a corrupt man." Another youth, pale, with a meditative face, wanted to correct something: "It is not just Fidel who talks about the New Man. It is the Revolutionary government." A second girl mentioned the purpose of her present schooling: "I am not only going to teach, but to educate. I am forming myself in order to form the people of the future. We will have to be ready to go any place we are needed—Argentina, wherever—if the *campesinos* there need us."

"The New Man will be different from the old man in

other respects too," the first boy added. "For instance, the *campesinos* didn't participate in sports before—now they do. The New Man will do these things. Boxers used to kill each other to live, sports and culture were *vicios*—not ways to build physical strength, strength of character, mental strength." A black youth with deep-set, intense eyes gave his opinion: "The New Man is a man who is ready to fight anywhere and defend the Revolution."

What will Cuba be like in twenty years? I asked them. What will happen when there are more things for people to buy? Do you think there will be conflict between you and your children as Cuba changes?

Miss Propaganda Secretary started to answer, then clapped her hand over her mouth merrily to let someone else be first this time. They all recognized "the generation problem" and acknowledged that there was conflict between parents and children. But they felt sure that educational content and methods would be changed to suit the times. Cuba would just go on developing, they said. "We'll make a machine with one engine, and then two engines . . ." "The Revolution has invested a great deal in livestock, for example—this will be paying off in future years." "The investments of today will pay off and we will have a full life. And Cuba will be a Communist country." All the students leaned forward as they spoke; their tone was excited, even passionate.

"Cuba," said one boy, "will be industrialized in all aspects." But so is the United States; can that be your model? "Certain characteristics exist in the United States which prevent all the people from enjoying the fruits of industrialization," he answered. "This will not be the case in Cuba." The meditative-looking boy added, "But we cannot live well while others don't." Another youth picked up: "We will send our experience, our machines, our technology to other countries. Anyway, Man faces many problems in overcoming nature. There will be problems to solve in this world for a long time. And then," he smiled, gesturing with his hand, "there will be work to do on other planets. There is no end in sight!" Everybody looked pleased with the prospect.

Minas del Frío had a system of *monitores*, outstanding students who tutored slower ones and helped the teachers in various ways. Ricardo was one of them: slim, white, looking about fifteen, with a sweet sort of manliness. It was hard at first not to see him in a Boy Scout uniform instead of the one he wore. He must also have been very bright: he had gone to an *escuela de calle*, an ordinary primary school, and then became a *becado* (live-in scholarship student), completing the last two years in one.

Everyone at Minas, when asked about his future plans, had said, "I will go wherever I am needed—wherever the Revolution sends me." So did Ricardo. Asked if he didn't have some preference, he seemed not to understand the question at first. He stood there, in front of a dormitory just before sunset, looking puzzled. At last he said, "I would prefer the Sierra." But he continued to have trouble speaking of himself as a separate identity. Each time he was asked for his own, personal opinion, he would answer "we." Or he might speak of the broad theory involved in the particular question. Finally he said, "You mean me, my personal opinion?" But the distinction seemed irrelevant to him. Later, another student explained: "We don't think in terms of 'I' and 'you'; we think in terms of 'we'—not only 'we Cubans' but the people all over the world. Even though we are telling our personal opinions, we use 'we.' We can't think of ourselves without thinking of other people."

Although Topes de Collantes was also a little city hidden away in beautiful countryside, it seemed different from Minas in many ways. A paved road led smoothly up through the hills to a genuine town with more than one life: tile and cinder-block factories for the construction of new buildings, a dam being built, a hospital, shops, and a non-student population of one thousand workers with their families. One huge, white structure, a dormitory, dominated the scene; with its flat, many-windowed façade staring out at the mountains, it looked just like what it once was—a private sanitorium.

Living conditions were less rugged than at Minas. Most roads were paved, classes were held in concrete buildings with large blackboards and real erasers instead of rags, the students slept in beds rather than hammocks, and the girls wore skirts. The program had more variation, with such subjects as music, dance, theater, and physical education added to the basic curriculum. There were also trips to the beach and movies. Students participated in the construction work, learned how to cut hair and do manicures at the barbershop, bake at the bakery, sew at the sewing shop. They had to do twenty days of unpaid agricultural work a year; some also went on their weekend time-off, voluntarily, to help out at a nearby *granja*—if extra hands were needed. The whole scene presumed more maturity. The *monitores,* for example, were chosen by the classes themselves, not by the teachers.

Topes opened in 1962 with a thousand students; by 1967, it had seven thousand, mostly girls. Minas had been a test for them, a number of the students agreed—that was its basic meaning, a test of fortitude, sincerity, aptitude. Their comments indicated that Minas had also implanted very firmly a readiness to go "wherever the Revolution sends me." Again, several had difficulty talking about "me" as something apart from "we." Their ideas about the New Man were similar to those of the students at the Oriente school, but they used political terms like "Socialist consciousness" and they spoke more specifically about Cuba's unsatisfied economic, social, and political needs, including the fact that "there are still many who don't understand the Revolution." When they declared the educational program to be the Revolution's most important achievement, it was with a quick, warm enthusiasm; they all came from *campesino* families and none of the girls' mothers had done any kind of work except household drudgery.

Then, with hesitant politeness, came the students' request to ask questions themselves at the end of our talk. They had given up lunch in order to talk during mealtime; curiosity about the United States must have been the reason. "Does the Ku Klux Klan work with the CIA?" "Are there any revolutionaries beside the blacks?" "Will you have trouble with your government"

—the most common question asked of any American in Cuba—"when you return?" "Can you publish what you want about Cuba, if it is favorable?" When they heard the answer to that last one—in some places, yes—they asked, "The clandestine press?" and looked confused to hear "No, but . . ." It was strange, trying to explain the American press on top of a mountain in Cuba.

The teachers at Topes de Collantes seemed more relaxed and self-assured than at Minas, both in their meetings to plan the next week's work and in the classroom. One history teacher, a handsome young woman, was lecturing with no prepared text or notes and with occasional flashes of humor. It was a final, crash lecture on contemporary Cuba, because this particular group had to leave before the regular end of the year to go on a special project.

As in most Cuban classrooms, the first action of the teacher was to write the date on the board and under it, "Year of Heroic Vietnam." (Every year has its name: 1968 became "Year of the Heroic Guerrilla," in honor of Che Guevara.)* Then she plunged into "The Construction of Socialism." Under that heading came a list of the principal tasks at this current stage of Cuban history, including "Readjustment of Administrative Organization." In discussing this point, she asked for someone to define *burocratismo.* "Spending money on people in offices when it could be spent on having people do productive work," a boy answered, standing to speak as was the custom. "Yes—but there's something else." She smiled encouragement. A girl tried: "Bureaucracy is when the planners don't go to see things on the spot, they just sit in offices." Fidel would have been pleased.

The teacher went on with the seemingly endless list of tasks and got to "Defense of the *Patria.*" "Why is that important?" the teacher asked. Whereas before many hands were usually raised but not all, this time every hand in the room went up. "To protect the country against attacks by imperialism." As

---

* 1969 was named "Year of Decisive Endeavor," an echo of the Revolutionary Offensive with its goal of a ten-million-ton sugar crop in 1970.

usual, the abstract "imperialism" was used instead of "the United States." (Cubans always emphasize the systematized nature of an enemy—that which makes it an enemy—rather than the group or nation in itself, which is why any talk of Cuba "teaching hatred" seems absurd inside Cuba.)

A quick historical review followed, beginning with the 1962 Second Declaration of Havana and going on to the October (Missile) Crisis, which the teacher discussed in terms of the many imperialist threats to Cuba's existence. She put considerable precision in all her comments: "You have to understand that not all activities against Cuba are carried out by the Marines," she said at one point; "those who came to Playa Girón were mercenaries." Her tone of voice, like her facts, was straight.

She dashed through the First and Second Agrarian Reform Laws, then the Declaration of Santiago of July 26, 1964. "The Revolution is not a finished thing," she concluded the hour; "it goes on every day. The goal is to make Cuba what it should be, and the most important factor in building communism is the *formación ideológica*. None of us can consider ourselves a Communist in the true sense of the word." Then another quick, bright smile, and she scooted off to a new class.

At the Makarenko Institute near Havana, the students began practice teaching. By now they were supposed to have acquired a solid foundation of Revolutionary conscience and *campo* understanding. They could serve as a vanguard in the struggle against selfishness and, old attitudes toward work.

These students typified Cuba but they did not tell the whole story about its youth. There were older students, based in Havana, who were expected to be more sophisticated in attitude as well as conduct. If you asked anyone from Havana University or an advanced student at the Art School what he planned to do with his life, he would probably not reply, "I'll go wherever the Revolution sends me"—at least, not in those words. They seemed undogmatic, aware and curious. At the same time, there was no question about their loyalty to the Revolution.

The majority seemed to come from poor families; they knew how their parents had grown up. It was rare to find somebody like the medical student who poured forth his disgust about life in Cuba during an open-air concert of *guajiro* music one night (his particular gripes were "that crude music" and "all those black people").

Fidel Castro has said many times that the Revolution wanted youth to think for itself; that brotherhood did not mean the denial of individuality. Nonconformity was a proclaimed value. Of course, it applied only to Revolutionary institutions and ways of applying or interpreting Marxist–Leninist theory— not to the basic validity of the Revolution or its broad Communist goals. It meant imagination and initiative, a positive force in building the society—not something which was "merely against." The man or woman who blindly followed procedure in a factory, who went out for agricultural work because it was the thing to do, who declared every production problem insoluble because of the American blockade, was not the kind of worker Cuba needed.

One of the ways in which youth functioned as a nonconformist vanguard was by creating what might be called centers of "cultural guerrilla action" ("Cultural Revolution" would be too strong a term). The Philosophy Department at the University of Havana was such a center. From time to time, Fidel reportedly came around to chat with students and teachers (or student-teachers) there; he would listen to what was on their minds, perhaps drop an idea which he would not present in a public speech, and leave them to raise a little hell. The subject could be the irrelevance of the university's economics curriculum to the nation's actual needs, the deficiencies of Cuban television programs, or old-fashioned sexual mores. Some of these young people, together with others from different departments, edited a magazine called *Pensamiento Critico* (Critical Thought). It began appearing in 1967: an attractive, imaginatively illustrated combination of political, economic, and social analysis by Marxist and non-Marxist writers. Its editors seemed Revolutionary, critical and humanistic: among the likely candidates to fill that need for better second-level leadership of which many Cubans spoke.

At Havana's School of Art, a little war was being waged against mechanistic, non-correlative education by a young teacher working with eight- and nine-year-old *becados* (live-in scholarship students). Seeking to interrelate the arts as opposed to teaching each in isolation, he had his pupils compose a story together—one beginning it and then each carrying the tale forward until the last ended it. The pupils then took the story and made it into a dance within a week, from choreography to costumes, without teacher interference. The final product was performed before and criticized by other students of the same age.

Another kind of "guerrilla center" had been created by a group of young journalists. In general, Cuba's press was not one of its greatest triumphs. From the viewpoint of news presentation, it lacked variety and depth. As for content . . . well, there was a Cuban joke which told how, for one of the annual January 1 parades of the Armed Forces, Fidel invited Hannibal, Caesar, and Napoleon. When the columns of soldiers marched by, Hannibal said, "Ah, if I had had an army like that, I could have conquered the world!" As the tanks and guns rolled by, Caesar said, "Oh, if I had had all that, the Roman Empire would never have fallen." When the rockets and guided missiles started coming, Fidel turned to Napoleon. Old Bonaparte had been reading a newspaper all through the parade and Fidel was baffled by his apparent disinterest. He finally burst out, "Listen, haven't you got anything to say?" "Wow," said Napoleon, "if I had had a newspaper like this, nobody ever would have found out about Waterloo!" In 1967, a publishing enterprise called *Juventud Rebelde* (Rebel Youth) was attempting to fill that kind of gap.

The offices of *Juventud Rebelde*, which housed a daily paper by the same name and several magazines, suggested the nature of the enterprise as a critic of the Revolution—within the Revolution. Photos of Fidel and Che hung in the reception room, with Lenin in the library, while a back room where the cartoonists worked had its walls covered with mottoes and satirical sketches: "This is a job for Superman" (in English), *MAD* magazine clips, mildly pornographic drawings of women, a drawing of a grotesque mouth with huge teeth and "The Voice of Truth" coming out between them in a balloon.

Of the publications which emerged from here, *Caimán Barbudo* was most notable for its seriousness and sophistication, its delving into philosophical or cultural issues not raised elsewhere. *Juventud Rebelde*, a daily with much flair in its format, acted as a voice for people's complaints about public services and snooped out bureaucratic goofs. "Why have these goods been on the docks for a year?" the paper asked one day, in a section devoted to raising such questions. The article went on to present long columns of facts and figures about the undelivered cargoes of eighty-six ships from different countries. Another story told about the six hundred metric tons of butter which spoiled in storage, and why. One article, headlined "And These Things—Why Do They Happen?" asked, among other dramatic questions, "Why did the Spam spoil?" It seems that some workers in a former Swift factory broke their backs to produce a large quantity of Spam, and then half a million cans had to be pulled out of distribution. (In 1968, *Juventud Rebelde* published few exposés of this type. *Caimán Barbudo* continued to cover cultural debates but the mass press had been mobilized behind the Revolutionary Offensive with its goal of a ten-million-ton sugar harvest in 1970.)

On the teen-age level, nonconformity in 1967 meant what might be called the Battle for the Mini-Skirt. Sitting in a Havana *cafetería* at 1 A.M., a sixteen-year-old student from a special science school explained this revolution-within-the-Revolution.

"We—my student friends here in the city—we like the *campo* but not its culture. Until recently, however, there was a ban on many 'foreign' styles, like modern music" (meaning everything new and popular in the West), "mini-skirts and short hair styles on girls, tight pants and long hair on boys. Then in July, there was a Party-sponsored *fiesta* at my school, where we had all those things and played tapes of modern music. It was the first such party. People have come to understand that those things did not have to be rejected just because they typify the *enfermitos*." The *enfermitos*, little sick ones, referred to a category of apolitical youth whose main concerns were clothes, hipness, and having a swinging time. Sometimes they were homosexuals, but not always. "Tight pants or modern music don't have to be a way of life," the science student went on, "they can just be enjoyed as pleasures."

A teacher at one of the language schools in Havana talked about how, at one time, the mini-skirt was a big issue among her students. "One girl, a member of the Juventud Comunista—they are usually sort of square—said, 'The others can wear mini-skirts if they want to, but I think they are immoral and I won't wear one until the Revolution tells me to.' A month or two later, she showed up in one." The so-called modern music was played now in the teacher's school, for fifteen minutes every morning in the classrooms before the beginning of the first period. And over the radio everywhere, night and day, came a non-stop flow of the Beatles, Rolling Stones, Charles Aznavour, cha-cha.

The Battle for the Mini-Skirt was tricky business. On the one hand, it would be easy to see the "modern" fashions as reinforcing the imitativeness and cultural penetration which typified colonial Cuba and still characterized the island in 1967: from the nationwide fascination with baseball to the special Sunday supplement for children with its little paper dolls to cut out and dress. Politically, the fashions could be seen as symbols of urban bourgeois status in the continuing class struggle.

On the other hand, the mini-skirt symbolized the struggle against a sectarianism that saw Western culture per se as decadent and counter-Revolutionary. After reaching a peak in 1961, sectarianism had continued to be a force in the society; the ending of opposition to Mod styles *because they are Western* reflected what should be its final waning.

But sectarianism was not just an invention of Escalante and his faction. It fed on popular values having nothing to do with "Western," such as *machismo*. These were the deeper sources of conflict. At that level, the Battle for the Mini-Skirt represented a struggle against taboos based on ignorance, against sexual hypocrisy, against old-fashioned notions of masculinity. Opposition to cultural nonconformity thrived on leftover values in the people themselves.

Fidel and other leaders did not care how long a person wore his hair or how short her skirt as long as it was not done in the Army or the classroom, and as long as the person was Revolutionary. This meant going to school or doing productive work. Vanguard workers could (and sometimes did) wear whatever styles they liked and get away with it; a girl in a mini-skirt who hung around the Capri all day and night, sometimes engaging in prostitution with foreigners or even in actual counter-Revolutionary deeds, would not. It wasn't a matter of opposition to Western culture but of Revolutionary demands that anyone living off the work of the people must be useful.

Fidel's position on cultural nonconformity was straight. But in the larger picture of Cuban youth and their schooling, some potentially troublesome contradictions appeared. The Revolution seemed to expect New Men with a creative, nonconformist mentality to emerge from an educational experience that was not nonconformist. In theory, there was nothing wrong with encouraging nonconformist thought within a broad Revolutionary conformity. Such a dialectic typified Fidel's style, the Cuban style. But it might prove difficult in practice.

An American student at Harvard College, Thomas Reston, spent two months in Cuba in 1967 and concluded that the guerrilla model held up to Cuban youth contained inherent contradictions which would eventually become antagonistic. The guerrilla should be both individualistic and disciplined, self-sufficient yet collective in his outlook. This duality, Reston said, is now stabilized by Fidel Castro who personally combines a bourgeois, civil libertarian concern for "individual freedom" with a revolutionary commitment to Socialist types of freedom. But can that stability be maintained? How to harmonize Che Guevara's guerrilla dictum of "Each man his own commander" and the slogan "Commander-in-Chief, give your orders!"?

The existence of such contradictions was suggested by some

comments of the sixteen-year-old science student talking in the Havana *cafetería*. He liked his school, an untypical institution which trained science researchers and teachers rather than technicians. Asked about the nature of such research in Cuba, he said, "There is no science for the sake of science here." He obviously meant that in Cuba science must serve humanity, but his single, flat statement showed no patience for going into the question. He discussed the Communist Youth League at the school, which included 71 per cent of the student body. "Those who work at the school—the teachers and other staff—have their own base unit. They do not belong to the student unit. That's not a good idea," he said thoughtfully, "because, although there is little difference in age and basic goals, there must be some conflict."

He, however, was not a member: "I was turned down because of being 'too *auto-suficiente.*' " The term means self-sufficient in the sense of unable to work with others, not adaptable to group decision-making, even arrogant. It did not seem a far-fetched criticism, given some moments in the discussion that night when he leaped to demolish other people's arguments before they had been fully set forth. "But they are going to help me overcome it," he added, "and I hope to be admitted soon."

He talked at length about his rejection and hope of acceptance. They concerned him very much, perhaps because of his background. "My family is very bourgeois," he had explained earlier in a hard voice. "Most of them have left. My father is working in a bank in Iowa. My mother is still here—she's very Revolutionary. But you know," he went on in another vein, "workers leave too—it's true, why should we hide it?" This was a complicated young man: trying too hard to prove himself with dogmatic statements, yet also intelligent and independent-minded.

In speaking of his own generation, however, he seemed at ease and secure. "We have a good relationship with the teachers. The students challenge them all the time—they ask questions during class and outside the classroom. A teacher may spend a whole class period answering one student's question. Or

130

a special lab might be conducted to prove who is right—sometimes the teacher is proved right, and sometimes the student," he smiled. "Also we have meetings with the teachers where we argue about everything from food to exams, and try to improve things . . ." The Cuban youth had no special respect for teachers as such, no special respect for older people as such.

"You know, this is a funny country," the student ended. "I just read *Don Quijote* all the way through, not only some excerpts in one of those terrible anthologies. And Cuba today is a sort of combination of Don Quijote and Sancho Panza—the idealist and the pragmatist. Our generation has a perfect balance of Revolutionary spirit"—enthusiasm, spontaneity—"and Revolutionary conscience"—discipline, selflessness. "I think the next generation will have more conscience and less spirit."

No one can yet say whether the Revolution will succeed in making something that can be called a New Man. Mass education began only a few years ago; economic problems place limits on what can be done and work still has a compulsory aspect. Yet even the present generation of youth is in many important ways a different breed from its predecessor.

The young people of Cuba had a sense of common purpose that amazed the most skeptical visitor to the island. This spirit was focused on both national and international ideals, with no conflict between the two apparent among the young. Nationally, they had a deep awareness of Cuba's situation as a tiny country with a colossus breathing down its back and allies of the colossus all around it. Playa Girón, subsequent CIA-sponsored operations, the Missile Crisis, and the blockade confirmed the obvious: the United States wished to see the Cuban Revolution destroyed, and Cuba would have to count primarily on itself for defense.

The motto for youth was therefore *Estudio, Trabajo, Fusil*—literally Study, Work, Gun, but usually translated Study, Work, Defense. The military aspect of that slogan showed itself mainly in the formations and marching by students at many schools, and in the compulsory performance of three years' service in the Army by young men between seventeen and twenty-seven. But the total picture was not as militaristic as this might sound. Many youths were exempted from the three years' service if they were students of medicine or in technical fields. If you were in certain work programs, which included extensive military training, you did not have to do an Army stint. In fact, so many students were getting military training as part of their educational or work experience that the Army did not represent a separate life style so much as one form of an activity in which everyone was somehow engaged—for reasons, beyond question, of defense only.

The dedication of the youth did not seem imposed from above, even in the didactic atmosphere of Minas del Frío. For one thing, Cuban history had a revolutionary continuity; Socialist Cuba could be seen as the current stage of a struggle for liberation—from colonialism and then capitalism—which formally began in 1868 and stretched over the next hundred years (with black revolts dating even farther back). Historic inspiration abounded. There was also youth's growing sense of personal investment in Cuba's survival and growth, acquired through the work they performed on the land. Finally, there was the current generation struggle.

Students and other youth all over the island told stories of ideological disputes with their parents. A girl described how she had gone to teach in the 1961 Literacy Campaign after long arguments with her parents and against their wishes; a boy recounted how his father told him that if he left home to do agricultural work, he could never return (the son did leave). Youthful rejection of parental ways and control coincided with the Revolution's needs. A striking degree of solidarity existed between the youth and the nation's leadership, parallel to the lack of identification between youth and parents.

The nationalism of young Cubans bore no resemblance to chauvinism. Cuba's geography, history, and culture had always militated against the arrogance of power; now socialism identified national ideals with international ones and Cuba's progress was seen as humanity's progress. In 1967, the youth seemed to be embracing wholeheartedly the idea that in the event of conflict between the goal of a higher standard of living in Cuba and the goal of aiding the world revolutionary struggle, the latter had priority. The idea, furthermore, had old roots. Fidel's message that "Cuba cannot be Communist until the whole world is Communist" was essentially a modern version of José Martí's words: "As long as there is one man who sleeps in the mud, there should not be another who sleeps in a bed of gold."

The internationalist consciousness of Cuban youth was developed not only in the classroom but by their total environment. Pictures, slogans, the names given to state farms and agricultural camps, all taught young Cubans to think of their lives as intimately related to revolution elsewhere—especially in the Americas. In the world where people carried on their day-to-day lives, there were light bulbs, thermos bottles, and mimeograph stencils from China; the wheat in a bakery from Canada; radios made in Cuba from Polish parts; alarm clocks from Russia and woven bags from Vietnam; medicines made in Cuba from Italian chemicals; buses on the street from England; trucks, jeeps, and planes from the Soviet Union, with trucks sometimes from France as well. All this created a much more favorable climate for internationalism than the days when almost every import came from one country—a nation now represented on the Cuban scene by an aging, carefully preserved Cadillac.

To say that Cuban youth bore no trace at all of ideas rooted in the former class structure would be false. And to predict what the next generation will be like in this respect would be foolish. The young people were surely more selfless and community-oriented than any preceding generation. They were also fascinated by consumer goods. They had money and couldn't spend it because almost nothing except necessities could be found in the stores. Also, Cuba was isolated from the world of teen-age goodies; few citizens could travel. When foreign visitors brought that world with them, even a cheap plastic pocketbook intrigued the kids because it symbolized outside contact. All this was truer of youth in Havana—where the visitors spent most of their time and where there were the most foreign movies and music—than in the rural areas. But still, where would it lead? The pull of continued scarcity on new ideas had unpredictable force, and the pull of human habit must not be underestimated.

Yet it was possible and beautiful to feel how human consciousness might be changed. After two months in Cuba, where the only advertisements to be seen or heard were for the Revolution and its values (with the exception of an occasional, small billboard about an INIT tourism facility or airline service), the sound of that Miami radio station with its long commercial for Jordan's Furniture Sale seemed to be coming from a very distant and unappealing planet. People could kick the habit of compulsive consumption, you felt, especially if there was nothing to buy—but more important, if there were other things to do which made life seem creative and exciting. To make a call from a public telephone booth without paying anything, as became possible all over Cuba in 1967, shook up your idea that the exchange of money was basic to modern life, and thereby brought into question old ideas about human relations. To see public transportation fares going consistently down instead of up—perhaps that's just too much for an American city-dweller to absorb. For the Cuban citizen, money has come to mean less in a real sense; the visitor, no matter how rich or poor, comes to share this feeling.

A moneyless society was not yet around the corner but it was planned and much discussed. Life already had a quality not to be imagined in capitalist countries—except, perhaps, in the dreams of some of *their* youth. "Here, you feel like a roll of dollar bills," said an eighteen-year-old American high school student from a small town on his return after a month's visit to Cuba. "What you are worth depends on how big the roll is. In Cuba, you feel like a human being."

Along with all the theories and institutions, there were individual educators in Cuba whose humanism and strength made it seem possible for a new consciousness to evolve. Fidel Castro has been mentioned; there were others. One of them was a director of the Ciudad Escolar de Camilo Cienfuegos in Oriente province.

The "School City" which he helped to administer turned out agricultural technicians. It deserved that name; twelve thousand youths lived in six compounds on eleven thousand hectares of ground, including farmlands and grazing areas for the rice and beef grown by the school. Almost all were sons of small farmers or agricultural workers from isolated areas. There was no scholarship standing required for entrance, only an age of fifteen years; some at that age had finished no more than three years of school. They studied the usual basic subjects and normally stayed four to five years, depending on their entrance level. When they left, they had finished ninth grade.

The director was older than most Cuban administrators—about forty—and looked lean and gentle, the classic professor. Sitting at a table in the small, well-furnished dining room of a guest house, he spoke slowly and emphatically about Cuban education. "Cuba has had to have 'a revolution within the Revolution' in its educational system," he said. This has taken place in accordance with the development of our present idea that an underdeveloped country is not simply one that lacks industry. It can also mean an agricultural nation which lacks the technology for maximum production. Before, we aimed to industrialize in the conventional sense of that word—now we have a new goal, the full modernization of agriculture.

"Look, all education serves the prevailing system. In a capitalist country, they must develop an educational system which serves the ruling classes—if they didn't, they would not only be making a mistake, they would be committing a political crime. Here, too, we must have an educational system which serves the ruling class. But here, that class is frankly meant to be the working class—the workers and *campesinos*. Here, therefore, the need now is to develop agricultural technicians as fast as possible in order to produce more wealth and give the people a better life."

"But what happens," asked an American student visiting the

school that day, "when experts are needed for that production yet promising students are not considered sufficiently pro-Revolutionary to be trained? Students have been refused entrance to the university for that reason. Doesn't Cuba's development require their skills more than their political loyalty?"

At first the man ducked the question: "As long as they do not harm the Revolution, they can go to the university." Then he said, "Look, it is the people who pay for those students' education—it is the people who grow the food they eat. What if we train those students for several years and then they leave? We have no assurance that they won't. We cannot take that chance when it is the people who pay." He paused. "And there is another point. How, we must ask, can an intelligent man see all the good that has been done in Cuba and deny it—unless he is, in fact, lacking in intelligence? In which case, he does not belong in a university anyway."

"We do not form technicians to go out and make money tomorrow," he went on, "but to be of service—to go where they are needed, including outside the country. *Patria* is a relative term. Fundamentally, a crime in Alaska concerns a Mexican and vice versa—a crime against man is a crime.

"When students first come here, they undergo a discipline which is almost military. Gradually we apply new kinds of discipline. For example, at first one student may say to another, 'Hey, fasten your shoe laces, here comes the *comandante*.' But that is acting out of fear—of being punished, like the fear of God before. After a while, he says, 'Fasten your shoe laces, that's not the way to go around here.' Some of the students cannot adjust and have to leave. But we believe in the New Man.

"It is like this. Our generation—my generation—is not free from the influence of laws and morality and customs which existed under capitalism. But the idea that you ate today and will eat tomorrow changes the attitude of a people. They realize that power is in their hands. If a man can work and eat and go to the hospital and get medicine free and send his child to school, he knows that this isn't thanks to God but to his own power. He is the state. The masses, the people of Cuba, also know that it is up to them to defend that state—that is, the Revolution. We intend the new generation to be free from the ideas which influenced us—and this will be the New Man.

"We have seen how new generations that did not experience the overthrow of a dictatorship might take the achievements of a revolution for granted. We have seen how this can happen in other countries," he said, without mentioning their names. "We have had some bitter experiences, such as during the October Crisis when some people"—mentioning no names again—"said, 'Butter yes, Cuba no.'

"But to accept the idea that Man must inevitably be corrupted by having things, is to deny the goodness of Man, to deny justice, humanism. Look, the United States has great potential but that potential is used for evil. Does this mean that the people of the United States lack goodness? No. Well, perhaps they have been so deeply infected by the system—almost like an epidemic—that it sometimes seems as though the sensibilities of the American people have been killed. They do not want to face the reality of what their system does to the peoples of the world.

"We cannot accept the idea that it is inevitable for Man to be evil. We believe we *can* develop in youth the goodness which Man contains—and that will be the New Man. He might develop naturally, just as there has been a historical development which took Man from communalism to feudalism to capitalism and now to socialism. But why wait? I think we must create him. Let us not talk only about Man as he is, but about his possibilities."

Colony Within the Colony

"Cubano es más que blanco, más que negro"
José Martí

White supremacy, another old idea rooted in Cuba's past society, is probably the most delicate and muddled issue that can be raised about the island today. Among Americans, particularly Afro-Americans, the issue can be a burning one. They look to Cuba both for perfection and weaknesses; the truth tends to get lost in the shuffle. For the truth about Cuban race relations has several, co-existing levels, like an ancient city where archaeologists uncover one settlement only to dig deeper and find another—and beneath that, yet another. The visitor can easily make the mistake of concluding that any one of the levels represents all there is to know.

At the first level of perception, it was clear in 1967 that racism as it once existed in Cuba had been wiped out. A liberation had taken place which no other multiracial society could match. On a second, deeper level, it was possible to conclude that certain forms of cultural racism still existed; that many Cuban whites still harbored attitudes which bore a chilling resemblance to those of paternalistic whites and sometimes outright racists in the United States. On a third level, the race situation in Cuba was to be seen within its Cuban cultural framework and its Cuban political context. One had to speak, finally, about Cuba and no other country: a Socialist, Caribbean, mulatto nation whose counterpart exists nowhere.

No outsider can understand the Cuban racial scene in all its complexity and perhaps nobody should attempt to do so without spending years on the island. But so many rumors have circulated in the United States, so many hasty judgments have been made, so much sensitivity has developed about the relationship between socialism and racism generally, that it is time for somebody to begin even a superficial analysis of the situation. One way to do that is by looking at each of those three levels in turn, as they might come into the outsider's view.

Before the Revolution, the blacks and mulattos of Cuba* endured the same types of exploitation as poor whites, but with the added oppression of racism. They formed a colony-within-the-colony of cane-cutters, maids, shoeshine "boys," and newspaper vendors, plus a small black bourgeoisie of doctors, lawyers, politicians. According to a 1931 census, black Cuban farmers owned only 11% of all land-holdings (compared to 74% for white Cubans), and these had less than 8% of the total value of rural properties. A young black woman might be in high demand as prostitute or cabaret dancer but little else. Blacks, in short, did the dirtiest work and for the least pay. At the very bottom of the scale were the Haitians and Jamaicans, who had been herded onto boats like cattle and brought to Cuba to cut cane. Housed in ghettos at the sugar *centrales*, treated like lepers by everyone, they received even lower wages than

* "Black" and "mulatto" are used here despite the fact that variations in skin color combined with variations in features make those terms inadequate. In this chapter, they often mean nothing more than dark and light brown.

other blacks and experienced a brutalization unmatched since the original enslavement of Africans.

At the parks, whites sat on benches while black people had to stand along the sides; in Santiago, there were separate clubs for white, mulatto, and black. Luxury hotels, restaurants, beaches, social and sporting clubs were closed to blacks. Interracial marriage led to ostracism.

With the Revolution, all overt forms of racism came to an end. Not only did social segregation pass away but, more important, racism in work relations. The first and second Agrarian Reform Laws changed life for thousands of black agricultural laborers and farmers. The Urban Reform Law put blacks into decent housing. Education opened up totally; the successful campaign against illiteracy was particularly important for black Cubans who had previously formed the largest group of illiterates. Thus the vicious circle of institutional racism (access to decent work, education, housing, and health facilities denied to blacks because of their poverty, which arose in turn from those denials) was broken once and for all. In the field of culture, the Revolution established many centers for the study of Afro-Cuban dances and music—despite the fact that their basis is religious, and religion is discouraged as being detrimental to the building of a modern, Socialist society. Fidel Castro also lifted the ban on the Afro-Cuban religious ceremonies.

Racism in the sense of the subordination of one racial group by another for the benefit of the oppressing group did not exist in Cuba in 1967. It was over, finished; socialism ruled out any such form of oppression. The Revolution had put the impoverished masses in power—and most blacks belonged to that class. The basic needs to which the state addressed itself were the basic needs of black Cubans. Conflict of interests along a color line was a thing of the past. Not only a decent life but a new dignity had become available to black Cubans for the first time. And whites began to be freed from whiteness. They stopped using words like *niche* or *macri* (nigger) and *negrada* (a bunch of niggers). Even better, the phrase *gente de color* (colored people) gave way to *negros* (blacks) among most whites. Where the previous society's institutions and authority had all stood behind racism, the Revolution stood against it. Fidel Castro established an equality based on fact and backed by moral force; more, he unified Cuba's people for the first time in history.

But something was still wrong.

You could see it almost immediately, in the posters. In a country where blacks constitute some 35 to 45 per cent of the population, black faces might appear when the picture showed a group but rarely when only one or two individuals were depicted. A typical sign was the big one on the road from the airport into the capital town of the Isle of Pines: "Welcome," it said, while a blond girl with Caucasian features waved her straw hat next to a slightly tanned white boy with similar features (the blond hair was doubly disturbing in this nation where even most white women are brunet). The pair certainly did not resemble the majority of youths actually working in the fields on the Isle of Pines.

There was something wrong about the illustrated certificate given to students graduating from secondary school, with its drawing of a prototype white kid. It did not help to learn that the artist was black.

In a summer, 1967, issue of *Mujeres*, Cuba's magazine for women, not a single dark face appeared among the forty-eight pages of fashion photographs and drawings.

Again, something was troubling about the top leadership. With rare exceptions like Juan Almeida, head of the army —long a province of blacks, for economic and historic reasons —that leadership was white. The same held true for the higher echelons of the Party. Lower down the scale, blacks were much more numerous; they held high posts in school administration, for example. But come to the bottom, there they were again: maids in the white folks' kitchens, street cleaners, ditch diggers. Whites and mulattos did this work also, but the honors seemed to go disproportionately to black Cubans.

Then you began to hear or feel it, a phrase or a look now and then. A passenger got into a taxi and the driver began talking about an accident he had just seen. "How badly was the person hurt?" asked the rider. "Oh, it was just a little *mulatto*," the middle-aged driver answered. An interracial couple checked into a small hotel; the elderly white desk clerk frowned violently while they registered and glared at them entering the elevator. A music student talked about how her mother "would just die" if she married a black man. A black singer in his mid-twenties told the story of how he had been with a lyric opera company in the province of Pinar del Río about two years earlier; as its best tenor, he was the obvious choice for the male lead in a planned production of *La Verbena de la Paloma*. Denied the role because the girl who would be playing the female lead was white, he appealed to the local Party office. That office upheld the decision for "aesthetic reasons."

Something was wrong, and it needed to be examined.

A quick glance at the history of Cuba suggests that it would have been impossible for any regime to stamp out racism altogether in a few years. The island saw its original, Indian population exterminated by Spanish genocide of various kinds (murder, overwork, imported disease), though not without a long, often heroic resistance; the importation of slaves, mostly from west and central Africa, beginning on a large scale in 1524; slave revolts starting in 1533 and not ending until abolition, over three centuries later. Slavery in Cuba presented a familiar scene. There were the bloodhounds and the whips; there were the mulattos begotten by white masters on black slave women.

A census taken in 1774 registered a population of some ninety-six thousand whites together with seventy-five thousand blacks and mulattos (both slave and "free"). In 1791, long-standing fears of a black uprising turned into terror when whites began arriving in Cuba from Haiti and telling of the slave rebellion there—an event that was to haunt white Cubans for decades. By 1817, the census showed free and slave blacks as 54 per cent of the population. Despite the official ending of slave trade, that proportion stood until about 1850.

It was in the first quarter of the nineteenth century that the slave trade reached its peak—and the movement against Spanish rule began in earnest. The growing number of slaves saw independence from Spain as a means of freedom for themselves; in fact, they started the struggle. But whites—the *Criollos* or Creoles, as they were called—remained divided for years. Many slave-owners and traders wanted freedom from Spain in order to achieve annexation to the United States, because they counted on the United States to maintain slavery in Cuba. They were frightened by the Haitian experience and feared the so-called *ennegrecimiento* (absorption of whites by blacks) of Cuba— "the black peril." The fact that a black man, Jose Antonio Aponte, led one of the first conspiracies against Spain in 1812, for which he was hung, made them not hopeful of change but more frightened. Other Creoles opposed annexation in favor of a reformed Spanish rule, but they too wanted slavery untouched.

Meanwhile, advances in sugar production techniques, and the climate of agitation, made blacks press harder. Slave uprisings and the number of runaway slaves grew. A wave of repression swept Cuba, its high point being 1844: "The Year of the Lashings," when the colonial hierarchy launched a campaign of genocide against blacks. It was only in the 1860's—also the time of the South's defeat in the American Civil War—that the annexation movement as well as reformism began giving way to those who wanted an armed struggle for full independence. They argued that slavery must be abolished, many of them because black troops were necessary to an armed struggle.

The War of Independence broke out in 1868 and Antonio Maceo, a "free person of color" in charge of guerrilla units in Oriente, began a brilliant career that was to last almost thirty years. The following year, slavery was abolished in the Central District, which the rebels by then controlled. But conservatives still pressed to appease the slave-owners. Meanwhile, blacks came to form a high proportion—some say 85 per cent—of the fighting forces; "The Lion of Oriente" (as Maceo came to be known), Guillermo Moncada, Mariana Grajales, would later be national heroes. Now, however, Maceo was slandered as favoring black soldiers over white and seeking domination of the island.

Spain fanned this fire with statements that the War of Independence was a race war; one Cuban historian says that Spain further tried to encourage disunity by spreading the rumor, after Maceo died in battle, that he had actually been murdered by a white compatriot. So powerful was this tide against Maceo that it halted the independence struggle at one point. Spain had compelled its opponents to sign a treaty, giving up their arms; Maceo announced that he did not accept the treaty and would fight on. He did, but in the face of racist opposition he could not save the cause. Cuba's forces were defeated in 1878, the end of the Ten Years' War; reformists and annexationists wearing a new dress called "autonomy" began to revive in the climate of defeatism. Then one of the few white *independistas* who spoke out against racism again and again appeared on the scene—José Martí, who rallied support for continued armed struggle. Martí died in battle against Spain, in 1895, but his dream of independence was soon to be fulfilled.

Cuba's status as a Spanish colony came to an end in 1898. Its status as an unofficial American colony began in 1902. What that would mean for black people became clear during the United States military occupation between those two dates, when blacks and mulattos were prohibited from joining the Havana police force—supposedly to avoid clashes with the Yankee troops, mostly Southerners. In effect, Uncle Sam sabotaged the push toward liberation by black and antiracist white independence leaders. Fear of "the black peril" diminished under Tío Sam. Then, over the years, Spanish immigration to Cuba became heavy as economic conditions in Europe worsened; before and during World War II, Jewish refugees also increased the white population. Thus the estimated 55 to 65 per cent white majority of today, although some black Cubans question that figure.

It should not be hard to imagine the racial attitudes and practices that Americans usually brought with them to Cuba—the cattle ranchers to Camagüey, the military men to Guantánamo, and the business types to Havana. Under their influence, racism settled in for another half century. Blacks remained poor or precariously established in the petty bourgeoisie; mulattos took their places according to whether they tried to pass (and could) or whether they considered themselves black and were thus treated. Two popular sayings told the story:

"Children are born to be happy; blacks are born to steal chickens."

"White is a career, mulatto is an illusion, black is coal that you find anywhere."

The Revolution thus inherited a mess: the mentality left behind by slavery, an old idea as lingering and resistant to change as any on this earth. Fidel Castro went to work against the past a few months after the overthrow of Batista, with his lengthy and historic speech of March 22, 1959, asserting "The Rights of the Black Man in Cuba." He emphasized above all the need to end racial discrimination in work centers: "It should not be necessary to pass a law," he said, "to establish a right which a person has by the simple fact of being a human being and a member of society. It should not be necessary to pass a law against prejudice. What must be legislated is anathema for and public condemnation of everyone who is full of prejudices from the past. . . . We are going to end racial discrimination in the work centers by making a campaign to end that hateful and repulsive system, with one motto: *work opportunities for all Cubans, without discrimination of race or sex. . . .* Let white and black unite to end racial discrimination. And thus we shall proceed, step by step, to create our new homeland."

From creating a new material reality Fidel went on to talk about the need to end an educational system which separated black and white and thus later separated them socially. "What should we do?" he asked. "Unify our public schools, bring to them all the necessary resources; not just buildings but also clothes for the children, breakfast, lunch, dinner too if necessary; build recreational fields in the schools where black and white will play together." His position was therefore not limited to general moralistic preaching about how everyone is really equal; he sought to change the actual conditions which bred the old attitudes.

René Depestre, a Haitian poet who had arrived in Cuba the

day before that speech after a long exile from his homeland, wrote a moving account (published in the Casa de las Américas magazine) about how he and Cuban blacks felt upon hearing Fidel's words—and what followed. Most white Revolutionaries welcomed it, he said, but many members of the petty bourgeoisie reacted as if Fidel had just invited all blacks to—what else?—marry their daughters, of course. Counter-Revolutionaries spread rumors to that effect. White ladies left the island, declaring that, ever since Fidel's speech, "those blacks have become impossible." Three days after the speech, Fidel went on television to reassure people that the Revolution wasn't going to tell anybody who to dance with—and then went on to blast "those who call themselves Christians and are racists; those who call themselves Martí-followers and are racists; those who think they are educated and are racists." He might have added, wrote Depestre, those who call themselves Revolutionaries and are racists.

The press followed up Fidel's speeches with similar declarations and articles. Then, as the early years of the Revolution passed, this kind of campaign waned. Since the institutionalization of equality had been achieved, it was apparently considered unnecessary to push further. That seemed to be the general position of the nation's officials, both black and white.

Officials often acknowledged that remnants of prejudice existed and that the economic position of blacks, as well as their participation in leadership, could stand improvement. But with less than a decade of equal educational opportunity, they argued, it was too soon for blacks to have overcome all past disadvantages. A generation or two of equality would wipe out that heritage. White prejudice, they said, was mostly to be found in older people. The youth were growing up free from such attitudes. As for the current leadership, one white *comandante* pointed out that most of it had inevitably emerged from the struggle against Batista and particularly from the July 26 Movement—which happened to be dominated by whites (often *criollos,* first-generation Cubans like Fidel whose parents emigrated to the island from Spain). The old leaders would be supplemented by new ones, including black ones, in due time.

146

Black students were indeed flooding into the schools under a system which made minimal demands for admission. They were also flooding out, into administrative and technical jobs rarely before open to blacks. With the acquisition of education and experience, as well as the arrival of a new generation, black political leaders should increase in numbers. In the Party, purely Revolutionary criteria were applied to determine basic admission, but education and experience played a role in deciding who got the higher posts. So while the Party had many black *members*, whites were more numerous in the upper echelons because of past advantage. This too probably will change in time.

The white officials were also correct in saying that young white Cubans were growing up with racial attitudes different from those of their parents. One among many examples of this was given by that young black singer who had quit his light-opera company because of prejudice. Now organizing the chorus of an agricultural camp on the Isle of Pines, he was asked if he could have encountered such prejudice on the Isle—which is dominated by young workers. "No," he answered immediately.

But to American ears, the officials' arguments could sound distressingly like all the excuses given to black Americans and other colonized peoples over the years—all the arguments about being "qualified" before you can hope for power, all the stalling and gradualism. It is difficult for North Americans to imagine a society in which the ideological forces mold *non-* or *anti*-racist rather than racist attitudes. At the same time, one can still ask: Will the new generation really grow up free of all racist values— especially in the areas of culture, aesthetics, and sexual relationships? What about the conscious or subconscious effect on young minds of those posters and other symbols? Shouldn't they be carefully examined and evaluated?

It was inevitable, and nothing to be ashamed of, to find remnants of prejudice after so few Revolutionary years. For centuries "black" in Cuba, as elsewhere, had been synonymous with everything bad: ignorance, witchcraft, "vulgarity," sin, and especially sexual aggressiveness. But should such deeply rooted notions be expected to wither away by themselves? Especially on an island surrounded by, or dealing with, nations whose more subtle racism could penetrate all sorts of images, books, songs, even the labels on their products—like the jar of hand cream from Spain that said "to whiten your hands . . ." ? It is a basic principle of the Cuban Revolution that a new mentality must be programmatically developed along with new production relations and other new material realities; that one cannot sit back and wait for it to emerge by itself. If this was needed to get rid of egoism, might not something similar be needed for racist ideas?

Cubans used to say, "Blacks are born to steal chickens"; now people happily quoted the old proverb, "Those of us who are not from the Congo are from the Carabalí tribe." But that was misleading insofar as it suggested that all Cubans fully accepted their African blood; that all Cubans would be happy to have thick lips and kinky hair; that all Cubans would intermarry without giving it a thought if they so desired. Certain gaps still existed between ideal and reality. Some black Cubans felt that those gaps needed to be explored in order to be closed, and that positive measures should be taken. They felt this even though Cuba had bigger problems to solve, and it would be easy enough to say, "How can the Revolution worry about such things when it is fighting for economic survival?"

Let's listen to what some of them had to say.

It was about five o'clock in the afternoon in a Havana theater during a rehearsal of *María Antonia:* the first professionally produced Cuban play that dealt with black life and culture and had a predominantly black cast. "People ask me," said Eugenio Hernández, its mulatto author, " 'Why did you write a play about *that*? It's so. . . .' They never ask white playwrights why they write plays which present white life and culture." Up on the stage, a few actors in the large cast seemed stiff or uncertain; it was their first time on a professional stage. In January, 1967, Aimé Césaire's play about King Christophe of Haiti had been produced in Cuba with white actors in blackface, supposedly because of the lack of black actors. But there were black actors, said the people working on *María Antonia*. In any case, this time they made up for whatever lack did exist by using nonprofessionals—several of them Jamaicans, who presented the additional problem of having to learn such things as the particular way Cubans move.

After the rehearsal, a small group of people went across the street to have ice cream on a café terrace. Three of them were black or mulatto artists and scholars; the fourth person was a young white man who did administrative work in the arts. In age they ranged from twenty-three to about thirty-five.

Their discussion of the play quickly broadened to the larger subject of racism.

Julio: Racism in Cuba is a very subtle thing—it's different from the United States. It is more subtle here and therefore it is harder to fight.

Jose: I'm not sure it is so subtle. There is nothing subtle about saying that thick lips or kinky hair are ugly and white standards of beauty are the only valid ones. Look, the whole world has been brainwashed about color for centuries. How can there not be discrimination?

Alicia: It exists even in the language. The other day a friend of mine was in a big crowd at the Plaza and there was some mix-up—a lot of confusion. The man next to her said, "What a black situation!" She asked him, "Why do you call it black—why not just say it is a bad situation?" He was very surprised.

José: The problem in Cuba is that there is a taboo on talking about racism, because officially it doesn't exist any more. And nobody, black or white, *wants* to talk about it. The whites have no understanding of what they have done and are sometimes still doing. A white woman told me the other day, "Oh, these blacks are so ignorant and badly behaved." I said, "But I am black." And she said, "You—oh, but you are an exception. I never see you as black." Well, I felt like telling her, "Lady, you need new glasses." And then there are the ones who say, "One of my best friends is black." *¡Ay!*

Julio: A professor of medicine I know, one of the few black doctors, tells me that when he is with whites he always feels under examination—that he has to prove himself better than the white professors of medicine.

José (laughing): Oh, you know how it is—blacks can dance and do sports but that's all. If they do something else well, hmm, look, my, isn't that wonderful. Another thing—the way white parents react to their daughters marrying black men. Since they cannot very well be openly racist any more, they always say the same thing: "Think how the children will suffer!"

Alicia: And then the black parents are so happy because they think their children are coming up in the world! A close friend of mine married a white man but now she is getting a divorce. In the end, the problem between them was largely racial. Things like the way he reacted when she went out at night . . . he would ask, "Where were you?" And she would say, "With friends." And he would just answer, "All right." She is very sensitive about equality of the sexes—but she told me that she would have preferred him to hit her! He was so polite and white and Western.

The fact is, only a few of the whites I know are really racist. The rest are just harmless little *blanquitos* who don't know what it's all about.

Julio: White Cubans can get very excited—really wild—about black counter-Revolutionaries. I think it gives them a chance to vent their racism, to justify it. Insofar as it is a right, black people have the right to be counter-Revolutionary too.

Alicia: There is a tendency to assume that the Revolution "gave" blacks their freedom—gave us the right to enter white society, to have the same things they have. It is an essentially paternalistic attitude. And it creates resentment.

150

Even José Martí had the idea of integration as almost assimilation. I do not want to attack him; he was a great man. But the record should be set straight. It was interesting to hear Stokely criticize Lincoln while he was here—that surprised many Cubans, who always thought he was a hero to all black Americans. Martí is a very different case from Lincoln, but his image should be corrected too.

José: Don't speak of paternalism without mentioning that wonderful word *folklore*. Ah, the Institute of Ethnology and *Folklore* . . . the *Folklore* Ensemble . . . Afro-Cuban culture is folklore, and that's it.

Alicia: The ballet is culture, but we are folklore. And in some circles, it is more *culto* to study the original Indians of Cuba— their culture and history has more prestige.

Julio: Look, it is just wrong. Folklore means a degenerate culture. The Afro-Cuban culture is a genuine, living culture.

Alicia: "Afro-Cuban" is a problem too. It is used to describe that culture in Cuba which has largely African roots—the religious ceremonies and their music, dance. . . . But "Afro-Cuban" implies that there is another, "Cuban," culture with which the Afro has been mixed. And such a thing never existed. Cuban culture as a whole is itself a mixture of African and Spanish, it is Afro-Spanish.

But words aren't the worst problem. The problem is that people won't let the whole issue come to the surface. I wish that Carlos Moore's article [a lengthy attack on Cuban racist attitudes, written by a black Cuban now emigrated to Paris, and printed in a 1965 issue of *Présence Africaine*] had been published here. It's a mixture of truth with many lies and exaggerations, but it should have been printed in Cuba; it should have been answered in that magazine and by a Cuban—not by a foreigner, a Haitian [this was René Depestre, in his 1966 Casa de las Américas magazine article].

José: There is something else. The Revolution says that Cubans and Vietnamese and black Americans are united in a

151

common struggle. But we are not yet there. Cubans like to say "everybody is equal, there are only human beings, not black and white." But this isn't true—look at my skin, it's black. His [pointing to Julio] is white. We act as though we have achieved the ideal of brotherhood when it is still an ideal. We can't achieve it unless we recognize that we haven't achieved it.

But when we talk to whites about all these things, they accuse us of being Fascists—"racists in reverse."

White practices and attitudes toward black Cubans in the past had bred correspondent black attitudes toward blackness. The group went on to discuss how some of the brothers and sisters thought and behaved as a result of being taught that White is Right for four centuries.

José: Look, many blacks don't even realize they are being discriminated against. A black girl told me today, "Whites are more intelligent than blacks." If she had been white, I would have—wham! But she was black and just did not understand.

Renaldo: I know black girls who try to make their faces whiter. And there was one girl, a real beauty, who thought her nose was too "Negroid." So she had plastic surgery—it ruined her beauty. Those terrible black middle-class types who try to be white. . . . I remember a black composer in Oriente whose music got whiter and whiter.

José: There was a Cuban who complained about being put in an anthology of literature by blacks. "I am a writer first," he kept saying.

Alicia: I was brought up as a well-educated girl from the black middle class. My mother has always been afraid that I would marry "a bum"—one of those blacks who belong to the secret societies and smoke marijuana. [Not uncommon among blacks and some white intellectuals, marijuana was illegal in 1967 although there appeared to be little prosecution of smokers.] And black people aren't supposed to wear bright colors—we must be dignified, discreet, *culto*. So I lead two lives—one with the people I enjoy, and the other in my mostly white professional world. When we blacks get together and talk, we always end up agreeing that we don't like most whites. I think blacks usually prefer to be among their own people.

Yet perhaps I am not entirely free from all the prejudices of the black middle class. I still won't wear my hair in the "Afro" or "natural" style, as many black American girls are doing. It's crazy—in every beauty shop there is one person who can do black hair, and that person is always black. But there aren't yet any middle-class black women in Cuba who will wear their hair natural.

A pretty mulatto girl arrived then and somehow the conversation got onto the subject of sex.

José: Listen, *chica*, don't you know that all white men want to make it with a black or mulatto girl? It is their dream. You are just a sexual object to them. They used to do it with their servants and now they want you.

Girl: I have felt that sometimes. But I will not have anything to do with that. There has to be real interest between us.

Julio: Listen, it's a complicated business. Sometimes I go to bed with a black girl and she asks, "Why did you make it with me?" I tell her, "Because I like you as a person, as a woman." But she is sure that it is because white men want a black woman. Then, if I go with a white girl, she will say, "I thought white men preferred black girls." Damn. Then sometimes I go to bed with black girls and they say afterward, "Oh, I thought all white men were cold—you are not."

Alicia: White women from abroad who come to Cuba often go for black men here. That was a big thing for the men at first, having a white woman. But after a while they quit in disgust. A white Cuban asked me, "Why is that?" I told him, "If you had ever been with a black woman, you would understand."

José (leaping up, laughing): Ha! That myth of black sexual superiority—what a myth that is. *I* know.

The aggressiveness of this group—their open criticism and defiance of whites on a specifically racial basis—was far from typical. The fact that they lived in Havana and Havana was the main center of surviving petty bourgeois attitudes, which included racism, largely explains their sensitivity. Most blacks—*campesinos*, workers, bureaucrats—seemed to accept things as they were. "We just prefer to be with our own people," said a secretary in a provincial city. Behind this attitude could sometimes be found a withdrawn quality—a shyness with whites—and sometimes traces of resentment. Ordinary blacks might agree that prejudice lingered but they rarely expressed any feeling that a big effort should be made to uproot remnants of racist attitudes. Yet latent awareness and pride turned up in many kinds of black Cubans, and especially during the widely publicized visit of Stokely Carmichael to Cuba in July-August, 1967.

From the Prime Minister on down, enthusiasm for Carmichael was tremendous. In his speech closing the OLAS, Fidel Castro spoke at length and with great warmth about the black movement in the United States and Stokely in particular. Everywhere I traveled, one question was asked by black and white alike: "What will happen to *Stokeh-lee* when he gets back to the United States?" But black Cubans demonstrated a special response to his visit and concurrent events in Detroit and Newark. Never before, they said, had they had contact with a young, fire-eating black leader like Stokely. On August 18, anniversary of Watts, Cuba held a "Day of Solidarity with Black People of the United States." Carmichael had left by then, but some sixty thousand Cubans showed up on two or three days' notice. They waved printed posters and also many homemade signs saying, "Carmikel, we are with you!" or "With our solidarity, we will protect Stokelis." The entire audience seemed enthusiastic but again it was the blacks who seemed to be watching and listening with particular intensity.

Typical of this response were the remarks of a black agricultural technician in his mid-twenties who came up to me one afternoon in the *campo* and started asking questions about the revolutionary consciousness of Afro-Americans, the lack of union support for the radical black movement, and related matters. His manner was formal and precise. Then suddenly he burst out, "That one—Stokely Carmichael. I like him! I like him." He shook his head in wonder, half-laughing to himself with pleasure. "I never thought he would say such things. He really gave it to them!"

Blacks said they felt inspired by Stokely and sometimes torn, for he made them race-conscious and race-proud in a country where such attitudes were not encouraged. What he did not do, however, was to bring to the surface any buried anger, bitterness, or desire for separation. Those emotions seemed to be absent from the Cuban climate. What the aggressive black intellectuals said about racist attitudes might sound all too familiar to American ears—but the tone of their speech did not. Their voices and faces felt different. It became clear that while similarities between the black Cuban and Afro-American experiences existed, there must also be great differences.

The first, superficial evidence of this was the color mixture in the population, the mere sight of which can be startling to American eyes. Cuba's population and culture have been characterized by a degree of *mestizaje*—crossbreeding, hybridization —to be found nowhere in the United States. This, of course, dates back to slavery and the fact that there was much more racial mixing because the Spaniards did not bring women with them as the American colonists did. There were other differences in the slave systems. The British gave local slave-owners a free reign, while Spain asserted a measure of central authority. Certain legal rights were reserved to slaves and the murder of one was a felony in Cuba. The Catholic Church frequently intervened between master and slave (the better to preserve the system, but still its actions offset somewhat the crushing of a people's spirit and flesh). White immigration was lower, so freed blacks could establish themselves in the skilled trades with more ease in Cuba.

Racism after abolition had much more of a class nature in Cuba than in the American South. Cuban blacks were not allowed into upper-class restaurants, for example, but there was no segregation on buses. Oppression never approached the extremes of the United States—Klan, lynchings, bombings—nor was discrimination written into the law. The many outstanding black leaders in the War of Independence provided images of strength—male images—for black children. There were also black political figures throughout the twentieth century; the leadership of the old Communist Party was dominated over the years by blacks. On another psychological level, the doctrines and ritual sensuousness of the Catholic Church did not encourage the attachment of moral and sexual hang-ups to race in the same degree as dualistic, puritanical American Protestantism.

Another crucial factor was the evolving but firm group culture sustained by black Cubans. A primary struggle of Afro-Americans has been to affirm a cultural identity which would restore the sense of collective integrity undermined by slavery. In Cuba, that need was fulfilled for most blacks by a relatively unified body of continuous tradition centered around the secret religious societies and including traditions of music, dance, food. The absence of wide-scale industrialization also helped to sustain the so-called Afro-Cuban culture. Today, there are even ordinary blacks who speak the Bantu and Yoruba dialects, and isolated villages whose life reportedly retains a strong African style.

Still another basic difference lies in the colonial experience. Afro-American militants view racism in the United States as analogous to a colonial relationship: the white mother country exploits the black colony. Also, a distinction is often drawn between exploited and colonized. While American whites may experience economic exploitation, they have not—as an overall group—been subjected to colonization. Exploitation can be more than a matter of dollars; in a capitalist, racist society, the white can overcome his oppression with money but the poor black has two counts against him and eliminates only one of them with the acquisition of wealth. Thus any colonized people is exploited, but not all exploited peoples are colonized.

This analysis has relevance for Cuba but it cannot be applied simplistically. The two-dimensional relationship of white mother country to black colony becomes, in Cuba, a three-way relationship. Spain, followed by the United States, played the role of external white mother country to *all* Cubans, while white Cubans played the role of internal white mother country to black Cubans. Black, white, and mulatto—not merely blacks— have been a colonized people and have experienced, for example, the cultural inferiority complex that forms part of the colonized mentality. True, blacks did form another colony within the colony; they were in a sense doubly colonized. The exploited whites were not exploited *because* of their color, as were the blacks (among other reasons). But sharing the colonial experience helped reduce the distance between the two.

For all these reasons and still others, racism in Cuba did not produce the physical and spiritual ghetto-ization of this country. Neither black nor white was as psychically distorted as in the United States. To say that black-white relationships in Cuba contained resentment, guilt, and fear but little hatred—for others or for oneself—is generalizing wildly yet seems to be confirmed by what people said and how they acted.

Lines had just not been so sharply drawn. Even at the height of racism, when it was customary at public dances to put up a rope which divided blacks from whites, they danced to the same band and thus shared a part of the same culture. Whites joined the Afro secret societies (during the nineteenth century, they could enter only by paying what it cost to free one slave but today everyone pays an initiation fee). "It really is possible to trust a white here," said one of the most black-conscious Cubans. "There really are 'white niggers,' those who have lived close to the black society." "The race problem here is mainly cultural, a matter of aesthetic standards," said another Cuban. Color in itself did not seem to be a big thing, as in the United States. But the black and brown women who were considered beautiful, and who might be seen as evidence of no prejudice, had Caucasian features—not "Negroid."

Still, no white Cuban ever exudes that special air of cold, blue-eyed superiority which white Americans at their worst can manifest; that imperviousness to the possibility of there being any other way to view the world than the Yankee way. Nor do white Cubans resemble the lower-class white American racist, less complacent and more twisted with fearful hate. Nor the edgy, self-conscious liberal. White Cubans are a Caribbean people and a once colonized people. They know, from both past and present, what it is to be a Third World underdog. In a sense, there is no such thing as a "white" Cuban except perhaps for recent immigrants from Europe and their children. Most of Cuba's white citizens shared with blacks a common mentality on certain subjects, common styles of talking and joking and mockery, along with their many cultural differences.

There is still a long way to go; black and white remain ignorant of each other in many ways. Sexual relations could be a problem for several generations; the mentality behind the old practices of black women commanding high prices as prostitutes and every big shot having his brown concubine did not disappear when those institutions themselves did. Blacks still show widespread and deep anxiety about sexual relations with whites, according to a series of informal interviews made by a young film-maker. But all in all, the possibility of honest, comfortable, *human* relationships between black and white exists in Cuba to a degree unimaginable in the United States.

Cuban history and traditions combined with the sweeping changes of the Revolution to make the racial situation not only far better in Cuba but different in basic nature from many other countries with a racially mixed population. Life seemed good enough to the black intellectuals that they saw their struggle primarily in cultural terms, complex enough that they disagreed about the nature of the cultural problem and about what needed to be done. (Inspired by Stokely Carmichael's visit, several black women in Havana got their hair cut natural. It was a small-scale "guerrilla action" but stirred up a storm in some quarters. People who had admired Afro-American women with naturals didn't like the style on Cubans; "it looks terrible," they said. But in at least one case, a white man's attitude seemed to change when the irrationality and cultural arrogance of his disapproval were pointed out to him.)

The group talking after the rehearsal of *María Antonia* discussed two kinds of needs: to stimulate a positive black consciousness among black people and to create among both black and white a new sense of what Cuban culture—in the full sense of a life ideology, not merely the arts—really was. To meet that first need, José believed that "we must change attitudes and images in the schools, in films, radio, television, theater. When my son watches television, he sees a popular white singer strumming away" (lively imitation of the singer) "and that's a hero figure—but how can my son identify with him?"

He went on, however, to say, "It is a very complicated problem. We have to beware of paternalism—that's the worst thing of all. I remember, right after the Revolution, they made a big effort to make up for the past. They did some ridiculous things, painting the faces of dolls black. A black singer gave a concert and someone wrote a very critical review of it. Another person protested, saying how could anyone attack a black singer. But she was *terrible*! They were also careful to put black people into the posters and signs.

"Now all this has stopped because supposedly the problem doesn't exist anymore. Or if people admit that it does, they say, 'Time will eliminate whatever vestiges remain.' But that isn't true. An effort has to be made. *And the black intellectuals must lead the way*, to avoid white paternalism.

"Because there is officially no discrimination, because there is no policy on this question, we have to work to break down racist attitudes by an individual approach. Each of us does what he can in his field. It's a form of guerrilla warfare." The play should stir up discussion, the group agreed; someone at the Film Institute was trying to make a movie to stimulate further discussion. Manolo Granados' *Adire y el tiempo roto,* a novel about an interracial couple and the complexities of racist attitudes, would soon be published ("Ah, there's a beautiful chapter in it attacking that myth of black sexual superiority," said José).

Courses in Swahili and Bantu were starting at the Art School.

The FAR (Revolutionary Armed Forces) had put out a history book on the people of Cuba which contained errors but at least gave some of the truth about African origins, Julio pointed out. The FAR magazine, *Verde Olivo*, had also published material along that line.

The group felt the need for a degree of cultural black nationalism, but even more for a cultural revolution whereby the true nature of Cuban culture would be affirmed. This, they said, was the aim of the play, *María Antonia*. A complex work functioning on several levels, *María Antonia* superficially presents the world of poor blacks living around the old Mercado Único in Havana: a lumpen world of *marijuaneros,* secret societies, *santería.* The characters speak straight-up street talk with flashes of poetic but spontaneous imagery. (The language alone would be startling on a Havana stage, where an essentially white and elite tradition has dominated—at least in the professional theater.) On another level, the play shows a woman hopelessly rooted in her world but trying to fight off the weight of its imperatives: the *machismo* which requires a man to kill when challenged to do so and the *hembrismo* which requires a woman to destroy a faithless lover, the relentlessness of sex, the apparent inevitability of violence. These elements are then enveloped in religious doctrine and rites.

When interviewed about the play's meaning, Eugenio Hernández said, "Let us leave aside race. The characters simply represent what is Cuban. The *machismo* in the play is not limited to a racial concept." The play, he said, was about anybody caught up in any losing struggle against what sociologists call culture-determined responses. But the author also made it clear that the play was intended "to create a conflict between the spectator and the image of himself which he sees in the play" —that is, to clear up the myths about black Cuban culture and thereby make white Cubans recognize the blend of primarily African and Spanish elements in their own life styles.

Culture in Cuba, as elsewhere in the Caribbean, was a mixture of Indian, European, and African elements—in which the African had been negated. Most of Cuba's pre-Revolutionary values had been imposed by white European (Spanish and United States) colonizers. Cultural revolution thus meant Cuba redefining its values, supplementing the new political unity with cultural unity. As the magazine of the Casa de las Américas editorialized, ". . . until the Cuban Revolution, the general progressive goal was to eliminate prejudice toward the black race as inferior to the white. Today, that attitude seems to us still paternalistic. Today it is a question of going farther: *assuming* all our true traditions . . . including of course the powerful African traditions." In this light, the issue was larger than racism.

But resistance to "assuming Africa" ran strong in some quarters, both white and black. It could also be argued that positive affirmation must precede assumption. There were, therefore, black intellectuals who had different ideas about what should be done—or at least, different notions about priority and emphasis—from those previously expressed here. When the various schools of thought came together one night in a Havana restaurant, it was sometimes like having LeRoi Jones, Bill Epton, and James Baldwin in the same room at the same time—and then again different.

José was on hand, and Julio, the white youth. Also Arturo, a mulatto scholar of Afro-Cuban culture. A young black poet, Luis, was present too. The four had just come from watching a class of *aficionados* practice various dance steps of Yoruba, Dahomey, Bantu, and Congo origin (the four major groups of Cuba's Afro culture) in an old working-class section of Havana. The class, which met for several hours five nights a week, was one of many in Cuba.

On the necessity for stimulating positive black consciousness through the recording of Afro-Cuban dance music, the four were in agreement. But then José began discussing why the dances performed by the class were not "pure" African. "The whole Afro culture in Cuba has been affected by time and space —by the Cuban environment," he said. "In the dance—when the man and woman bump the pelvis, that was originally a fertility symbol. Now it is just love, sexual attraction. The *form*

—the movements—of a dance may be the same, but their content has changed. There is no such thing as a separate African culture here. Or a Spanish culture, for that matter."

"You're an assimilationist!" Arturo exploded. "And there is no use our talking about it." A silence fell; this was obviously an old argument between them. Then he said, "My position is what you might call *mestizaje positivo* as opposed to *mestizaje negativo*. The first means a blending of cultures in which there is equal respect for both. The second means that a minority culture is absorbed—as an inferior culture.

"There is something very wrong," he pronounced slowly, "there is a terrible sickness created, when a black child receives a doll with white flesh and blond hair. The child aspires to be something it cannot be. This has to be uprooted before you can have a positive blending of cultures. Until it is uprooted, we must protect our African culture as separate. Otherwise, we might as well all take pills to become white."

José was insulted, and looked it. "If you think you need to tell me about that doll, about the need not to straighten one's hair, about taking pills, then we cannot possibly talk. I know those things. But I am talking about something else. I am talking about what is *culture*." In the presence of Arturo, José sounded much less militant than on previous occasions. But the issue was more complicated than "militance."

"Culture is not just the dance, music, and religious rites," José went on. "It is a totality of life and ideology. We must *de-mythify* this whole business of African origins. *Negritude* has many weaknesses. Listen to me, *negritude* is the big thing of the President of Senegal because he has nothing else to offer. It is a political ploy. We must de-mythify *negritude*. The black people in Cuba—or in the United States—are first of all Cubans, or North Americans. There must be a wider vision than black consciousness. There must be more ideological development . . ."

"He is in love with Marx," said Luis, the poet, smiling, after José and the others had left. "And he makes concessions to white Cubans. I am somewhere between him and Arturo.

"The guerrilla approach won't do, I think. There has to be an active *movement* of black intellectuals. There are already a number of good writers—some of them white. But it is not a movement yet, we just get together once in a while. When Juan Goytisolo [the Spanish novelist] was visiting Cuba, he told some of us, 'But you are Spanish—and nothing else.' That is the kind of thing we must resolve.

"Look, we have to push to *take over* Cuban culture. That sounds extremist—well, we have to be extremist for a while to balance things. Swahili and Bantu will be taught—not out of some kind of phony negritude, but to enrich a person's background. The whole educational system is Europe-oriented, starting from the first grade. We must get away from all that . . ."

"I want to be integrated but not assimilated," Alicia said at one point in our talks. Her words summed up the attitude of these black intellectuals, for whom the issue in Cuba could not be assimilation versus separation, as in the United States. "And I love the Revolution. There is no basic conflict between those two feelings. In fact, it was the Revolution that made my present feelings possible."

For all their criticisms, these black Cubans felt that socialism was the only basis upon which a nonracist society could be built in Cuba. None believed that the present gap between reality and ideal invalidated the Revolution. As Alicia said more than once, "My raising these questions would have been impossible without the Revolution. I could not have begun to think this way otherwise." For all their different ideas about where to go from here, they agreed that "we had to get rid of the racist basis of our society first." That opened the door to talking about the liberation of Man on all levels. They could not have disagreed more strongly with Afro-American militants who say "socialism is irrelevant to our struggle." They rejected the position that because racist attitudes continue to be found in certain Socialist countries, socialism is no better than capitalism.

One black woman, who had experienced racism brutally in her childhood and was very sensitive to the issue, saw white prejudice in Cuba as a remnant of the whole, petty bourgeois mentality. Prejudice would disappear, she said, when that mentality disappeared. This would come only with the end of the class struggle, which would be communism. The very term, socialism, by definition included continuing class struggle. No nation had yet seen the end of the class struggle; therefore, no nation was yet free of racism.

While agreeing that class plays a basic role wherever racism exists, other black Cubans felt the need for a less mechanistic and more revolutionary application of Marxist theory. This, of course, opens up a whole larger chapter of Cuban history as well as a subject much debated by black, brown, and white radicals in the United States: the relationship between Marxism-Leninism and racism.

As spelled out by its founder in his particular time and place, Marxism was Europe-oriented and viewed the urban proletariat in the capitalist centers as having the greatest revolutionary potential. It did not anticipate the importance of national liberation struggles in colonized areas. Neither did it theoretically exclude them. But in the vacuum of discussion left by Marx—and despite writings of Lenin, Stalin, and the Chinese—certain misinterpretations emerged falsely bearing the Marxist label. As scholars have been recently pointing out, these un-Marxian Marxists held that the key to world revolution lies in the class struggle within the Western, affluent nations; that oppression in colonized areas would be ended only by revolution in the metropolitan nations; that racism and colonialism would automatically pass away under socialism. In their mechanical (and paternalistic *and* racist) application of a purely class analysis to racism, they construed "Workers of the world, unite" to mean that black people must support the white proletariat against capitalism and wait for liberation to materialize, rather than whites joining in the fight against racism. Anything which weakened proletarian unity (including black nationalism, in their opinion) should be discouraged. This became the position of various Communist parties, including that of the Soviet Union. It also helped produce the gradualist, legalistic approach to social change called revisionism.

In Cuba during the early sixties, to summarize a long and complex story, the Soviet Union and its East European sisters became the key to Cuba's economic development. This relationship was accompanied by ideological influences which, among other effects, strengthened the hand of elements from the old Cuban Communist Party (Partido Socialista Popular) that sought increased power in the new regime. Anibal Escalante was the leader of this faction, battling Fidel to establish an authoritarian, Soviet-oriented party and society. (An ironic footnote to this struggle is the fact that the old P.S.P. leadership had over the years been predominantly black.)

The problems encountered in Cuba in the early sixties by Robert Williams, black advocate of armed self-defense who had fled from the United States, can be explained in part by this sectarianism. Cuba had welcomed Williams (unlike the American Communist Party, which was still damning him in 1963), but Williams came to disapprove of the Soviet Union's position. Also, *burocratismo* was rampant in the early sixties and Williams could not always accomplish what he wished in the desired time. Blacks in Cuba who knew him further attribute his difficulties to the man's own character, as they saw it: his lack of political sophistication at the time. The cultural gap also created problems, intensified by the fact that Williams did not learn Spanish during his three years in the country. Che Guevara tried repeatedly to mend the breach that developed from all these circumstances but too many forces operated against his efforts.

Escalante lost that first round of the struggle, in 1962, but the influence of "the Soviet line" lingered. The beginning of a breakthrough could be seen at the first Tricontinental Congress in January, 1966, when Cuba came out firmly for armed struggle and for the Latin American revolution—though it also took the side of the Soviet Union against China at that meeting. At the OLAS conference of the following year, however, Cuba criticized the Soviet Union for giving financial and technical assistance to oligarchic Latin regimes, blasted certain Latin American Communist parties as reformist advocates of peaceful change and coexistence, and praised the Afro-American revolutionary movement.*

So one can hope that the Soviet Union's diminishing influence on Cuba, together with the Cuban Revolutionary insistence on a non-mechanical application of Marxism, will lead to a rejection of the pure class analysis of racism: the view that blacks are simply one more element among the oppressed millions, by chance black, and that racism automatically disappears when exploitation ends. Although a class analysis may work better for Cuba than other nations, it still misses the mark. It fails to take into account the long-range effects of the double colonization of blacks, the variety of exploitation from one race to another, the fact that racism cuts across class lines. It cannot fully explain the traditional prejudice of the *guajiro*—the white *campesino*. It needs to be balanced by what James Forman of SNCC, in a 1967 speech at the Western Regional Black Youth Conference in Los Angeles, called a "skin analysis": the view that blacks are oppressed solely because of their color.

Neither the class nor the skin analysis is adequate by itself, as Forman pointed out. African history denies the pure skin analysis; so does the history of other nations, including Cuba. Scholars describe how, in 1876, the Spanish Governor of Cuba organized a plot together with the President of Haiti to assassinate Antonio Maceo, the future hero of Independence, then exiled in Haiti. Friends saved the life of this black man from another black man, allied with a white colonialist. More recent Cuban history shows politicians playing on race purely to win black votes.

---

* The new put-down of Escalante and his faction in 1968 reconfirmed this stance. Also in 1968, an interesting indication of the different capabilities of Soviet and Cuban intellectuals to understand racial issues emerged—in a poetic debate. A Soviet poet wrote a tribute to Martin Luther King after his assassination in which this line appeared: "His skin was black but his soul was pure white . . ." Cuban poet Nicolas Guillén, a mulatto, composed a sharp reply concluding:
> "Why shouldn't the heroic Pastor
> have harbored a black soul?
> A soul as black as eoal."

Failure to look beyond the skin analysis, as Forman said, makes it difficult to guard against reactionary nationalism. It creates the danger that Frantz Fanon preached against, for Africa: lack of an ideology. Only a combination of the two analyses can explain the total reality of racism and point the way to full liberation. This would be a truly dialectical, *revolutionary* analysis.

Cuba has an ideology and that is its great strength in dealing with racism. But just as some Afro-American militants have found it necessary to look beyond the strict skin analysis, Cubans might do well to expand that ideology beyond the pure class analysis.

Using a revolutionary analysis, Cuba could make a conscious examination of all those symbols which might perpetuate unconscious racist values. Scholars could re-examine what has been written and correct the myths generated by racist historians as well as by un-Marxian Marxists. (The one-hundred-years' anniversary of the War of Independence, celebrated on October 10, 1968, did see some efforts toward this: in Fidel's speech and in a *Granma* article on the role of blacks in the independence struggle. The latter concluded: "They had been ready for a liberation movement for some time. Their suffering and their bloodshed had already paved the way for the epic struggle for freedom.")

Educators should take another look at Cuban textbooks, including one used at the Minas del Frío school in 1967, which criticized the Independent Party of blacks and mulattos in the early 1900's because it failed to appreciate that "the poor white was as exploited as the poor black" and thus "encouraged Cuban divisiveness." It would be good to find out more about blacks like Nicolás Morales, who in 1795 organized what was apparently the first conspiracy against Spain's rule. Some of Martí's statements should be set in their context of time and place. Beyond the borders of Cuba, a revolutionary analysis could bring some new thinking about the potential of the lumpen proletariat (usually black) in Latin America. The door is wide open to ideas and actions which would not only deepen the humanism of Cuba itself but help to achieve her political dreams for the whole continent.

A few days after the end of 1967, some fourteen hundred intellectuals met in Havana to prepare for the 1968 Cultural Congress. The statement they issued contains a comment on racism that points toward a new and useful position for Cuba:

Racism is not, historically, a product of modern imperialism; it is an ideological vestige of the past that imperialism inherited and shaped to its own ends of domination and exploitation, turning it into an essential part of its own system to such an extent that a prior condition for the disappearance of racism is the disappearance of imperialism. The experience of Cuba is a clear ratification of the need for armed, revolutionary struggle and the later development of socialism in order to eliminate racism. However, in the ideological field, the painful effects of racism will continue for some time, as will other negative carry-overs of the old society. The New Man will not know racism.

One might wish they had said, "The New Man *must* not know racism," rather than taking it for granted. But in the end, this is a problem for the Cuban people themselves to solve. They are agreed, black and white alike, that their Socialist Revolution is the only possible basis on which to proceed to clearing away all the forms of sickness in human minds and human relationships. The way has been opened; the problem of lingering racist attitudes waits to be resolved—in its Cuban context, by Cubans, and in a Cuban style.

Those of us living in countries plagued by racial oppression will watch this unique situation with more than interest. Like the single star carried on its flag, Cuba stands alone as the only black-and-white nation which could in the near future destroy racism altogether. The end of the long nightmare seems so close there; perhaps that is why so much is asked.

The Longest Revolution

On a shady side street of Havana, in an old residential area, there stood a business establishment called the Pin Pon: "Instant Photo Service," all types of I.D. pictures taken and printed on the spot. The Pin Pon was housed in a green frame hut which sat by itself in front of an open-air coffee counter and a small grocery. It looked like a gypsy shop—as though it could be picked up and moved to another location in a wheelbarrow at any time. The personnel consisted of the photographer, a taciturn young man, and his helper, a busy little old gentleman. The old man handled the customers, graciously inviting new arrivals to be seated on the crates that lay around and reassuring others that their photos would be ready in *"un minuto, señorita"* (he was not of the *compañera* generation). He also dried the photographs as they were printed: laying them out on a corroded iron surface, putting a cloth on top, lighting a small flame underneath, and pressing the pictures flat with his slow, trembly hands. The Pin Pon was an island in Revolutionary time-space.

About six o'clock in the afternoon on a gray day in September, there were several persons waiting quietly for their pictures: a woman with her teen-age daughter, two middle-aged men, another mother with a boy of about six. Two young militiamen, who appeared to be on no particular mission at the moment, had sat down to chat. Then a girl in a *mini-falda* walked in from the street and up to the public telephone at the coffee counter. A hum rose from the group and people stiffened slightly; one sensed that a discussion of consequence was about to begin.

"The *mini-falda* is all right for Europe, because men are more faithful there," said the plump, middle-aged mother of the six-year-old boy. "But in Cuba, a man is here today and gone tomorrow. Things are bad enough without mini-skirts."

"Listen," said one of the militiamen, "the trouble is, Cuban women are very jealous."

"Huh," replied the mother of the teen-age girl, addressing nobody in particular, "he says that because he's a wild one."

"Listen, I'm telling you, Cuban women are very jealous."

"Well, yes," she smiled, "they *are* jealous. The other day I was waiting at the bus stop. It was hot and a man waiting there said to me, 'What a terrible heat—it's suffocating.' Just then his wife came up. You should have seen her standing there with her hands on her hips—like this—and what a look on her face! 'Tell her you have children!' she shouted at him."

"Look," began a man of about thirty-five or forty, "the other day I was waiting to get in the movie. There was a woman in the line near me. She began talking with the man behind her. Just then the man's wife came along to join him. She gave the woman such a look! He kept trying to explain that they were only talking about the difficulty of getting into a movie on Saturday night. But his wife would not listen."

They all laughed while the six-year-old boy smiled vaguely. Then his mother turned to the middle-aged man. "Tell me, would you let your daughter wear a mini-skirt?"

"No," he replied instantly, "no, I don't think it's right."

The new batch of photographs was ready. Everyone crowded around to watch the old man iron the pictures, and to see how they looked. He served the ladies with special care and they beamed. The girl in the mini-skirt had left; quiet again descended over the Pin Pon.

"The most interesting question in Cuba today is the new relationship of men and women," said a young painter named Tomás. "Imagine, all my married friends from 1960 have been divorced since then. But it is basically a healthy sign."

Comments similar to the painter's could be heard all over the island. Old ideas in the area of sex—in particular, about the societal roles of women and about relations between men and women—were a subject that came up all the time. The society showed many contradictions between the present, Revolutionary liberation of women and oppressive attitudes hanging over from the past. Along with a New Man, there was also a New Woman to be created. Like the black, she had an extra distance to travel.

Pre-Revolutionary Cuba assigned three roles to women: man's slave in the home, mother, and pleasure object. Life was simple, in a sense. Middle-class girls, after a due amount of chaperoned dating, were turned over by their daddies to husbands—with hymen intact, or the deal was off. From then on, life meant four walls and the double standard. Work, of course, was something that "nice girls" never performed. Poorer city girls, who were not nice but still needed to eat, did go out to work: at night, in the streets of Old Havana or along the waterfront of Santiago, "Hey, meester, you want to sport?" As for poor women of the *campo,* they always worked—in the fields and the home, bearing innumerable children and looking fifty at the age of twenty-five. In essence, the position of the Cuban woman before the Revolution was that of women in any non-industrialized, capitalist society. Oppressed as a group, they differed from the women of industrialized, capitalist societies mainly in that proportionately fewer Cuban women had the opportunity *also* to be oppressors—as individuals, in the middle-class.

The status of Cuban women, like that of the blacks, had local characteristics differentiating it from patterns in other Western countries. These derived mainly from Catholicism and other Spanish institutions, the Latin *machismo* tradition, and African elements in the culture: all three being influences which were mostly negative yet sometimes positive in comparison with other cultures.

The Catholic Church gave special strength to the equation of virginity with decency and of marriage with child-bearing; *machismo* supported the double standard and the sexual reification of women. But Cuba also had a matriarchal tradition, rooted in slavery and poverty. This, combined with certain Spanish traditions of female authority, made woman a central figure in the society. There developed the cult of the Martyred Mother and the cult of the Gritty Grandmother, two formidable figures. Furthermore, the Afro-Spanish culture did not make woman per se into a symbol of evil temptation as had Anglo-style dualism. All in all, Cuban women had a more defined and even more aggressive personality than the white Western female coming out of a patriarchal, puritanical culture. At the same time, the basic subordination of women to men was absolute in Cuba.

Strong women played an important role in Cuba's struggle against Spanish rule. One of them, Ana Betancourt, was already demanding equal rights for women at a meeting of independence leaders—the Assembly of Guaimaro—held shortly after the war with Spain began. She tried (and failed) to have women recognized not only while the war was on but also after. History records her heroism on many occasions, such as the time when she was taken before a firing squad and ordered to write her husband, also in the struggle, to surrender himself. She refused, but lived. Years later, in the same period when American suffragettes were marching and going to jail, Cuban women renewed their struggle for civil rights. They won the vote in 1934—some seventy years after Ana Betancourt's original demand—and other forms of official equality followed.

During the insurrection against Batista, women played important roles as far back as the Moncada attack. Haydée Santamaría and Melba Hernández, who had done time in prison for their part in that assault, were soon joined in action by a host of nurses, teachers, and organizers; a full Rebel Army battalion of women combatants, named after Maceo's mother; messengers like Lidia and Clodomira, serving Che Guevara and Fidel Castro respectively, both of them murdered on a mission in Havana. There were also women in the urban Underground, like Ursula Díaz Baez. A pretty girl of eighteen, planning to become a doctor someday, she carried out a number of sabotage and other disruptive operations. These included immobilizing the "Ten Cent" with a time bomb and ringing all the church bells in Havana one night to interrupt the mass and agitate among the people. Then came another night, in 1957: she was killed when she set a faulty time bomb and it exploded immediately.

The most prominent women in Cuba when I was there—Celia Sánchez, Haydée Santamaría and Vilma Espín—had all been active since that early period of the Revolution. They also related to the rest of the current leadership in some specific ways: Comandante Celia Sánchez as administrative secretary to Fidel, Haydée Santamaría as the wife of Party leader Armando Hart Dávalos, and Vilma Espín as the wife of Raúl Castro. The two married women are known by their maiden names, the usual practice among women in Cuba.

Vilma Espín headed the Federation of Cuban Women (FMC), which was set up in 1960 and swung into action the following year with 90,000 women participating in the drive against illiteracy. By 1967, the FMC had 750,000 members. In the words of its director, "The Federation prepares women educationally, politically, and socially to participate in the Revolution. As an arm of the Revolution, its main functions are the incorporation of women in work and raising the educational level—including political consciousness—of women." The FMC provided help on government projects when asked, and also ran its own projects: all coffee work in Oriente, for example, was turned over to the Federation to administer. It directed a major program of voluntary work by women during the sugarcane harvest, during emergency military mobilizations, and in other periods when additional labor force was needed. It trained women for new jobs.

One of the proudest achievements of the Federation has been the *círculos infantiles* and *jardines,* two types of free day-care centers for children which enable women to work. (Children can be brought to them from the age of forty-five days.) It seemed impossible to find anywhere in Cuba one woman who was not enthusiastic about the facilities and atmosphere that these centers offered. "The children receive *todo, todo, todo,*" they all said. "Everything" meant a program of play and learning, three meals, medical attention if needed, and notably affectionate attention. "But women still have problems studying and working," said Vilma Espín. "The economy cannot yet afford to provide everything in order to free women from drudgery. There are not yet enough day-care centers and boarding schools." As of 1966, only an estimated 150,000 women had become regular wage-earners since the Revolution. Most of them, furthermore, were not in production—like the volunteers —but in service work (teaching, staffing nurseries, etc.).

The size and the nature of that statistic, however, is deceptive. Getting women out of the kitchen, whether on a permanent or temporary basis, whether to plant coffee or teach, had produced what Fidel called "a revolution within the Revolution." Not only were women going out of the house for the first time; they were staying out overnight—on guard duty—and even leaving the country—to study in distant places like Russia. They were also becoming less dependent economically, thanks to new work roles and the many free services offered by the Revolution. Even having a child out of wedlock no longer had to mean financial disaster. Women's new participation in sports was making a small dent in old ideas about femininity (and class): the idea that "nice girls" don't get sweaty.

Women were visible everywhere: as workers, teachers, administrators, government representatives. They directed important projects and delivered keynote speeches at important events. The landscape of Revolutionary Cuba was not a man's world. No longer were women the janitors, caretakers, and consumers of the society, but its producers and organizers.

Vilma Espín told an anecdote which suggests the problems that this revolution-within-the-Revolution was destined to face. During the struggle against Batista, a precious and inadequate shipment of guns arrived one day at a location where both men and women were fighting. A few of the Revolutionaries on hand, in a spirit familiar to women from any of the movements in the United States, maintained that the guns should go to the men. The women protested; male supremacy went down in defeat. But while it may have lost the battle, the war was far from over.

That war has been two-pronged: daughters versus virginity-obsessed parents, and women versus men prone to jealousy, or to resentment when dinner isn't ready, or just plain unnerved by the new economic independence of "their" women. Most young women active in the Revolution had some story to tell of opposition to their involvement. A girl who had wanted to teach in the 1961 Literacy Campaign went through a long hassle with her family before she left, and when she did, *"Vaya,* that was a blow in my house. It was typical of the Revolution. And for the first time I began to value a certain kind of freedom for myself." As for wives, a young woman who signed up for two years of agricultural service on the Isle of Pines was threatened by her husband with divorce if she went. She did, and the divorce papers arrived not long afterward. "The changes have been *traumatic* for Cuban men," said Tomás, the painter. "The hard thing is that they cannot legitimately oppose the changes. A woman who goes to work or on guard duty is doing it for the Revolution. The men would have to be counter-Revolutionaries to oppose it."

Nevertheless, some did oppose the changes. "A lot of Cuban men wish they could put chastity belts on 'their' women," said a Cuban journalist. Beatriz, a tall and handsome *mulatta* of about thirty-five, was a Marxist but had to work out her own guidelines to break the sex barrier in her profession. "It was very hard at first—men treated me as either a sex object or an inferior. I made a point of going to cover the most difficult stories, things like hurricanes, and going up in the mountains. I refused to do 'women's stories.' Now, most of the men accept me as a colleague and like me—some don't, mostly because I made them look silly about their prejudices at some point.

"There is real contradiction between the theory of the equality of women and reality," she went on. "A high value is still placed on virginity." Marina, a young translator, spoke on the same theme. "Girls who have had lovers will tell their husbands that their hymen was broken from horseback riding or something. I even know of girls who have had surgery to restore the hymen. A lot of this is ignorance; people believe that if there isn't a pool of blood on the wedding night, the girl can't be a virgin—and so she is no good.

"Many young men still ask permission from a girl's father to be her *novio,* 'go steady.' In a small town, it would be impossible for an unmarried couple to have relations without the town knowing—and being, for the most part, scandalized." This last comment, like all her others, applied mainly to the urban middle class or petty bourgeoisie. Poor couples of the *campo* have for years lived together and raised families without benefit of ceremony.

The elaborate establishments where the surrender of virginity could be made official told something about the importance attached to that event in Cuba (they also, perhaps, reflected a desire to compensate for the lost glamor of a church ceremony—the reason why the Soviet Union has similar establishments). Several Cuban cities had, or were acquiring, a Palacio de Matrimonios. Havana's Marriage Palace occupied the former Spanish Casino, an exclusive club for Spaniards only. The first floor contained a large waiting room with marble floors and two groupings of richly colored plush chairs in gilded frames— chairs so enormous that eight of them filled the entire space. Off to one side was a shop with rings and necklaces laid out on black velvet, perfumes and cosmetics in other cases; then offices where a couple could arrange to have photographs taken, discuss reception plans and so forth. A flight of wide marble stairs led to the Golden Room: an Italian Renaissance-style ballroom of giant size, with paintings all around the ceiling, crystal chandeliers, gilt fixtures, massive pieces of carved and gilded furniture along the walls, every item dazzling-bright. Then there were the Green Room and the Rose Room, only slightly less impressive; dressing rooms for the bride; banquet rooms, in one of which a wedding cake and champagne glasses stood ready for a party that afternoon. The rooms, the marble stairs, every bit of space was lined with sculpted cherubs, statues and paintings of lovers, Dresden or pseudo-Dresden shepherds and shepherdesses kissing, stained glass windows. Glenn Miller's "Sun Valley Serenade" played in the background and all was for free except any food or drink served.

The Palacio also had some less overwhelming rooms; in one small chamber, a very young couple was getting married. The notary, reading aloud the legal article of marriage, got to the part about "Is there anyone opposed to this marriage; if so, speak now . . ." After a few minutes of silence he pointed to one of the guests. "You over there—are you opposed?" "Me?" the man answered, startled; "No." "Then why do you look so sad?" The notary, unmarried, was a sweet sort of joker; "I don't do that with everyone," he said. "You know, not with the couples who have been living together for a long time." The Revolution inspired a rise in the marriage rate, with a 300 per cent increase in the province of Oriente; much of this represented couples who had been living together for years but now had the opportunity and financial prospects to make it legal.

After the wedding, there were some beautiful and imaginative places in the countryside especially designed for honeymooners. Two provinces of the island had resorts with real tree-houses as rooms and a main dining hall for meals. Playa Girón offered housekeeping cottages on the beach. The romance of marrying remained a solid institution in Revolutionary Cuba—though some were more equally married than others and the double standard still flourished. "Men don't like their women to go out, even in the daytime—even to the movies with another woman. They are supposed to stay in the house and take care of the man's needs," Marina continued.

Not surprisingly, infidelity remained the most common cause

of divorce—more so than political differences or disagreement about Revolutionary involvement, according to Cuban press reports. (The only official grounds, however, were the same as before the Revolution.) The divorce rate had tripled between 1958 and 1965, although at that high point it was still only one divorce per thousand Cubans. The procedure was that if both persons wanted to divorce, they announced their intention in a civil court, returned in a month to state they had not lived together for that time, and soon after the papers were finalized.* If contested, a judge stepped in. Men still paid alimony; support ran less if any children were in the day-care centers.

Contraceptives were available in Cuba without restriction in 1967. These included the diaphragm and an intrauterine loop called the *anillo* (I.U.D. in the United States); the pill was still considered too dangerous. Any woman, married or not, could go to a hospital and be fitted with an *anillo;* should it fail and the woman become pregnant, she could have an abortion free of charge. She could also have a free abortion if she reported to a hospital within a month after becoming pregnant—but her family would be notified, which acted as a deterrent. Abortion under any other circumstances than these remained illegal. A woman who was over thirty-eight and had had five children could have a free operation to tie up the uterine tubes.

The state did not actively disseminate birth-control information for several reasons, including the prejudice which still existed. A woman was offered an *anillo* or diaphragm at the hospital after she had had her first child, but a lot of women didn't get to a hospital. (The Federation of Cuban Women urged them to go; if that was impossible, it helped them to find a midwife.) A 1967 issue of *Granma* did carry a three-page spread telling about the availability of contraceptives and abortion—an information service which, Cubans agreed, would have been hard to imagine in their country even a short time earlier. But the majority of women still did not use any method of birth control. In addition to the specific drawbacks of the I.U.D. and

* In 1968, the waiting time was even further reduced.

the diaphragm, there were the economic, educational, and psychological obstacles common to underdeveloped areas. It was startling to find a woman like Beatriz the journalist, who said: "Once my daughter was playing with the sons of a neighbor and their mother came to me complaining about something going on between the children. I talked to her and said that I would give contraceptives to my daughter when she finds a man who pleases her. She was very shocked. But look, *el pipí es mío*—personal matters are personal."

Cuba had no sex education program at the time, although its first—via radio—was in the planning stage. It would be interesting to see how it handled the question of woman's role in bed. "The idea that sex is for the woman's pleasure as well as the man's—that is the taboo of taboos," various Cuban women agreed. "Less change has taken place in this area than any other."

Old ideas about masculinity, which made babies needed to prove manhood and which made men feel threatened by loss of control over a woman's body, also explained why contraceptives were not in wider use. "The husbands of women who get the *anillo* will say, '*Me molesta*,' and the wife then has it removed, although it can't possibly be felt by the man," explained Conchita, a young Havana artist who didn't look as though she would go along with that bit of male double-talk.

Conchita was hurrying home at that moment for her child's birthday party. Being a good Cuban, she wasn't in so much of a hurry that she couldn't take time out to complain about a life in which she worked all week and still had to do the week's washing together with other household chores on the weekend. "My husband helps, but it is still too much," she said. There were other women who talked about the new "double exploitation." They used the term only half-seriously, but the gripes were real enough. "I know women who get up at four A.M. to make dinner before going to work," said Marina, "because their husbands get furious if they come home from work and don't find dinner ready. Even intellectual men and women get hung up in things like this."

These women's comments indicated that it was male chauvinism in the realm of interpersonal relations that most preoccupied them. Few talked about how men dominated the leadership. (This was true even in lower political strata; among the thousands of delegates elected to Local Government, for example, only about 11 per cent were female.) Few women complained about job discrimination as such, although Conchita did mention that some men still had the habit of saying, "Women get sick, have babies, they'll be away from the job." Also, a kind of indirect prejudice functioned in the choice of who got sent abroad to study. "There are plenty of qualified women but they don't get sent because of fear that they will marry and stay there, when their skills are needed at home." Conchita, who was pretty hot on the subject of discrimination, paused a moment and then said, "Listen, do you realize no woman has ever been executed as a counter-Revolutionary?"

Enjoy, enjoy, some would tell her. The problem was, too many Cuban women did. They accepted not only outright male chauvinism but also being patronized. "Sometimes," Conchita said, "the women are as much or more opposed to their liberation as men. They like to talk about themselves as long-suffering martyrs, all that." According to a philosophy student, "More men than women oppose equality for women—but a lot of women have a low consciousness about it. That is mainly because of lack of education and much lingering puritanism. Also, many Cuban women who assert their rights and complain about male chauvinism expect men to treat them in the old, courteous ways." An American-born girl who had lived with her husband for several months before they got legally married told of how "some of the women I know were shocked by that. But then they would say, 'I wish I could do it.' Women are stupid here—no, not stupid, just afraid to shake off old customs."

In this respect, Cuban women seemed to be quantitatively but not qualitatively different from women of other nations. Their attitudes reflected the long process of conditioning to which most of the world's women have been subjected. Briefly, and only in terms of recent centuries, that conditioning served to support male-dominated, capitalist societies but was rationalized biologically. Women were taught to value above all the institutions of marriage, nuclear family, female chastity, and then monogamy—essential under early private property systems and important as a panacea for the poor, who had no other area of power. They were taught to be privatized, to be isolated in their emotional lives or in the home, away from the collective—where they might swell the working class and thus become a threat to its rulers (not to mention the rulers' egos and convenience). They were taught to define themselves and their worth in terms of men, particularly in terms of their ability to catch one. They were taught to live vicariously and believe that was the only way to live. They were taught from birth to embrace a condition ranging from slavery to second-class citizenship and believe it to be their only available form of security. The sexual caste system, like the racial caste system, delineated the life roles of its subjects and shaped their minds to accept those roles. "Feminine" in Cuba as elsewhere thus meant home-oriented, passive, needing to be guided and protected. The old definitions stuck, even when their economic origins and biological justifications had altered.

Cuban women, like their sisters in more "modern" countries, had difficulty perceiving their psychological oppression. Knowing one's place could seem to have its merits, and major changes could seem threatening. For middle-class Cuban women, marriage in pre-Revolutionary days meant a meal ticket as well as subservience; some Cuban women in 1967 hinted at a fear that their new status could bring about the loss of that meal ticket should they want to stop working. More profoundly, the incorporation of women in work—accompanied by new institutions like the *círculos infantiles*—might alter the finding of identity in housewifery and motherdom. What, then, would give a woman a sense of importance? The Revolution had answers to that question, but it would be hard for women to overcome fears about giving up old roles through which they knew how to obtain a certain measure of power, security, and identity.

The tides of change were in motion, however, and not to be

stopped. Some members of both sexes had begun to break with old sexual mores. Most Cubans, for example, still tended to think of the *posadas* (hotels where rooms could be openly rented by couples for a few hours) as whorehouses but a University of Havana student casually mentioned his visit to one in a general discussion about the nuisance of waiting in line for so many things. As usual, Havana's middle-class elements provided the main pressure for new mores. The educational level and the proportion of middle-class people ran higher there; 40 per cent of the Local Government delegates elected in the city of Havana were women, in contrast to the national proportion of 11 per cent. Havana was also most open to "modern" cultural influences in general. A *Juventud Rebelde* spot survey of 1967 showed that about half of the men and women interviewed were ready to accept the idea of virginity not being a prerequisite to marriage, and of a man and woman in love living together for a while as being an intelligent preface to marriage. (The big, double-page spread was illustrated by a drawing of a girl in mini-skirt with fishnet hose and a boy in "tight" pants.) These were all *habaneros*.

Outside the big city, attitudes were more often like that of the *campesino* who dismissed the chances for new sexual styles, saying, "Ahhh—we men are just too dirty-minded." Women tended to be like the pregnant *campesina* in San Andrés who moved from hanging laundry to heating water to child care all day long without complaint, while her husband did a bit of farming. But women doing agricultural work in the Plan of Banao, far from Havana, were making some interesting discoveries about their own attitudes toward themselves, and finding a new sense of identity away from home.

Under the impact of these changes, the Cuban man's behavior ranged from hostile to confused to liberal. Among the latter was a young teacher in the Art School who affirmed that the students should have relations with each other whether married or not. "I told that to one of the directors and he said, 'That's terrible—the boys will just go from girl to girl and never get married.' And I answered, 'But meanwhile, everybody will have had a wonderful time!' " This same teacher, however, got upset when his American-born wife went to the movies alone.

A very few men saw that "the woman question" also involved "a man question"; that the liberation of one sex from old ideas should be accompanied by a liberation of the other. As the painter who had spoken about the traumatized male said, "Cuban men will have to find new ways in which to be men." But *machismo* still had a firm grip. Cuban men would brake their cars to a screeching halt in the middle of traffic in order to ogle a well-built woman, and it was hard to be sure whether they did so because they were truly overwhelmed or because they felt it was required. The men probably didn't know either, for their conditioning had been almost as deep as that of the women.

All in all, the status of women and sexual relations in Cuba was a curious but not so surprising mixture of past, present, and future; of Revolution and conservatism; of the situation in some highly industrialized countries and the situation in some very undeveloped ones. Giant steps had been and were being taken toward the liberation of women. But if that liberation is defined as freedom from old roles and definitions, with full availability of alternative life patterns, then it would be more accurate to define the changes which had taken place thus far as the basis for a total revolution rather than the revolution itself.

The anomalies could be wondrous. Havana's special school to train women for directing traffic, for example, startled one member of the American liberation movement when she visited it in 1968. During the morning, the trainees learned how to handle a gun and even more rugged forms of self-defense. In the afternoon, they had a class in how to apply cosmetics—as if they were back in the days when woman's role was to "please" men and femininity meant competing with other women. Many men may find this contradiction harmless or even nice. But it isn't, if one realizes that the Cuban woman was still in the process of being accepted and of accepting herself as "equal to" or "as good as" men—a patronizing concept similar to white liberal attitudes towards blacks (equal rights being something else again, however). Most Cuban teachers were female, and no one seemed ready to imagine men staffing the day-care centers. Even more than in the case of racism, the old structure which supported oppression was gone—but the ideology lingered on.

The policies of the Revolutionary leadership on women's liberation combined unqualified support and compromise. Equality of the sexes was actively taught. A group of boy and girl students at Minas del Frío, asked if they could imagine a woman as Prime Minister in twenty years, all answered "yes" instantly. "Women will have the same rights as men, we will be able to do productive labor and we will be able to pick up a gun like men," one girl added. "Women will not be the tool of a corrupt society," affirmed a young man. Their discussion of woman's future was enthusiastic, if predictable.

In the area of sexual mores, the Revolution again faced conflicts created by trying to deal simultaneously with material and mental realities rooted in the past; again, it had to make compromises. The scholarship program exemplified this. In order to get students out of their homes and into the boarding schools for training to help modernize Cuba, the Revolution had to offer assurance to the parents that their children (daughters in particular) would remain virtuous. Leaders remembered the exodus of 1960–61, when anti-Revolutionary propagandists spread the idea that children were going to be grabbed from their parents and put in boarding schools where God-knows-what would happen to their "purity." Thus the sexual segregation and strict mores applied to the *becados*, with a few cases of students expelled for having had relations. Poet Allen Ginsberg, during his rather turbulent visit to Cuba in 1966, was moved to ask bluntly, "What's your program for these kids—masturbation?" But the problem bothered some Revolutionary Cubans too.

"Fidel recognizes the prejudices that exist," said one man, "but too much open encouragement of sexual liberty could make tremendous propaganda for the counter-Revolutionaries. Also, it would disturb many parents." The Revolution therefore followed a policy of fine distinctions. Among young agricultural workers who had signed up for two years, for example, long-range abstinence was not demanded. The only taboos were adultery and promiscuity. Generally and unofficially, the same policy prevailed—toward adults—in the neighborhood C. D. R.'s, which had influence on such matters as a person's admission to the Party. As for the Party itself, "It is willing to examine these problems, since it is pragmatic and interested in *la masa*" (the masses), Beatriz affirmed. "You couldn't propose that all mothers give contraceptives to their kids—but the sectarianism has ended. There was a terrible period when an unmarried woman could be expelled from the Party for becoming pregnant. People were scared to make mistakes and there was a lack of qualified people. But now many people in the Party are using their heads—which is what Fidel always told them to do."

Fidel himself was a big supporter of "woman power" in the areas of work roles and attitudes. In his speech at the 1966 National Convention of the FMC (Federation of Cuban Women), to mention only one example, he spoke at great length about women's achievements in agricultural production: the superiority of women workers in the Plan of Banao to men workers in terms of discipline, sense of responsibility, enthusiasm, vocation. He told how a woman had become administrator of the Plan of Banao (noted for its production of asparagus and strawberries)—"the first time a woman had been assigned a task of that nature . . . and it seems to us a reasonable thing—more, a good thing—that the director of a plan in which thousands of women are working should be a woman." He also said, "If women think that they have attained an optimum situation in the society . . . if they think that their Revolutionary purpose in the society has been achieved, they would be making a mistake. It seems to us that women still have to struggle a great deal . . . to attain the place they should occupy." Inequality still existed, officials affirmed; the present represented a transition period, with many women still subject to "housework slavery" while being incorporated in the society's work.

The Prime Minister was way ahead of most Cubans in his

position on the equality of women but some women felt that even he did not altogether understand the problem. He did tip his masculine hand a bit, in that same 1966 speech, when he spoke about the lack of adequate facilities for the freeing of women to work. In the absence of more workers' dining rooms, and so forth, he asked, "Who cooks for the men when they come home from work?" But, *compañeros:* women have to eat too, when they come home from work. Fidel himself acknowledged, however, that ". . . if someone had once asked me if I thought I had prejudice, I would have answered absolutely no—because I really believed that. . . . But what has happened? . . . What is happening is, in reality, that the potential strength of women is superior to what the most optimistic of us could ever have thought. And for this reason we say that perhaps at bottom, unconsciously, there was some prejudice or some underestimation . . ."

The Federation of Cuban Women was generally silent or conservative on the thorny issues. The FMC did work hard to liberate women from the home and from ignorance, by many means. In a typical issue of its magazine, *Mujeres,* an article appeared on women in agriculture and also an illustrated piece about a woman who photographed the birth of her own baby (astounding for a Latin country). But of the ninety-eight pages in that issue, forty were devoted to fashion and thirteen more to recipes, embroidery, hair styles, child and household care. Nor did the FMC explore the changing sexual mores. "The Federation isn't on the same wavelength as the younger generation," was one comment. "The Federation is mostly older women."

The Revolution was not rocking the boat on the question of new definitions. For example, women were often assigned to certain types of agricultural work that called for patience and meticulousness—on the grounds that the female excelled in those qualifications. Even if someone had questioned whether women really have an innate predilection for the tedious and the painstaking, few Cubans of either sex would have been concerned with the answer. Such work was vital to conquering underdevelopment and Cuba had to use the best available personnel. Furthermore, the women themselves took pride in their skill and enjoyed a sense of group unity.

In its position on homosexuality, the Revolution also seemed to be acting in a spirit of compromise. In the early days, when dogmatists like Anibal Escalante held a certain power and the existence of heavy counter-Revolutionary activity could be used to justify harsh measures, some rather underdeveloped policies had been adopted toward homosexuals. It was argued that homosexuals tend to form un- or anti-Revolutionary cells; without debating the truth of that contention, we know that it was often applied dogmatically and sometimes with unpolitical motives. By 1967, official policy seemed much more sensible and humanistic than before—and probably ahead of much popular thinking. The nighttime raids to catch homosexuals *in delicto flagrante* were over. The practice of sending homosexuals, along with military-age delinquents considered unsuitable for regular Army service, to compulsory labor camps called UMAP (Military Units for Aid to Production) was also ending if not already past. The novel *Paradiso*, with its explicitly homosexual passages, had been published.

Although homosexuality was still illegal, actual policy came down to a restriction of homosexuals from contact with youth as teachers and supervisors, and from practicing medicine, where physical intimacy occurred. In general, the humanity and flexibility of people like Fidel or Haydée Santamaría (director of the Casa de las Américas) had prevailed over both popular prejudice and sectarian dogmatism on this issue. Furthermore, Fidel indicated in at least one interview (with Lee Lockwood in his book *Castro's Cuba, Cuba's Fidel*) that the Revolution was continuing to explore the homosexuality question.

The overall picture of Revolutionary policy on women and sexual relations indicated that, even if the men who ran the country were willing, Cuba's economic and political needs inhibited a revolution in certain areas, mostly outside work. The conquest of material underdevelopment had top priority; polit-

187

ically, people had enough gripes about things like rations for the regime not to take an unpopular position on gut issues like femininity and masculinity. But a few Cuban women were already pushing for new definitions.

As with other old ideas, the task of examining the more complex aspects of women's liberation was a province of youth. On one level, women scholarship students at the University of Havana were putting up a fight in 1967 against the regulations which required that they be back in the dormitory an hour ahead of the men every night. On a broader level, philosophy students and teachers at the same university were discussing in seminars the problems created by the changing role of women, and conducting various forms of "cultural guerrilla activity."

Among them were two young women, Josefina and Sarita, both in their twenties. Their main concern was the anomalies created by this fast-moving Revolution: the coexistence of semi-primitive ignorance with "free love," for example. They were troubled that sexual liberty was coming about in a vacuum. "There is no orientation, no position on it taken by the leaders," they said one night. But the two young women were also looking beyond the purely sexual aspect of "the woman revolution." They saw one big obstacle as being woman's own attitude toward herself. This idea was spelled out in a paper then circulating among teachers, students, and others interested in the issue.

"Economic independence is not enough. It is not a matter of a woman being able to pay her way but . . . of being able to transform her attitude toward life . . . the problem will not be solved simply by the incorporation of the woman in work. Extracting her from the role of housewife will not automatically change her attitude toward life. A woman working for the collectivity can continue to view problems through the prism of subordination and passivity.

"Change of occupation is only the basis for the transformation of women . . . her whole attitude must change. It is a process of personal realization, which does not lie merely in dedicating herself to a creative task but in shifting the center of interest from the limits of one's emotional life and events within the nuclear family, to a much broader area . . . which goes beyond individual interest: the interest centered in social activity. A woman realizes herself as a person when her viewpoint transcends egoistic interest."

Their position thus resembled one wing of the radical women's movement recently emerging in the United States. They did not view men as The Enemy: ". . . the true feminine struggle is the rejection of all those childhood teachings, all those family pressures during adolescence, and even the dominant social thinking which affects her as an adult . . . the idea of femininity, of womanhood, as meaning the dedication of one's life to finding and keeping a companion, generally at the price of being his satellite."

These two young women recognized that women had been oppressed both culturally and economically; that, as in the case of racism, the cultural factors had acquired a force of their own so great that their automatic disappearance under socialism should not be taken for granted. But socialism provides the only basis for the true liberation, they believed. Only a collective society offered the possibility—if not the assurance—of women shedding their privatization and reification to become fully human.

"The 'woman problem' in Cuba is now fundamentally cultural rather than political or economic," Josefina pointed out. "Griping about the status of women—like race—is something that has begun only with the Revolution," said Conchita, the young artist. "Men will find new ways in which to be men," the painter, Tomás, had commented optimistically, "because the basic society is better." In Fidel's words: "The basis for discrimination—the exploitation of Man by Man—has disappeared."

The ending of overt white supremacy opened the way for blacks to explore and attack its covert forms; the freeing of women from the kitchen (though still partial) catalyzed an awareness of deeper problems. Both new forms of liberation had created what might be called "rising expectations." Or, to put it more sharply, they had brought Cuban blacks and women to the point of challenging "the man" way down deep. In the same way, the ending of bourgeois supremacy—the creation of new class relationships—brought into focus many problems having to do with how people related to their fellow workers, to work itself, to government. Each upheaval left its own vacuum of values.

In clearing away the social structure of oppression, the Revolution opened a Pandora's box of human problems which developed under capitalism and colonialism but have roots older than both. Ironically, the very act of placing power in the hands of the poor, the rural masses, meant placing it in the hands of those Cubans whose life values were most conservative and resistant to change. From the way a campesino *showed respect for city people, to his feelings about intermarriage, to his prejudice against long hair and homosexuality, he asserted his conformity. This was just one of many newborn contradictions to be worked out in the long Revolutionary process. Liberation had been won, now freedom had to be forged.*

The New Man and Woman would emerge from the interaction of several forces: changes in the societal structure, specific efforts to uproot old ideas, the particular nature of Cuba's culture and people, and whatever it is that can be truly called human nature. The Cubans themselves said that the New Man was not to be forged in some eternal, frozen image. He would change with the passing of time, with new technology, the mobility of human imagination—a constantly "unfinished product," as Che put it. The name of the game was dialectics; its only unbreakable rules were Marx's favorite maxim, "Doubt everything," and: "Keep the faith."

The Campo

PART THREE:

Two Weeks on the Isle of Youth

Revolution creates the conditions for a true cultural mutation. That is why in the Third World . . . the revolutionary experience is the only valid foundation of the 'cogito.' It provokes an exalting unity of thinking and social being. To make a revolution . . . brings us to a new postulate of reasoning: I make the revolution, therefore I am, therefore we are. . . . We cease to be the zombies of history.

René Depestre,
Haitian writer
in exile in Cuba

Two Weeks
on the Isle of Youth

Youth at work in Cuba: the phrase can conjure up poster images of a sturdy young man with hoe in hand, gazing across newly planted fields into a boundless future, or a smiling girl displaying a sack of freshly picked coffee beans and not one drop of sweat on her pretty face. But Cuban posters are usually better than that, and Cuban youth at work isn't like that at all. It is, rather, a stirring and hectic and live phenomenon, involving people who are not quite "New Men" nor old ones either. To work with them for a while is to understand how the Revolutionary present has one foot in the past and another in the future—yet its own separate identity as well. That was one reason why the Isle of Pines, now being renamed the Isle of Youth, seemed to me the single most exciting place in Cuba.

The Isle of Pines, the largest land body in an archipelago of 350 islets and cays, is about the size of Delaware and lies some fifty miles off the southwest coast of Cuba. Squarish in shape, it vaguely resembles an old schooner with sails hoisted. Christopher Columbus landed there in 1494 and claimed it for his patrons, but Spain virtually ignored the island during the next three and a half centuries. It became a refuge and rendezvous for high-class pirates like Francis Drake, Henry Morgan, and John Hawkins as well as for some lower-class buccaneers. The last pirate in the classic style was Pepe "El Mallorquín" who took over the island in 1822. Some years later, Robert Louis Stevenson wrote a book about those days; in it, the Isle of Pines became Treasure Island.

Pepe "El Mallorquín" was reincarnated as Tío Sam following the end of the Spanish-American-Cuban War, in 1899. The United States sought to profit by the fact that Spain had not officially considered the island part of Cuba, so that it did not come under the terms of the Paris Treaty, and thus to arrogate sovereignty directly to Washington. With this expectation, an 1899 Department of the Interior map showed the Isle of Pines as part of American territory. "A little Texas," some optimistically called it. But annexation attempts met with strong Cuban opposition.

A familiar-sounding plan to bring about and justify United States annexation was concocted in 1905, when American landowners on the island announced that they had a six-thousand-man "liberation army" ready and were going to rise up. The United States Ambassador in Cuba then asked Washington to dispatch a warship "to protect the lives and property of American citizens." The conflict dragged on for years, with the United States virtually in charge of the island while Cuban university students spearheaded a movement for recognition of Cuban sovereignty. In 1925, the United States got its base at Guantánamo and relinquished control of the Isle of Pines, whereupon Cuba's President thanked Washington for its "generosity."

The American landowners stayed, however. In the days of Batista, say Cuban historians, the whole southern half of the island was owned by an absentee landlord known as Mr. Davis, who got it from a Mr. Hedges, who got it from Nobody-Knows-Who. Certain Cubans didn't do badly either. A cattle rancher named Goyo held a great hunk of the north, while three or four other friends of Batista carved up what was left. In general, these gentlemen spent little time on their property. Except for small amounts of citrus fruit and cattle, the island's great resources went untapped: marble, tungsten, gold, copper, iron, hardwoods. The rivers and subterranean lakes were not utilized for irrigation. Nobody built roads to the long, beautiful beaches along the coastline or to hardly anywhere else. The offshore lobsters and sponges lay undisturbed. Vast tracts of land remained empty.

Even people did not grow on the Isle of Pines. In 1819, after more than three centuries of Spanish rule, the island had less than two hundred inhabitants. The slow pace continued for decades; by 1960, there were still only 10,000 people or about three souls per square kilometer. Half of them were—in addition to the landowners—agricultural workers, fishermen, and charcoal-makers, together with a large floating population. Nueva Gerona, the capital and a free port with no export or import duties, attracted some of the latter: gamblers, contrabandists, and prostitutes. About an hour's drive from there, Batista built a luxury hotel—the Colony—which attracted another class of visitors: American tourists and wealthy Cubans, drawn there by a casino, the discreet location, and an abortion clinic. "And then there's the Gun Club, with eighteen superb French pointers," said one travel poster.

The other half of those 10,000 persons inhabited the Presidio Modelo, Model Prison, which had been built between 1926–29 by the detested tyrant, Governor Gerardo Machado. During the reign of its first administrator, five hundred men were reportedly murdered—many of them under the pretext of attempted escape. Subsequent directors of Cuba's largest prison appear to have been only slightly less brutal but much more corrupt. The last administrator before the Revolution was Major Juan Capote: an enterprising fellow who got his job by supporting Batista's *coup d'état* and grew rich on it. He first went into the real estate business, selling and renting parcels of land attached to the prison or acquired by influence. Then Capote became a landowner and cattle rancher; soon, he added bricks, marble, and stone (produced with prison labor) to his profitable catalogue. Like the administrators before him, he also did nicely by supplying prison labor to the large landowners at low cost to them and total benefit to himself.

Those incarcerated in the Presidio, as well as most of the free population, were located in the northern half of the island: a flat, tame area humped occasionally by a low mountain or some strangely shaped rise of rock. The south, on the other hand, was a verdant and beautiful wilderness, often jungle-like in land-scape. A huge swamp divided the two sections, and no roads for four-wheeled traffic connected them before the Revolution. So different were the two parts, and so isolated from one another, that people in the south acquired the habit of saying, "I am going to the Isle of Pines," or "the island," when they headed north. Another oddity of the southern area was several settle-ments of Cayman Islanders, such as the town called Jackson-ville. Composed of eight extended families of fishermen orig-inally from the British territory, the people of Jacksonville often spoke only English and retained many of their Cayman customs —including the myth of a promised land where there are plenty of coconuts and no hurricanes ever blow.

With the Revolution, some road building started on the Isle, and plans were made for other kinds of development (it seems curious today to learn that, in 1959, Fidel talked about estab-lishing direct flights to bring tourists there from the United States). Then, in 1966, hurricane Alma devastated the island and thousands of youths from the Communist Youth League went there to help pick up the pieces. They became excited about the island's possibilities and proposed that its development be made a special youth project. Enthusiastic about their idea, Fidel began embellishing it with plans for the building of dams, a causeway connecting the Isle with the mainland to solve the severe transportation problem, and other elaborate undertak-ings. The project was presumably approved by the Party's one-hundred-man Central Committee and the eight-man Political Bureau, with details hashed out there and in other agencies.

The first waves of youth came in the spring of 1967. Many of them set to work first to make the island more hospitable for the thousands who would follow. With the July 26 anniversary as a target date, they worked around the clock building or expanding dormitories and dining rooms for the various *campamentos,* camps in which people would live. They helped construct new centers for the artificial insemination of cattle. A large group worked to complete new eating and recreation facilities in Nueva Gerona: an ice cream parlor—named Coppelia, like the one in Havana—a pizzeria, a seafood restaurant. By September, there were thirty-four camps and all kinds of young people on the island. (A year later this figure had risen to sixty, plus four family work camps. As of December 1968, there were 42,000 new workers on the Isle.)

The largest group was the forty-five hundred *columnistas,* who had signed up for two years; if they wanted to leave before the end of that period, they could, but very few did. The *columnistas* received room, board, medical and dental care, work clothes, transportation, and eighty-five pesos a month. That sum, intended for personal items and treats, was only a few pesos less than the full income of many Cuban workers. Then there were the hard-driving *guerrillas,* who had volunteered for two months of unpaid labor and set themselves a goal of working sixteen hours a day. Also, groups of students came to the Isle as the place to do their required, forty-five-day stint of unpaid agricultural work. Finally, there were a number of construction brigades who came and stayed as long as it took to do a given job.

The main types of labor performed had to do with citrus fruit and cattle. The Communist Youth League was responsible for recruitment and ultimate supervision of the manpower. The overall project in which the youth worked had been named "Camilo Cienfuegos Special Plan for Development" and functioned somewhat like a small ministry. It had its own budget and staff but worked closely with existing national ministries and government agencies in many fields.

The Isle had set particularly high goals for its citrus-fruit production. As one agricultural engineer told me, "We have a long way to go and many problems to solve. I made a tour of the United States, went to several universities, studied the citrus cultivation. They have very good, very advanced methods. But we are going to produce fruit as good as Florida, Israel, Spain." Other plans called for the creation of four thousand *cabellerías* of pasture and converting the south, much of whose soil was pure rock, into tillable land. A dam capable of irrigating forty thousand hectares had already been completed in mid-August, 1967.

Economic development was not, however, the only purpose of the Special Plan. Most of the people who signed up for two years had been neither workers nor students before; they were uninvolved, nonproductive street kids and the Plan thus formed part of a national effort to integrate this category of youth in the Revolution, obviously no easy task. "The conditions of life here are difficult, the work is hard and often completely new for many who come," said the First Secretary of the Communist Youth League on the island. That, in the late summer of 1967, was an accurate understatement.

A sign in the capital town of Nueva Gerona indicated another goal: "Why shouldn't this island be the first site of communism in Cuba?" The method for building communism there was to follow the same principle applied in another Special Plan, that of San Andrés: gradual elimination of money and the mentality that goes with it. Over the years, the Revolution would increase the goods and services given to workers while simultaneously —and proportionately—decreasing the wages paid, until the former took care of all needs and the latter disappeared completely. The Isle had certain characteristics which made it an interesting candidate for becoming "the first site of communism." Before the Plan, the Isle had no population to mention (considering its size); no entrenched classes; not even a school to teach acceptance of the status quo. With the elimination of a few landlords, its slate had in a sense been wiped clean. Only a fraction of the land on the Isle remained in private hands; almost all development was being undertaken collectively. By virtue of its very emptiness, the Isle offered the possibility of starting fresh—of building from scratch.

Still another aim of the Plan was that large numbers of those who came to the Isle for two years would settle down there and populate the still empty island, thus enhancing not only the national economy but also military security. To this end, new housing was being constructed for couples and families. The population had already leaped, since 1961, from ten to forty thousand, with ninety thousand expected by 1970. The traffic between Havana and the Isle ran heavy; almost every hour during the day, going and coming, a full plane made the twenty-five-minute flight (it was also possible to travel by bus across Cuba and then ferry to the Isle).

I went to the island the first time partly out of curiosity and partly because some American friends were going anyway, to make a documentary movie. At the small airport, a guide and two cars hired by the film-makers stood waiting. The guide was Malena: a handsome and unusually poised girl of twenty-three from the province of Oriente. She had Indian features and coloring, brown eyes, and short brown hair with a slight kink in it. There was a lisp in her low voice; like most Cubans of her age, she spoke no English. Her inexpensive clothes looked well put together: trim white pants, bright blue overshirt, matching scarf and shoulder bag. Her manner was warm, humorous, efficient.

On the long ride to the Colony Hotel, where foreign visitors still stayed, Malena talked a little about herself. A *militante* of the Communist Youth League, she had studied Russian and become a translator at a time when Cuba's economic emphasis was on industrialization. With the shift to agricultural development and the existing labor shortage, as well as her *militante* responsibility to set an example, she had begun to rethink her life and eventually decided to come to the Isle. "At first I wasn't so keen about signing up for two years," she said. "But since getting here six months ago, I am very, very happy. My only problem is that I am anxious to get back to my camp and agricultural work. I am a temporary guide, because there are so many visitors now." That night in the hotel, she stayed up until four o'clock in the morning making arrangements for the American film-makers. Three hours later, our group began its three days of travel around the island.

We passed many times through Nueva Gerona, the capital, because the roads leading to different parts of the island—and there were still few of them—all passed through it. Nueva Gerona felt like a frontier town: laid out in neat squares, unmellowed, bustling with people and movement. The scarcity of telephones on the Isle (and girls—only one to every fifteen males) gave social contact a particular intensity. Every place for eating, every cafe, seemed to be jammed every evening and offices as well stayed busy until late at night, with jeeps pulling up and leaving again constantly.

But the town's finest hour came just after dawn and again around five or six in the afternoon, when open trucks packed with workers would pass through on their way to the fields or back to the camps after work. Then all the children, and some adults too, stood in front of their homes along the road to cheer and wave at the workers, who cheered and waved at them. The passage along the roads was a grand procession, spontaneous despite its many repetitions. Girls on the trucks would sing along the way, alternating love songs and Revolutionary anthems indiscriminately, so that one minute it was *"Tu serás mi baby"* or *"Me enamoré"* and the next it was "Arise, ye prisoners of starvation" or "Forward, Cubans . . ." When a truckload of girls from one camp passed a truckload of girls from another, there was a great calling-out to individual friends and shouted demands for the latest information about so-and-so. When a truckload of girls passed a truckload of boys, a wild kind of cheering rang out and the boys' arms stretched forth toward the girls longingly until they were far apart again.

We visited a dozen camps of different types in different parts of the island, each with its particular qualities and atmosphere. Patria (Homeland) was a trim cluster of cinder-block or wooden buildings enhanced by flowers, with a pleasant, open-air dining hall. As in many camps, the toilets were Turkish and a shower was a bucket of water—but that did not seem to hurt morale. All the two-hundred-odd girls did a specialized type of work: grafting citrus plants. In addition, they were all from Havana and most had been on the island for several months. Thus when they came marching home from the fields at the end of the day, singing, or sat eating around the long table at night, an exceptional pride and congeniality filled the air.

"Free Algeria Camp," on the other hand, was one where former delinquent boys had come (voluntarily) to do various types of ordinary fieldwork. Recruited by the neighborhood C.D.R.'s, they received forty dollars a month instead of eighty-five dollars (but that included cigarettes) and they studied three hours a day instead of the usual one or two. Discipline, which had been strict when they first arrived a few months back, was more relaxed now, yet still stricter than in other camps. When I asked a quiet youth what he planned to do after his two years on the island, he replied, "I will go wherever the Revolution . . ." and was reluctant to say more. There were also young men like the cook: a seventeen-year-old boy with a thin, merry face, who chatted in a relaxed way. "I never worked as a cook before— they suffered at first, I'm afraid," he said, stirring his pots jauntily. The camp's spirit seemed tentative, still in the process of crystallization.

Yet another feeling pervaded the camp of male students from Havana's Art School, who were there for a forty-five-day stint of volunteer work. They had put up signs all over the camp's roughhewn buildings: "Coppelia" on the battered frame dining hall, "Hotel Habana Libre" on the dormitory, and "Private Bath" outside the communal toilet. They did the usual, backbreaking fieldwork—hoeing, scattering fertilizer, weeding —but in the evenings they put on musical and dramatic performances around the island. This was the cool camp of the Isle.

Like Patria, the camps of *vaqueros*—cowhands—had a special atmosphere of pride and unity. Herding the cows out to pasture, bringing them in at milking time or lassoing a calf, the youths—mostly under twenty—rode their horses with an air which combined Western cowboy style with Latin *machismo*. The boys who milked the cows or cleaned the stalls had less swagger but worked with equal concentration. One of them pointed to some F-1 calves, product of the first crossbreeding between Cuba's Cebu and the Holstein: "We call them 'the sons of Fidel.' " The name came from the fact that this crossing had been Fidel's idea, and that the animals represented the future of the nation—in a literal sense. "Fidel knows all their names," the *vaquero* went on, "not just here but all over Cuba. And he supervises all the crossings." "Do you think he'll still know all the names when we get to F-4?" another youth asked as he walked in from lassoing some strays. In the *vaquero* camps, where the workers were responsible for animate creatures, there seemed to be a kind of involvement absent in camps where people related only to plants—and often weeds at that.

At the camp called Revolution, we were almost startled when the blond girl *responsable*—person in authority—welcomed us with miniature bottles of rum, to be drunk on the spot. That was part of the generally more relaxed and mature scene at "Revolution" and also at "Liberty." Most of the camps had an all-boy or all-girl population; these two were integrated. "If it works out well," the *responsable* said, "future camps will be mixed too. But we couldn't start all of them that way." The workers at "Revolution" and "Liberty"—who included a few married couples—were fewer in number, somewhat older, and had a higher level of education than the people at the other camps. They did the same kind of work out in the fields but the atmosphere at the camps themselves was more like that of a college campus, with recreation halls, libraries, and even a beauty shop at "Liberty" for the residents.

Neither camp had the degree of semi-military discipline prevailing elsewhere. This discipline generally meant division of the workers into *pelotónes* (platoons); morning and evening formation for announcements; marching on the way out to work and coming home. At all camps, the day began at about five; work hours ran from around seven-thirty until about five. After dinner, something was always happening: a class or a Ping Pong contest, perhaps an evening of drawing cartoons about imperialism. By eleven, lights were usually out in the dormitories. Once a week "Pass Day" rolled around: work stopped at about eleven in the morning and everyone was on his own until curfew some twelve hours later. For segregated campers, this was the only time in the week when the sexes could mix legitimately: at other times, men and women were not even supposed to speak together except by permission or under unusual circumstances. Every forty-five days, all workers had five days off plus travel time in which they could go home to visit family and friends. But sometimes their leaves were postponed—Malena, for example, had not been able to take hers yet because of all the visitors she had to show around.

Schedules were always subject to adjustment for an emergency situation. At eleven-thirty one night, we went to the grapefruit packing plant; a freighter was leaving for Europe in three days and two shifts of girls were working almost around the clock to meet the goal of a five-hundred-ton shipment. The man in charge had been born on the Isle of Pines, a rarity, and ran this plant before the Revolution. He had a fairly complex operation on his hands: unloading the fruit as it came in from the groves, maturing it in dark, dry rooms for three days, washing and polishing it, then sorting and packing it by hand into cardboard boxes marked "Treasure Island—Grapefruit" and *"Île du Trésor—Pamplemousse."* Only the best went abroad; rejects were set aside to be sold in Cuba or juiced. The girls worked seriously and steadily as the belt bringing the grapefruit down for selection clanked on through the night and the boxes filled with fruit piled up.

On the last day of our visit, we went to the old prison once called "Model."

The Presidio had continued to function after the overthrow of Batista, as a place for those caught in counter-Revolutionary activity. The Revolutionary administration was decent, an ex-prisoner working in Nueva Gerona said, and the three-stage "Re-education Program" initiated by the state led to the early release of many. Re-education meant lectures, reading, and especially working, although the desire simply to get out and be with one's family seemed to have been a strong motivating force for becoming "rehabilitated." The ex-prisoner with whom we talked sounded that way. A bakery owner before the Revolution, he had joined a clandestine sabotage group in the early sixties. Then he was caught, served three years of his ten-year sentence, and had been released after a year in the Re-education Program. Now working as a bakery supervisor, he didn't sound very converted to Revolutionary ideals—but he had become a productive citizen and no more was demanded.

Yet despite these reforms, Cuba still did not feel comfortable about continuing to use the Presidio, with all its evil ghosts. Construction of an enormous new rehabilitation center was begun, as a sort of antidote. Then came the plan for the island: the Presidio had to go, period. By February, 1967, it was shut down completely as a prison and the men still left inside transferred to other penal institutions, sent out to work on farms in the Re-education Program, or set free. On June 7, nine men went to work on the Presidio with blowtorches. In twenty-seven days they ripped out every grill of bars from the windows, every cell door, every cot, every removable trace of the past.

In August, 1967, the old cell blocks of the Presidio must have presented one of the world's strangest sights. Walking down a central path, we first passed the rectangular "Selection" buildings for good-conduct prisoners. Just beyond them were two giant rotundas called *circulares,* for ordinary convicts, one on each side of the walk. Some distance away lay a small, low building for bad-conduct prisoners. On the ground surrounding all of these structures lay piles of barred grills and doors: a single window perched askew on its side here, a door lying flat over there. They had been left where they fell after the blowtorches struck. In the white walls of the stripped buildings, the old nail marks looked like stigmata.

The *circulares* were haunted houses. A dim light came through the small cell windows. On the ground level you could still see some of the pipes which had brought in water for the showers and toilets there. Five tiers of cells, connected by two staircases, ran around the entire circumference and height of each building. The cells faced out on the open, central area: pure cubicles, without doors or door frames now, each with a number inscribed above it. There were enough cubicles for at least a thousand men. Rising in the dead center of each *circular* was a guard tower, reachable only by a tunnel leading from outdoors; one guard could stand on top of that tower and control the entire building. High above, the roof was lost in darkness. Hundreds of invisible birds had moved in there after the prisoners left, and their raucous, echoing song made the emptiness seem even more vast. Whether you stood down on the ground or on one of the walks running along each tier, you felt surrounded; you knew the fear and hopelessness which must have been instilled by this giant honeycomb.

In all of the Presidio, a single cell still had its original, barred door: the one in which Fidel Castro spent three months after the abortive Moncada attack. Others caught in that attack had also been put in the Presidio—like Juan Almeida, who would climb up to his cell window and sing out the July 26 anthem (for which he received a beating and fractured arm). But Fidel's cell, located by itself in the hospital building, had been retained as a museum with a small exhibit of Revolutionary photographs and mementoes. In striking contrast to the *circulares,* this cell contained two rooms of decent size and a shower. "Well," a guard explained, "Fidel's family was large, and some of them were influential . . ." Later, someone else said that the purpose had been to isolate Fidel from other prisoners. Probably both explanations were true, but the guard's directness provided one of those small, pleasing moments that often occurred in Cuba despite all the reasons Cubans have to be cautious with American visitors.

The administration building of the Presidio, a tolerable-looking structure which hid the *circulares* from view as you arrived at the prison, now housed a new school: the Rebel Youth School City. Close to a thousand young men were already there, studying to be agricultural technicians (plans called for that enrollment to be expanded to twenty thousand). Their fields: citrus fruit, cattle, hydraulics, soil conservation—all particularly relevant to the Isle. Meanwhile, architecture students from the University of Havana were working to redesign the buildings— especially the *circulares*. What they could do with those sinister beehives, nobody yet knew. "But they must look different, absolutely different," school officials agreed.

On the road leading from the Presidio back to the main highway, we passed a large building with a new sign in front of it that said, "Campamento Juvenil Livia Gouverneur." I asked Malena, the guide, about it and she said, "That is *my* camp. Unfortunately we have no time left to go there. But it is the most interesting camp on the island," she added, a little mysteriously. "You should come back and see it." Then she rode with us to the airport and seemed genuinely sad when the plane was ready to take off. She stood on the observation deck, smiling and waving her blue scarf for a long time, even after the plane had lifted high and turned north toward Havana.

Ten days later, I went back alone to Malena's camp to live and work for two weeks.

Friday, August 25

The Livia Gouverneur camp was one of the largest on the Isle, with 416 workers at that time. It was known informally as Escuadrón—the Squadron—and its physical appearance must have been one reason why. Turning right off a main highway some ten minutes' drive from Nueva Gerona, you proceeded up a road heading straight for the old Presidio. Just before reaching it, there was a precise, right-hand turn. A short, arrow-like drive led directly to what had been the barracks of a military unit attached to the prison and was now the camp. In front of the main building lay a sort of traffic circle. On it stood a semicircular, concrete barricade with slits to fire through at any enemy coming down the drive.

The building itself was a large, stone rectangle of two stories, with side wings not visible from the front, the whole thing painted white with gray and yellow trim. Its long façade had been done in a style that might be called Late Spanish Military. At each end rose a windowed and crenelated tower. A veranda ran the entire length of the façade, faced with arches; above it, a second-floor balcony also ran the length of the façade—a fine spot for generals to stand and review the troops. The total effect of this establishment was geometrically precise, many-eyed, more boastful than impregnable. Perhaps, I thought, the place will at least be cool and breezy: the temperature had gone over ninety and remained there.

It was six P.M. when I arrived, and a large group of workers had just arrived from the fields. They marched in from trucks parked out on the road, passed the traffic circle, and headed around the left side of the building toward the back. They were a raggle-taggle lot: mostly young women of fourteen to about twenty, many in flimsy pants and torn blouses, others in dresses with shabby brassieres showing where a button had been lost or a seam ripped, a few girls neat in the gray pants and shirt uniform of the *columnista*. A young woman almost six feet tall counted cadence on the way. Then the *pelotónes*—platoons containing twenty-six girls each—halted in a giant courtyard at the back of the main building where a young woman stood ready to make some announcements.

This was Cacha: a buxom Communist Youth League *militante* of medium height with brown hair and expressive hazel eyes, nicely dressed, animated, a good-looking girl from the Midwest if she had not been so Cuban in shape and gesture. As the current *responsable* of the camp, Cacha did not have absolute authority—the camp was run by an Executive Committee composed of Communist Youth League members—but her manner and the respectful stance of the audience suggested that her word carried unusual weight.

In a pleasant, husky voice she first introduced me to the crowd, who gave a loud and tongue-twisting cheer: the camp's version of "Two, four, six eight . . . rah, rah, rah!" I was the only foreigner staying at the camp then and the first American to work there; Cacha told them my name but during my stay most would call me *"La americana."*

Then she got down to business.

225

"I am happy to announce that twenty *compañeras* are leaving the camp tonight to become nurses. They will study in Havana. This is a great honor and I know we all wish them luck.

"Now, there is something else. Look behind you at the laundry." On the far side of the courtyard was a line of low buildings: the outhouses, showers, kitchen, and an open-air laundry which doubled as a washroom. "Look at all the clothing which has been left in the laundry. It looks very bad. It should have been hung up to dry immediately. And there is something else. Some people have been taking clothes which belong to others, without asking permission. Perhaps you do this at home. You take your sister's dress when your own isn't clean, perhaps without asking. But you cannot do it here—take something without asking, or take it and leave it for the person to find, dirty.

"I know you are waiting to receive your camp clothing. Unfortunately, it has not yet arrived—many other camps have been waiting even longer than you. In the future, each of you will receive a specific set of items and we will be able to make a proper inventory. But now," she paused, looking determined, "the pass will be canceled for tomorrow unless your conduct improves and all items of clothing are restored to their owners by then."

The crowd began to murmur. "You know I have never canceled a pass before on the island," Cacha continued firmly, "but the situation is very serious. I want to ask you how you feel about what I have proposed here. Do you accept it?"

Cacha's style with the workers was based on a modern, "masculine" appeal to logic rather than the old maternal approach of "Look how you are upsetting me, you must behave," which would have seemed more Cuban. Whether that confused or pleased the girls, they all shouted *"Sí"* as though they meant it and dispersed quickly to take showers.

In a few minutes the two broad stone staircases leading to the second floor, one at each end of the building, became thronged with girls rushing up and down. On the second floor I found a huge open area jammed with double-decker bunks.

Almost all of the four hundred workers slept there. They had no cabinets or storage space for clothes and personal possessions; things had to be draped over bedsteads or kept in boxes under the lower bunks.

Someone took me to my place in a small room, off the main area, where only sixteen women slept. The room, located in the northern tower of the building, was bare except for the bunks and a few pieces of clothing in view. A window at one end faced the top of the tree in front of the building; if you leaned far out and stretched, you could glimpse the sea in the distance—the northern waters of the Isle. A single light bulb burned high in the ceiling of the room. On the back of the door hung a sheet of yellowed paper, which no one had bothered to remove. It was a list of the soldiers once housed there and their schedule of who was to clean the room on what day.

Several women were sitting on their bunks now, waiting for the lines outside the showers to diminish. "Did you just come from Havana?" one of them asked me eagerly. "Ah, things are so well organized there now," she said, addressing the room at large. "Before, everybody used to fight to get on the bus, and fight inside it. Now, people line up to wait—and move quietly inside too. Can you imagine such a thing?"

Almost all of the workers in the camp came from Havana or its environs, but they had rarely been born there. Their parents often turned out to be *campesinos* who had formed part of the constant migration from the countryside to the city and brought them along as children. Among these was a girl of twenty, who now began to ask questions about my travels around Cuba, about the United States. Her nickname was China, which is pronounced Cheena in Spanish, and she looked like an Indian princess: small but strong, with brown skin and a full head of black hair, a high forehead which protruded slightly, prominent cheekbones, eyes set wide apart. Unlike most of the others in the room, she did not chatter but spoke briefly and with care.

When she asked a third question, another girl who had been talking to me earlier interrupted in a resentful tone. China replied, the girl answered back, and finally China said in a serious

227

voice: "Look, *mí amor,* we must all talk to any foreigners who come here. We must all relate to them. You cannot expect to have one all to yourself. That is not being a good Communist—how will we ever achieve communism that way?" One or two of the others nodded; soon everyone had left the room to bathe or eat.

It was still light outside. In front of the building two different groups of workers were dancing. About a dozen white and two or three black girls, laughing and shouting, did a sort of square dance in a prim circle around the flagpole. Out in the large basketball court which lay to one side of the entrance drive, a host of only black and mulatto girls were doing a way-out rumba while a curly-headed teen-ager pounded on a conga drum. The girls wore raggedy shirts and tight cotton pants with zippers often held together by safety pins; their heads were covered with curlers improvised from the cardboard centers of toilet-paper rolls. They moved in pairs or sometimes alone, hips punctuating the drum beat, proud and cool. For a minute, I forgot that this was an agricultural camp in an old Cuban prison; it was really a Saturday evening at Rockland Palace, the girls were dressed to dazzle and doing the bougaloo, on, on, on, without pausing for breath.

Inside the building, the administrative office was chaos. Cacha sat behind a desk or beside it or on it, as a stream of girls came to see her: one had somebody's clothing to turn in, another was leaving for Havana in an hour to study nursing and had no money for the trip, another wanted to show how bad her mosquito bites were, then another piece of clothing, then a request for change of a ten-peso bill. Somehow, Cacha remained cool and attentive to everyone. A girl brought coffee to the office; Cacha gulped it down, holding her cup with one hand while pleading for order with the other. After an hour the turmoil lessened and she jumped up. "Let's go to town," she said to me, "I have to see someone at the Communist Youth League office."

With three hitches—jeep, bus, jeep—we got to Nueva Gerona and discovered that a fashion show was being held in a theater there. Cacha negotiated another jeep ride back to the camp; there, she loaded up a truck with girls and brought them in to see the fashion show—perhaps to boost morale after her threat to cancel the pass. At the theater, she paused briefly to admire a bathing suit, then ran to the office and settled in a jeep again to return to camp. Her boyfriend was driving, and she finally seemed to relax.

"Who was Livia Gouverneur?" I asked, "the woman the camp is named for?"

"She was a Venezuelan martyr," Cacha answered. "With the first group of girls who came here, we had a meeting where these things were explained. But most of the girls who are here now came later and we haven't done that yet. With them, we have to establish discipline first.

"These girls come from the worst possible background—really poor homes. Many come just for the money. Those are all things from the past and you don't wipe out the past in a day, it takes years and even then you do not always succeed. Many of these girls have been here less than a month. They have a superficial knowledge of political things. They are Revolutionaries, yes—because they have *seen* what the Revolution has done, the changes it has made." She pointed to one of her eyes, as Cubans often did to emphasize the truth of a statement. "If you ask them, What would you do if someone killed Fidel or if Cuba was invaded? they know. They wouldn't have to be pushed into fighting. But if you ask them, What is OLAS? they have no idea. One thought that Douglas Bravo [the Venezuelan guerrilla leader] was a baseball pitcher. If you ask, Who is Armando Hart? they will say 'a Communist.' They don't know what he does or how things work. You won't see many people reading the books here in the library.

"In my own life, I grew up with everything I wanted. We were not rich, but I never lacked a doll or enough food. I was seventeen at the time of the triumph of the Revolution and I didn't understand much. My brother said it was a bad thing and I thought about that." She pointed to her head, another common gesture. "Then I began working for INIT, in the accounting department. There was a colleague who had been in the original assault on Moncada, and another who was also a Revolutionary. I talked with them a lot and my ideas changed. It became unacceptable to me that some people should have plenty to eat and others didn't have enough . . . you understand? It was hard for me—I remember one day when I came home from work and there was no food in the house, none. I cried!" She laughed at herself in retrospect. "But my ideas changed; and when the October Crisis came, I decided to join the militia. That was it. Later I came here—I feel so much more useful and happy than in that office!

"My brother left. Then he wrote a letter saying he didn't like the United States, the people were not like the Cubans, they were not so helpful, so open, so ready to get involved in your problems, to share. I didn't answer. Then, one day while I was visiting my mother, he called. I didn't want to talk to him, but she begged me to—it was her son, after all, and all that. She is a Revolutionary but she is also a mother. It's hard. So I took the telephone. He said that he wanted to come back to his homeland and I said that this was no longer his homeland. He began to cry, he was so sorry he had left. I couldn't talk to him so I hung up." Cacha's face was serious but without pain as she ended the story.

Back at the camp, people still stood waiting in line to eat although it was after ten o'clock. I wandered around the first floor for a while. Besides the administrative office, an infirmary, sewing room, a dozen empty rooms (some with blackboards), a large dining hall, and a lounge were located there. Girls hung about, talking for another hour. As I passed, they would cluster around and ask questions about the United States, American prices, clothes. Five of them bummed cigarettes; not with a "please" or "do you have?" but just "give me." When I went to wash up at the laundry tubs, a girl admired my American toothpaste tube and asked to have it when it was empty. Cubans of all classes speak more directly than other Latins—far more than the Mexican middle class, for example—but these girls were unusually brusque. Not inimical, they had been schooled in a world where "please" was never much of a word in the vocabulary. They also seemed disinclined to believe that I, as a foreigner, could speak Spanish, and since I didn't speak it the way they did, that further encouraged some of them to insist on sign language. I felt at home and among friendly people, but also like some kind of freak.

Up on the second floor, most of the bunks were filled with sleeping bodies. The small, side room was dark, silent, stifling. I lit a match to find my bed and discovered gratefully that somebody had put a mosquito net over it. All around, mosquito nets rose like tents to veil the motionless shapes entombed within. A faint breeze began to blow in through the single window; outside, there was no moon and the fields in front of the camp lay still. I'm in some crazy kind of boot camp, I suddenly thought. No, a cross between that and a Girl Scout camp. I tried to fall asleep but the mosquitoes buzzed outside the net all night long.

Saturday, August 26
   "*¡De pie! ¡De pie!*"
   On your feet! On your feet! It must be a mistake, I thought, it's night outside, what the hell is going on? I fumbled to lift the mosquito net and peered out at the room full of thin, fat, tall, short, silent, chattering figures dressing under the bare, dim light bulb. One or two bodies, still in bed, let out soft moans. It was five o'clock in the morning and I had just fallen asleep.

The main dormitory seemed to be heaving with horizontal bodies crawling out from under sheets and bent-over bodies pulling on shirts and pants and vertical bodies heading down-stairs to wash. One girl was complaining about a hole in her shoe as she dressed, talking, talking, talking. A lot of people still lay in bed. Outside, in the courtyard, no trace of a sunrise showed yet. I went to the well carrying a borrowed bucket; a dark figure silently took it, filled it, and handed it back with a smile.

It was late by the time I reached the dining room and the line had vanished. In the hall—a bare and high-ceiling room—

crumbs of bread littered the long, concrete tables. Someone pointed to the serving counter, got me some hot milk with a sort of malt flavoring and two large chunks of plain white bread. Norma, a middle-aged woman who had the bunk next to mine upstairs, appeared and asked, "Do you want coffee? Come with me." It was she who had put up the mosquito net the night before and offered her bucket that morning. One of six Party members assigned to work at the camp, Norma played Den Mother with solicitude and an almost constant stream of advice or comment. Most of the girls called her *Tia,* Aunt, the common form of address for a woman over thirty (above forty, it was Old Woman and after fifty, Grandmother).

She led the way now to the kitchen, a one-room building with several iron grates over open coal fires on the ground. Just outside stood more grates with coals still glowing under them. Huge tubs lay here and there, with drops of milk clinging to the bottom. Several young girls and an older woman were already scraping corn husks for lunch. The girls smiled at me and then resumed their gossip about different people at the camp.

"She's doing it for the pay, that's all . . ."

"She said she wasn't going to work this morning because she just didn't want to. So she reported sick."

"Imagine, she came down here last night and asked for milk. I asked her why she didn't come at mealtime—this isn't the time to come to the kitchen for milk, we have things to do."

"She took my shirt, godammit, and I'm going to slug her!"

"I had guard duty last night—in this blouse, with no sleeves. Look how the mosquitoes have bitten me. And worse, I had no cigarettes."

Out in front of the main building, a little gray showed in the sky as the *pelotónes* formed around the circle. The platoons, organized according to where people worked, stood at ease. Rosa, the six-foot top sergeant, was delivering a long lecture on how to march. She moved back and forth constantly in front of the different groups, an angular and graceful figure. "First, I will show you how *not* to do it. Look, this is 'the slouch.' " She demonstrated it, slumping around the circle. "Now, this is the goose-step—no good either," and she did a high-stepping imitation, her long legs flying, once again around the circle. "Now the right way." She straightened up and began striding around the circle in a free, almost natural walk. But this time, Rosa kept on going—out into the entrance drive and up toward the road, her figure becoming smaller and smaller until it looked as though she didn't intend to come back. Several girls laughed. "Why did you laugh?" Rosa shouted, walking quickly back to the circle. "This is serious, you understand? Let's go." She blew her whistle and everybody took off for the road where the trucks usually lined up to take people to the fields.

They had not arrived yet and the mosquitoes were snapping fiercely. China tapped me on the shoulder. "Do you want coffee?" She led the way to a small store and counter by the road, where a dozen construction workers already stood silently in line facing the big, shiny coffee maker. When it was ready, the woman behind the counter filled the little cups with the strong, rich, black liquid. China insisted on paying for both of us.

Five medium-sized, open trucks arrived just as the sun began to rise. The driver lowered the tail gates, China heaved herself up lightly, and then turned to hold out her hand to me. She walked to the front and stood looking out over the side. Flat, empty land stretched toward the east where the sky was filled by that amazing Cuban dawn: giant-sized and distinct rays pointing out from an orange circle into a rose sky scattered with wisps of gray and blue. *"Ay, qué lindo,"* exclaimed China, with a shiver of delight. "How beautiful it is. Look how you can see the rays! I would like so much to paint it. Before, we used to paint the Virgin with rays like that around her head. We don't do that anymore." She paused and then sighed, "Oh, I love the dawn here." Her face was filled with a wide-open, dreamy smile.

Packed tightly into the trucks, the workers finally left for their different destinations. The roads were full of people from other camps on their way to the fields. Every few minutes a truckload of young men or women would pass the truck in which I rode with China and, as always, the shouts would go up. From the roadside homes, naked children waved and old men watched, looking both pleased and sad, as though their own youth or perhaps a youth they had never had was flashing by them for a second. The place of work for our truck and three others that morning was El Abra, a citrus nursery encompassing several large fields of orange and lemon seedlings, plants, and trees.

The trucks unloaded at a frame shed with a roofed, open area in front of it. Everyone jumped off and milled around a few minutes to receive instructions before going to work. It was a jumbled lot of girls in their various forms of dress, with one girl ready for the muddy fields in spike heels. The girls from Patria, the camp of grafters, also worked at El Abra, and so there were over three hundred workers in the area that morning. China was one of the two *responsables* of my platoon: leaders chosen for their industriousness and sense of responsibility. A little like foremen, these *responsables* were sometimes—but not often— also Communist Youth League members, who were expected to be the best not only in work but also in group relations, study, and other areas.

I followed China out to a field where the work for that day was weeding, by hand. A heavy rain had made grass grow high around the tiny orange seedlings, some of which were less than an inch tall. It was soft but tricky work: you could easily uproot a seedling by mistake. "Remember, *compañeras,* what counts here is quality—not quantity," Norma kept repeating in her high-pitched voice. Most of the girls did not know each other's names and would call out, "Hey, you in the red pants!" or refer to somebody as "the one in the big hat." Bits of conversation drifted across the field; from time to time one worker would scold another for some carelessness or inconsideration: "That's no way to be a good Communist." Or you would faintly hear an argument in another field and suddenly the word *socialismo* would sail across. As the morning passed, a remarkable amount of complaining about physical ailments took place until finally a hard-working girl in a nylon stocking cap, who looked pure Congolese, burst out: "This one has a headache and that one has a backache and the other has a toothache—what a bunch!"

After two hours the sun had reached full strength and seemed to scorch the land as well as everything on it. I stopped working for a minute to look around. On one side stood a range of low mountains, mostly green but with rose-colored bare spots where marble was being quarried. On another side, just beyond the last field, a reddish tile roof and bits of whitewashed wall poked out of the greenery on a hillside. It was the house where José Martí had been a political prisoner at the age of sixteen, under a special arrangement made by a rich gentleman of the Isle with the Havana prison authorities. From the baking fields, the large farmhouse in Southern-French style with its surrounding of handsome old trees looked like an oasis. Someone told me that the name El Abra was in fact the name of this old estate.

Then the sky darkened. Because this field was so far from shelter, everyone headed in to reach the shed before it rained. And then it did not. Some workers went back to the fields, while others stayed behind in the shed and trimmed orange shoots for replanting. They had to be cut to a precise length, measured out by a guidestick, and each leaf trimmed slightly more than half. A man in his mid-twenties, one of the few professionals around, proposed an *emulación* to stimulate the work pace. So there was a contest between a group of girls from Escuadrón and a group from Patria, and everybody went like crazy with their clippers for twenty minutes.

Another professional at El Abra was Arthur Rivers: old, white, weather-beaten, an emigrant from Gran Cayman. He had come to the Isle of Pines in 1907, he said, and at first worked clearing land. "In 1909 I planted the first grapefruit tree on the island—the first to my knowledge. Then, in 1916, I helped pick the first grapefruit. The next year, there was a terrible storm which destroyed all the fruit. Most of the land was owned by Americans then—I worked for a family from Michigan from 1916 to 1926. Got along with them fine. Then

235

there was another big storm, which cleaned out that family—after ten years. Well, I went on working in citrus until 1943, and then I did all kinds of work—on the railroad tracks, fishing, collecting charcoal. Many Americans left in 1960, after the Revolution."

Then he looked out at the fields and the workers. "They used to use prison labor here. That was no good—the prisoners didn't care about the work, and they even sabotaged it, so the fruit was no good. Now there are enough plants right here to fill the entire island when they mature. Where will they put them?" He shook his head. "All the island's soil isn't good for citrus. And the girls aren't taking proper care of the plants. They aren't careful enough," the old citrus hand fretted. "This work requires a lot of skill. You see that fellow over there?" He pointed to another "old" man, about thirty-five, who was also a supervisor. *"He* has forgotten more than *they* know. Huh. And look how slow they work—I'm eighty-one years old, and I can do better than that. But when *merienda* comes, watch them move!"

Merienda was snack-time; it arrived just then and indeed they did move. Half a dozen types of iced cakes and cookies were laid out on the bed of a truck, with a supposed ration of two apiece, but girls would go back into the line and get two, four more. Another twenty minutes of work, and the trucks arrived to take everyone back to the camp. This was to have been Pass Day and, although final cancellation of the camp pass had not been announced, everyone assumed it would be. "We are not going to work this afternoon," someone explained, "even though the pass is canceled. We never give work as punishment."

On the truck, no one seemed very depressed. Half of the way home they all sang "Downtown" in Spanish; then a fat girl with a fine soprano voice started *"Que linda es Cuba,"* and everyone joined in the chorus at full volume as the truck tore down the highway. Back in the camp, the dormitory filled with girls setting their hair and dressing up even though they were going nowhere. Holding mirrors—sometimes only pieces of mirror—they would apply eye makeup with extreme care or fuss over one curl for ten minutes. Lunch was a little meat, a heap of rice with beans, bread, some stewed fruit, all dished onto a metal tray with depressions, and milk. No talking at table.

Dancing and drumming began again in front of the building as China asked if I wanted to go into town with her. It seemed unfair, when the others could not, but I agreed anyway. China herself was free to go because of her special status at the camp. There had not been enough experienced *responsables* during this difficult, breaking-in period; China had therefore been borrowed from Patria, along with Cacha and several others. "How long will your group be here?" I asked her while we rode into town on the bus.

"I don't know," she said. "It depends on how things go."

"And how do you think things will go?"

"It will be all right," she answered. "You should have seen the girls at Patria a few months ago. They were worse than the ones here. Now they have a good spirit. I like Patria so much. Two weeks ago there was a call for people to work at night as well as during the day. People were asked at a meeting to volunteer by raising their hands—and every hand went up! There was a Swiss girl working at the camp then, she could hardly believe it."

"And what were you like a few months ago?"

"Oh—well, I come from a very poor family. My father was a *campesino*. But he was very honest, he taught us what was the right thing to do. I think that helped me," China said quietly.

In Nueva Gerona, the street scene was like Saturday afternoon in the Wild West. *Vaqueros* in their jeans and cowboy hats, construction workers, and agricultural workers lounged on the stoops and porches, gossiping or making comments on the women who passed. "She must be from Havana," they said about one whose skirt was an inch above the knee, "look at the mini-skirt!" China ran into many friends and left them all with the same words: "See you at Coppelia." We got to the ice cream palace finally and stood in line for three quarters of an hour to eat giant sundaes. China suggested going to the movies; it was a film from Spain of *La Verbena de la Paloma,* the light opera, in

237

color and panavision. Sitting in the balcony of the town's only theater, China seemed less enthralled by the old-fashioned story of love and jealousy than the rest of the audience. A young militiaman next to her kept passing a bag of candy until she finally had to say, "Please—no more!"

It was night by then, but not difficult to hitch a jeep ride back to the camp. There were three men inside, and one of them began to make suggestive remarks about how they could be reimbursed for the ride. China protested mildly at first and then, as the man insisted, more vehemently: *"Compañero,* you are being very rude. Besides, this is no way to act toward a guest in our country. My friend is a foreigner."

"And I'm an Englishman," the man shot back without humor. China asked the driver to stop, but he would not. As the jeep sped on, she became upset and half-pleaded, half-shouted, *"Compañero*, please let us out! Immediately!" The driver finally pulled over and stopped. The spot was not far from the camp.

Walking back there in the moonlight, China looked miserable. "I feel like crying, he said such bad things. It was terrible. Cuban men are so *ligero,"* she said in a troubled voice—so lightweight, flirty, unserious. There was a pause as she glanced up at the Caribbean sky, filled with brilliant stars. Her mood shifted slightly.

"I want to think about profound things. I would like to study art. But I don't want to make photographs," she added, beginning to relax at last. "I realize that you must make art for the people, not for yourself. But I want to convey something, to make people feel what I feel. I think that gives them more." Then she stopped talking and we trudged on in silence toward the lights of the camp.

Inside, she led the way to the lounge, a spacious room decorated with bright-colored draperies and artificial flowers. There was a small library: *Crime and Punishment* and *The Grapes of Wrath,* in Spanish, sat beside a *History of the Middle Ages,* the collected works of José Martí, books on film. China pointed to a dozen abstract charcoal drawings hung on the walls. "What do they mean?" she asked. We looked at each picture, talking about some of them, and when we finished she glanced at me and nodded—not smiling but content. The jeep incident seemed to be far away for her now.

Sunday, August 27

"Anyone who wants to say something," Rosa announced to the platoons, "has to step forward, salute, and say, *'permiso para hablar.'* " She acted out the three-step procedure. "No more of this 'Rosa! Rosa! Rosa!' from all over the place." It was Sunday, six-thirty in the morning, and the platoons stood around the circle in the blackness. Although she had been working the night before until after one in the morning, Rosa looked fresh. Her dark pants hung neatly, her long-sleeved blue shirt was unwrinkled, her heavy work-shoes polished.

The work that day at El Abra was confusing and hard. The *responsables* kept shifting the work locations, and each time the girls began at a new spot it took them ten minutes to settle down. "Hoe there." "No, don't hoe there, hoe over here." "Use your hand, not the hoe." "Use your hoe." The grass to be weeded was waist-high this time and it could take four or five blows with a hoe merely to loosen the roots of the weed. There were the usual little arguments and then one girl asked where a certain worker was. Nobody knew, but they all clearly suspected the missing girl was goofing off. "Well, maybe she'll show up for *merienda*," someone offered. "Now, what sort of capitalist motivation is that?" the *responsable* asked.

When lunch arrived on a truck, everyone collapsed in a grove of trees too young to give any shade yet. The large metal pots, trays, and cutlery were unloaded while long lines formed. There was a little meat, rice and beans, sliced cucumbers, guava, and cold water; the truck had brought a large chunk of ice along with the food. The driver, a lean, taciturn fellow whom everyone called Grandfather, sold cigarettes to the workers and sometimes a special item like sandals. He counted his money carefully, and then took off to deliver another load of food at another location.

After eating and then sleeping for an hour, everyone went back to work. At one end of the fields, under a tree, a small group gathered around a muddy area and began packing citrus branches for transplanting. Two girls raked mud out of the water; others cut up burlap sacks with machetes to make wrapping; still others were already packing the branches in mud and rolling them up in burlap. Rosa approached, sat down, and began pulling out the stitching of a burlap sack with surprisingly long, sleek fingernails. "It's for a sheet," she explained in her matter-of-fact voice, "to sleep on the ground and not get so dirty." Her brown hair fell forward as she bent over the bag, working silently.

I asked about her family but she only said that her mother was a housewife and her father was dead. When the other workers began quizzing me about the United States, Rosa did not join in; she just listened, leaning forward eagerly, beaming and nodding at me. Now and then she would jump up to show someone how to use a machete more efficiently or the right way to wrap the burlap around the mud.

After saying nothing for more than an hour, Rosa began talking about how she and others had worked to get various facilities ready in Nueva Gerona for July 26. *"Vaya,* that was a time— for about two months, we worked from seven in the morning to seven in the evening and then again until one or two! We got the Coppelia finished in forty-five days and the pizzeria too. We slept only a few hours a night, but we could do it because of all the enthusiasm." She glowed with pleasure at the remembrance, then fell silent again.

When she had finished with the burlap, she folded it neatly and stood up. "Would you like to see the roses?" she asked me. "Did you know there is a garden here?" She led the way through several fields, toward the highway. Passing one group of workers, she called out to the *responsable,* "Take a twenty-minute break at—let's see—at four-fifteen," and strode on. The day had reached its hottest hour and the air did not move at all. Suddenly Rosa paused and looked down at her feet. Without a word, she motioned me to come and look down also. Then she touched a plant looking like a small fern, and its fine leaves quickly contracted in self-protection. She smiled and walked on.

Finally she came to the garden. "The roses go to Havana to be sold," she explained. "Small teams work here, grafting and caring for the plants. There are all kinds of grafted roses. Look." She dashed across the field as if she knew what she was looking for, paused at a bush, took out her knife and cut a flower. Then she came back with it: a rose with petals which were peach-colored on the inside and yellow on the outside. She handed it to me, then went striding off between the plants again and picked here, picked there, sometimes beckoning me to come look and sometimes bringing a flower back to be examined. There was a red rose of the familiar type/ a pink rose with the strongest perfume of all/ a cluster of baby roses, reddish-orange/ another pink rose, with a yellow center and petals spread flat/ a new kind of rose "which doesn't go like that," she moved her finger in a circle, "but like this," she indicated the crinkled spread of a carnation/ more pink and yellow roses/ a rose with petals that were peach-colored on the outside and yellow inside, "the reverse of the first one." All of these she placed in my hands. Then she spotted something else and moved swiftly toward another part of the field. This time she came back with seven kinds of daisies: pink, orange, white, fuschia, orange-red, Chinese red, dark orange. She handed over each one with a brief explanation of the grafting process. My hands were overflowing, but she had not finished. Near a hut— "a Japanese lives there and he chases the girls away sometimes" —she found a frail, white flower and cut some of these too.

Walking back to the shed, I asked Rosa if she had always known so much about flowers. "My father and mother had a little piece of land outside Havana. My mother liked roses so I learned a little then. But of course I know more now." I asked her what she planned to do after her two years on the Isle were up and when she answered I realized that I had known what she would say. "I will stay. I love it here," she said simply.

An hour later, the trucks arrived to take everyone home.

Rosa sat up front in the cab with the flowers, which she had put in water in her tin cup; it would have been impossible for me to keep a firm grip on them in the back of the truck. At camp, everyone piled out and lined up to march in. I went to buy cigarettes at the little store and when I returned everyone had already reached the courtyard. There was Rosa, still holding the cup of flowers, marching around and calling out orders. "Company, halt! Right face! At ease!" The flowers flashed as she moved: the old and new kinds, the magic ones and the duller ones, the successful new types and the less successful ones, all the experiments, the profusion and confusion of color. Rosa seemed to be holding a whole revolution in her large, gentle hand.

Monday, August 28

On Monday morning the marching was smarter and there were no lectures from Rosa or anyone else. The trucks arrived late; everyone had been waiting half an hour before they came. At El Abra, I worked with the curly-haired girl who had been playing the drums for the group of black dancers that first day at the camp. Her name was Josefina but everyone called her Cusa. She was short, compact, and wore a small-brimmed straw hat with "Cusita" embroidered across the front. It came down low on her forehead, making her look like a don't-mess-with-me street kid and hiding the fact that she was very pretty. Cusa had a younger brother in one of the camps of deliquent boys. Her family had been poor whites from Oriente; the father now worked as a projectionist in a Havana movie theater.

"What do you like to do?" I asked her while we sat face to face on each side of a row of lemon seedlings, weeding.

"Sports. Especially swimming. I'm crazy about swimming. I can swim underwater for a long time, oh, from here"—she squinted across the field—"to over there." It looked like almost a mile. "No, I can't," she grinned mischievously.

"Do you like this camp?"

She shrugged. "Not as well as where I was before. That was the Korea—right across from the Escuadrón. But they moved everyone out of Korea and it's closed now."

"So you probably won't stay here after your two years are up?"

"I dunno." She cocked her head and asked abruptly, "Hey, do you know how old I am?"

"No."

"I was fifteen yesterday," she said looking pleased with herself.

When the day ended and the trucks arrived back at the camp, I was surprised to see a man of about twenty-five standing on the veranda. Militiamen often dropped by on errands and the workers were sometimes visited by their brothers or fathers in the evenings, but a civilian male at that hour was a rare sight. He turned out to be the chess teacher, back from vacation. Classes in various subjects were to begin that night after dinner.

Cacha addressed the platoons in the courtyard. "Things are getting better," she said. "We are pleased with your work. You are doing very well.

"But there are still things to be improved. Last night we had another problem. Two *compañeras* were found in a truck at two o'clock in the morning with two *compañeros,* in a way that was not correct." Her voice was flat and straight. "They have been expelled. So have the *compañeros*. Also, one girl stayed in town all night. She has not come back to the camp yet.

"We cannot make this island the first site of communism in Cuba with such people," she said more emotionally. "I would like to know what you think about the matter."

A girl spoke up from the back. "Well, I think it's all right at the movies perhaps—but not in a truck."

Cacha looked startled and then smiled faintly. "Look, we are not trying to make you into nuns. We are human and we expect you to see your boyfriends. But this was not a matter of a boy with his arms around a girl, you understand?" There were a few titters from the audience.

"Listen," she went on, "this camp should be the most prestigious camp on the island. On October 21, the anniversary of the founding of the Communist Youth League, we want people to say 'Livia Gouverneur is the best camp on the island.' We must all work to achieve this. We must work very hard. Now, it's time to bathe. Rosa . . ."

And Rosa took over, dismissing the units.

Around the building, people talked about the expulsions. "The problem is that there are only girls in this camp," said one; "it's better in the mixed camps." One of the Party women declared, apparently with some accuracy, "The problem is that there wasn't a good selection process. In the haste to get the maximum number of youth on the island they did not process people carefully. They didn't explain the situation here well enough. For example, many of the girls did not know about the semi-military discipline." Susana, a *mulatta* with a Shirley Temple face, announced ferociously, "Some of the girls here are terrible—there are a few who should be stood up against that wall and shot." She waved at the side of the building. "If I ever lost my morality, I would want someone to shoot me!" Her rosebud lips were set in a tight line, her blond curls were bouncing.

Although no one seemed upset that a foreigner had witnessed this seamy business in Revolutionary Cuba, several tried to explain it with mild embarrassment. "These things are inevitable," said one girl, "when you bring together so many girls—many of them from families of shoeshine men, people who live off the streets. They grow up in *solares,* with six people in one room and the children see everything. Some of their mothers were prostitutes."

I assured her that I wasn't shocked; anyway, the United States had its own problems with youth—"bigger problems than what happened in the truck." She looked surprised and then thoughtful. "Perhaps," she asked hesitantly, "that is because the youth are not building anything—not making a revolution?"

Classes were held that night, the first time for many workers. In the empty rooms on the first floor, classes in basic subjects had started for some. Everyone who had not gone beyond the sixth grade was taking math and Spanish tests in the dining hall to ascertain their level. In the lounge, girls who had done secondary study were gathering in discussion groups. A worker in the camp who had grown up in Marseilles began teaching French to one group of workers. Out on the veranda, a bright-looking boy of thirteen had just arrived from the Art School in Havana to teach music.

Among those studying the basics, a mutinous spirit set in. Many of the girls did not want to go to class and they sneaked out of the rooms at every opportunity. China, who had been gone all day to see the dentist in town, went up and down the hall stopping girls as they dashed out of the classrooms and convincing them to go back. As we passed one room, a girl sitting by the door grabbed my arm. She was wearing a black leather motorcycle jacket and dark glasses: a mean chick but looking a little lost right now. "I don't like to study," she groaned. "I can't read and write much. I just like to *work*." She was the *responsable* of a platoon and worked, in fact, harder than anyone else in the camp.

The classrooms quieted down after a while and Cacha appeared, hustling less than usual. She had a few minutes to spare and we went off to talk on the veranda.

"My mother is coming to visit tomorrow," she said. "Things have been hard for her. She is a very strict person, very *severa*. You know what importance is given to virginity in Cuba—if you're not a virgin, you are worse than trash. She was always opposed to my going places alone, or going out at night. Once I went out with a boy, and came home at midnight. That was absolute immorality—but seriously! One day, I just had a talk with her and explained that if I really liked a man, I would go with him. She had to accept things. Now I am here for two years—that took a long time for her to accept.

"Many people, including Cubans, think that the Revolution —the Party—is very puritanical. But it is not true. A girl will not usually be expelled from the Isle for sleeping with a man or even for having a baby. There was a girl here who got pregnant and miscarried. We took her to the doctor, he fixed her up and said, 'Don't have relations for fifteen days'—and that was it. I could have a baby and it would be all right. The one thing which is unacceptable is going with more than one man at a time. You can't have one today, another tomorrow, a third the next day. That isn't a human way to relate to people. Also, you cannot go with a married man who has a wife and home. But I am single and my boyfriend is single—and there we are."

I asked her why, then, had the two girls in the truck been expelled.

"Here in this camp, we have to establish a climate of discipline at the beginning," she answered. "In other camps, they have parties with boys—they drink and dance and everything is all right. At Patria, on July 26, we had a party with boys and music and cognac. But the girls at those camps are mature. Can you imagine what would happen in this camp if we had a party like that now? And yet, the girls who are now at Patria used to be worse than the girls here.

"Look, we know the youth have to be young, to love, to be *alegre*. We want them to be. We don't want to force them into Revolutionary attitudes. We believe in education through work —and through the idea of transforming this land. When someone is expelled, when someone fails to be convinced, I feel terrible. I feel a great sense of failure. It is not her fault but that of her background, and I have not succeeded in helping her to overcome it. We want to convince, not to compel. We do not want any prisoners, any jails in Cuba. And if we have to shoot anyone at all twenty years from now—when there is a whole, new generation—then we have failed terribly. . . ."

Just then, someone walked into the office to announce a new crisis. A *militante* of the Communist Youth League had struck another girl. The mediator, the *militante,* and the girl who had been struck came in and sat down. It was Cacha's opinion that the *militante* should lose her status, but she decided to send the girl home for five days first. "Then we will discuss the situation."

She leaned back and stretched. "Oh, we had a fine time three weeks ago at Patria," she said. "Fidel came to the camp. It was his birthday and he sat around talking with us until three in the morning. The American folk-singer, Barbara Dane, played and sang. I did not want to meet Fidel—I just wanted to look. He is such a brilliant man, such a fantastic person. Finally I did meet him. When he looked at me, I cast my eyes down like this," she said, lowering her eyes. "It was too much! Then he put his hand on my shoulder and—oh, I didn't want to take a bath for days!" She let out a whoop and then jumped up from her chair. "Let's go see what's happening."

It was midnight; the exams and classes had ended. Cusa came down the hall, her hat tilted forward, walking on her heels like the hero in a Western after a good rumble. "I got a hundred on the math test," she announced. "I was the only one to get a hundred." Her face was a mixture of pride and be-cool but her eyes were shining. She took me to the dining hall to meet the teacher who had given the test and who was still helping students with their work. "This is my friend," she said to the teacher; "tell her I got a hundred." Then she sat down at the long table in the hall and asked me to spell out my name and address in the United States. She began to copy it until she could write the unfamiliar combination of letters and words by memory; after three times, she did it right. Cusa could probably have done anything that night.

Tuesday, August 29

It was a memorable day.

Between ten P.M. and midnight, a special assembly took place in the courtyard with the entire camp present. The executive committee had prepared a list of ten girls and various infractions they had repeatedly committed: two of them, stealing; one, "indiscipline and lack of respect for rules"; two, pulling up many citrus seedlings deliberately; three, "bad attitude toward work"; one, unauthorized departure from the camp. The accused were presented for trial by their peers. Different girls spoke up, some to give testimony supporting the charges and others to express their opinions on the seriousness of the misdeed committed. Nine of the accused laughed and chattered through the long debate, and had nothing to say for themselves. One remained serious, though also silent. It was Cusa, who had been charged with "indiscipline."

Finally the camp voted unanimously to expel them all. Cacha said: "This represents a defeat for the camp. We hope these things will not happen again. If we succeed in that, we will have once again won a victory."

Cusa broke into tears and begged to be allowed to stay. Cacha told her, "We will discuss things further tomorrow."

Wednesday, August 30

It turned out that the ten girls expelled were not the only ones to leave the camp during the past ten days. Another six or eight had left unannounced, for different reasons. The platoon distribution had been affected enough to require reassignment of people and tasks. Thus China's platoon went to work in a new place: an experimental citrus station known as La Casa Americana—the American house.

A long, paved entrance road led off the main highway past empty fields, curved to the right, and stopped in front of a sprawling, ranch-style house of pure United States vintage, red brick, in the forty-thousand-dollar bracket. A carport big enough for two automobiles separated the main building and what must have been the servants' quarters. In front of the main building, a tiled patio faced a nice shade tree. The house, both front and back, had "picture" windows of heavy, louvered glass —its one concession to the local environment.

Indoors, a ceiling-high stone fireplace separated the living room from the large kitchen with its wall oven and other modern fixtures. There were exposed brick walls, a copper chandelier, practical tile floors for the children—everything that *House and Garden* would have approved. A pine-paneled hall led off from the living room to several small rooms, closets, bath, and then the master bedroom. The house contained no furniture now except for two work tables, a few wooden chairs, and a blackboard covered with data on grafting, from classes taught by a Bulgarian technician at night. But a walk-in closet, paneled with cedar, was full of old books lying in a pile: the Miami telephone directory; *What Policemen Should Know*; *the Layman's Legal Guide*; *Official Rules of Card Games*; *Ele-*

ments of Surveying; a paperback introduction to psychoanalysis; *Taps for Private Tussie*, a best-seller of the forties. It was not so hard, then, to imagine the American family that once owned this place.

"They came here from Miami for only two or three months a year," said the old man whom everybody called *Abuelo* (Grandfather) or Julián. His real name was Septimus Williamson; a strong-looking Jamaican with a back bent by long years of labor, he supervised the work done at the experimental station. "There were only a few houses in this area then, and they all belonged to Americans. After the Revolution, the man who owned this place left. Then the house was given to some Cubans for a while. They didn't take proper care of it, you understand. Did you see how all the things have been ripped out of the bathroom and kitchen?" His wrinkled black face curved down with disapproval. "Yes, ma'am, they even ripped out some of the wood in the walls. Then, oh—two, three months ago—this experimental station was opened here. The house was in terrible condition. China can tell you—she was one of the people who cleaned it up. It took five days.

"Fidel put me in charge of this place because of my experience with the citrus. Fidel personally, yes ma'am," he beamed. "When he comes around here, he always speaks with me."

During his fifty years in Cuba, Grandfather had forgotten more of his English vocabulary than had Arthur Rivers, the old man from Gran Cayman, but his Jamaican intonation rang through clearly. When he spoke Spanish, he became a different person; the words pelted forth like machine-gun bullets, all run together in what was almost a monotone. He barraged the girls now: "Get to work, get to work, pine trees must be planted to protect citrus seedlings from hurricanes, hurry, hurry, why you so lazy? I do twice work in one hour as you in one day . . ."

There was only one *pelotón* working at La Casa Americana, and everyone fitted easily into the truck that was waiting to go pick up the pine trees at another location. The ride there took almost an hour. I stood on the truck with another worker, just above the tail gate, while the others, down on the ground, carried the baby pine trees from where they stood over to us. It was fast, hot work: picking up the trees and rushing to stack them at the front of the truck bed, then back to get more, then to the front again, trying to keep up with the twenty workers on the ground. As the bed became full, the job grew easier and finally all of the two hundred and fifty trees needed were loaded.

Back at the Casa, we unloaded the pines beneath a giant tree about a hundred yards from the house. It was a *jagüey:* that mysterious tree which seems more like a house, built from what appears to be an infinite number of gray trunks, all entwined in a chunky mass, with a solid roof of green above. The *jagüey* has a shape and a darkness like few other trees; it looks as though you could never uproot it and you cannot feel hot in its shade. Sitting in that shade now in the late morning, everyone ate slices of sweet, juicy watermelon which China had brought from somewhere, while a light breeze drifted across the land. The smallness of the group created an entirely different atmosphere from that of El Abra. Almost everyone knew everyone else's name; at lunch, later, the line was short and all the workers sat together on the patio or in the shady carport area. After eating, we all listened to articles from *Granma* read aloud by one of the workers or dozed off in the peaceful afternoon.

Then a blond girl named Ramona asked if I would like to see the river which she had "discovered" that morning. A short walk across a long, hot field led to a grove of trees, and there was the river: small and shadowy, with a pretty little waterfall. "I love the water," Ramona said romantically. On the way back she talked a little about her life. "When I was a child, my father owned some sugar lands," she recalled, looking and sounding a little ashamed. "There was a refinery owned by Americans. I remember that the name of the boss was Mr. Harry. Well," she said, "*se acabó* Mr. Harry." No more Mr. Harry.

When we reached the house again, everyone was inside sleeping on the tile floor, so I lay down too and fell asleep instantly.

That evening, back at the camp, there was *pelotón* drill for an hour. Someone said that Cusa had been allowed to stay. I found her on the veranda, waiting to play Ping Pong. She said, dead-pan, "I'm leaving." Then she grinned. "No, I'm staying." But she did not want to talk about it more than that.

Thursday, August 31

At the Casa Americana, the day began peacefully enough. The pine trees had to be planted in three rows along one side of the entrance road, thus serving to protect the citrus plants in a field beyond and also to embellish the approach to the station. Lines were to be laid, Grandfather explained, holes dug at certain intervals, and the trees dropped in. It was a pleasant task, with a certain rhythm and sense of progression. While working, the girls talked back and forth along the rows, first just a remark here and there but then more animatedly until they were all going at once and the voices became a cacophonous blur. *"Ay, mi madre,* one at a time!" someone finally shouted. The chattering subsided temporarily; a few minutes later, a familiar barrage of questions about the United States began to fly in my direction.

"How short are they wearing skirts?"

"What kind of music is popular?"

"What kind of cigarettes do you smoke there?"

"Is it cold?"

"Do students work in the *campo?"*

"Do you know President Johnson? You *don't?* You never talked with him?" He was not, they decided, like Fidel.

"How beautiful it would be if the United States were Socialist," exclaimed a thin girl who rarely spoke. "We talk about that all the time. It is such a rich country!"

China, who had been listening to the dialogue with varying expressions of amusement and interest, took up the theme. "The United States is so developed, it has everything. There would not be the problems we have here of underdevelopment. If the United States were Socialist, it would be so easy to make a wonder there!" China leaned back and sighed, smiling in her dreamy way.

"I would like to go to the United States," said one girl, "to

251

visit, that is—not to stay." "Me, too," said several others. "I would like to *stay,"* snapped a girl nicknamed Rubia. The name, meaning Blond, referred to her pale skin, blue eyes, and curly yellow hair streaked with dark brown. Rubia had a sharp little face and sometimes waspish manner.

"Oh, *negra,* you wouldn't really," another girl answered. On the Isle of Pines, *negra* was often used regardless of a person's color.

"Yes I *would* like to go—yes, man!" Rubia threw back vehemently. "You can buy such nice things there."

"Some people in the United States say that's all you can do there," China put in, "work and buy, work and buy."

"And what is there to do here?" Rubia asked.

"Build a new society . . . recreate this island," China said, more intensely than usual.

"And what is that but work?" Rubia demanded. "Oh, how I want to go to the United States. I want so much to die there when the time comes," she ended, in a gentler voice. It seemed a strange thing for a seventeen-year-old to say, and this time China just threw up her hands.

"I don't want to go," a very young and pudgy girl piped up, speaking to me, "but please send me some *chicle* and cigarettes? Don't forget—*chicle* and cigarettes. You can put them in a letter."

Susana, the *mulatta* Shirley Temple who had wanted to be shot if she ever lost her virginity improperly, had a lot to say about people who had left Cuba for the United States. "My father is a Communist. His brother, my uncle, has gone over there. Before the Revolution, he had everything and we had nothing. My father fought in the Sierra—we didn't see him for three years. Batista's soldiers used to come and abuse us because we were his family. So my uncle lost some of his wealth and we have everything we need. He told my father that he should come to the United States too, but my father just said, 'Are you crazy? I fought for three years and now I have a good life. Why would I leave?'

"I came here, although my father didn't want me to leave

home, because I love the country. I love to produce things, so that when I see somebody eat a grapefruit or an orange, I can say, 'I worked to make the fruit you are eating.' I would never betray the Revolution, I could never betray it unless it became something else—unless Fidel sold out. And that he surely won't do!"

A young woman of about twenty-four, from the Party, began telling stories about people who had left the country expecting to return some day. One of them was the former owner of the house in which she herself now lived. "This person left rings and gold, embroidered sheets, all sorts of expensive things, with an old woman in the same house. The old woman stubbornly hangs on to every item; she says, 'in case they come back.' I asked her, 'How can they come back?'' And she says, 'Well, just in case.' " The young woman shrugged. "*Vaya*, such people are just ignorant."

The time came for the morning break and everyone trudged back to the house to sit in the shade a while. China looked tired. "I'm all right," she said. "This is nothing. You should have been here during the October Crisis—I was doing guard duty. We slept only two hours, and one night I fell asleep on duty. Someone came up to me, and I was so startled that I dropped my gun. *¡Ay, mi madre!*" She grimaced at the remembrance.

After everyone had settled on the patio, some sitting and some lying on their backs, China announced that there would be a meeting. She then turned the discussion over to Dora, a soft-spoken black girl who was the second *responsable* of the platoon (but not under China's authority; they shared responsibility). Dora explained that October 21 was approaching: the official anniversary of the founding of the Communist Youth League. There would be a special October 21 seal awarded to youth in work centers, state farms, and camps all over the island, if they met certain requirements between September 1 and that date. For the camps on the Isle of Pines, the requirements were: no infringement of discipline by anyone at the camp, no unjustified absence from class by anyone at the camp, fifty hours of voluntary work performed by each person, five sports activities conducted at the camp, reading and discussion of Fidel's July 26 speech. "It would also," Dora added, "be a good idea for you to read the speech he made here at the opening of the Heroic Vietnam Dam, because although many of you were there, you didn't hear it." She smiled wryly and then there was pandemonium.

Everybody talked at once about the impossibility of doing fifty hours of voluntary work. The grapefruit packing plant had no night shift going now; how could they possibly accumulate so many hours in less than two months? Some complained, others answered the complaints, others answered the answers, everyone was shouting simultaneously. One girl, somehow, slept through it all. China hollered for order and told the girl to wake up. She opened one eye, and China asked, "What are we talking about?" "I don't know." "I was sleeping," the girl added rather unnecessarily. "Well, *chica,* we won't get the seal that way," China replied in a firm yet friendly tone. Then she began explaining how it would be possible to build up fifty hours apiece.

"If we give up the midmorning break, we acquire half an hour every day. Then, if we also work an extra half hour at the end of the day, we already have an hour. Another hour could be picked up on the Pass Day . . ." The people listened a while, then began to add out loud; everyone came up with a different sum and began to shout again. Finally the group quieted and China called for a performance by the platoon chorus. "We haven't had time to practice," they protested, and another quarter-hour of chaos followed. At last they lined up in the driveway; the fat girl with the nice soprano voice began singing the verses of a melodious ballad about Revolutionary heroes while the others followed her lead and sang the chorus. Although it was the first time they had done the song together, they sang with vitality and skill. China looked happy; the day seemed to be improving.

Dora and I sat for a few minutes more before going back to work. She told me about how she had formerly been a student at an art school, preparing to become an artisan in marble because marble work produced exportable goods which would bring

Cuba hard currency. "I liked it very much," she said, and began to explain some of the techniques she had learned. "But then I decided that agricultural work was even more important for the Revolution. So I came here." Another girl sat down with us and told a similar story. She had formerly worked in one of the *círculos infantiles*, and loved taking care of children. "But this seemed more important."

Walking back to the field, I thought about what they had said and the matter-of-fact way they had said it. Then I realized that had been my first real conversation with black girls at the camp. At other times and places they had asked a question or two in a friendly relaxed way and then gone about their business, except for one sixteen-year-old girl who always wanted me to sit with her at meals. In general it was *mulattas* who had sought me out and with whom I had become closest—girls of about my own color. I thought this might be just a case of like-gravitating-to-like; that seemed to be the pattern with other relationships in the camp. But right now, back at work in the field, there was no such grouping. Black, brown, beige, and white chattered and planted pines together in one easy rhythm.

The workers finished planting another row of pines before lunch. Afterward, some lay on the floor of the carport drawing what they called "the propaganda": cartoons of different camp vices, including a picture of a girl in bed asleep after reveille— still a major problem every morning in the dormitory. A few girls leaned against the walls and napped. Others lounged on the floor and steps, talking with Grandfather. Somehow the conversation turned to love and jealousy.

"Once I was betrayed," said the romantic blond Ramona, "and I couldn't eat for two days—not breakfast, or lunch or dinner. Two days!"

Dora looked up from the cartoon she was drawing in disbelief. *"Ay, mi madre,"* she murmured, "I could never be so upset by a man that I didn't eat."

"I would like to be *friends* with a man," said Rubia. "Not just have it always be sex, sex, sex."

"What do you think love is?" bellowed Grandfather, the old

realist. "What do you think you are the product of? Especially you, with your hair like that," he added, nodding toward her blond head streaked with brown.

"That's a lie!" Rubia screamed. "I am from Spain, my family is pure Spanish." She had forgotten about love and was talking now about race: she meant that she was no *mulatta* and it was obvious that she also would not want to be one.

A young, black militiaman who had dropped by on an errand stepped in front of Rubia and addressed her in a clear, deliberate tone. "José Martí said, 'Black, white, yellow—a man is a man,'" he began slowly. Everyone grew quiet and he repeated the words. "Now, do you believe that a black man can become a professor?"

Rubia, who was sitting on a barrel, looked up at him and nodded silently. None of the workers said a word; the militiaman had clearly embarked on a speech.

"Well, the problem is that in Cuba today we have seven million people—but perhaps only four million of them have a Revolutionary conscience. The rest contain vestiges of the past." He enunciated every syllable carefully. "In the past, a black man in Cuba was discriminated against—just like the blacks in the United States. Do you know that there, if a black man is on a bus and a white gets on, he has to give up his seat?"

"That's not true!" Rubia shouted. "That's not true!" Members of the audience began to shout too. The speech broke down; Rubia asked me if what he had said was true, but nobody waited for the reply and the wave of heated talk rolled on. Grandfather stepped forward to tell a long anecdote about his own experience of racism in Cuba before the Revolution; the militiaman told another story. But Rubia refused to concede that there had ever been such a thing in Cuba or the United States.

Finally, the militiaman turned to Rubia and said in a slow, firm voice. "Your hair is blond, *compañera,* but your mind is dark. Your mind is much darker than I am." There was absolute silence.

Ramona sought to break the tension. "Well, we all have

different ideas. If the whole world thought the same way, it wouldn't be the world." She was smiling, trying hard to smooth things over.

The militiaman listened and then turned back toward Rubia. "Your hair is blond, *compañera,* but your mind is dark," he repeated.

There was nothing more to be said. Everyone headed back to the field except two of us who stayed to clean the house and yard. I began mopping the tile floor of the patio when Grandfather said, "You know, these girls—well, they talk to me, they tell me everything about their boyfriends. That Rubia—she told me once about a boyfriend she had loved very much. She said he betrayed her and she would never love anyone again." He shook his head and smiled. "Never going to love again—and she is seventeen years old. You should have seen me at that age!"

Grandfather had left Jamaica at the age of sixteen because he wanted to travel and be on his own. He came to Santiago first. He did odd jobs for a year, mostly cutting cane, and worked his way to Holguín. "I hadn't had a woman in a year when I got there," he chuckled. "They offered me a man—huh, I didn't want that. Then a woman, for ten dollars. Too expensive! Finally I got a Frenchwoman for five dollars." In his late sixties now, Grandfather still had a gleam in his eye as he chatted on about that day. "Yes ma'am, a Frenchwoman.

"Then I came to the Isle here, twenty-one years ago, intending to go home to Jamaica. But I stayed. I worked for the Americans, different ones, as overseer. They treated me fine, the white folks, yes ma'am. In the fifties, I got three dollars a day plus a big meal—a big meal. Now, of course, I make—oh, two hundred and fifty or two hundred and seventy-five dollars a month. It's by the hour. But once I had my own farm. I grew cukes. Then the American market dried up. One day a man came and told me not to ship my cukes—there wasn't any market. So that was the end of that. I've had my ups and downs. But I never married—no, ma'am. I still live on my own, and I like it that way."

A jeep drove up just then; the driver, a young agricultural

technician, took Grandfather off to discuss an irrigation problem. I sat on the patio for a moment, idly watching two workers approach the house; people often came in from the fields to use the bathroom or rest if they felt sick. One of the two was a fragile, white girl whose nickname meant Amiable. The other was a tall, sexy-looking black girl nicknamed Dynamite. The two stopped at the tree in front of the house and Amiable started to sit down on a wooden crate which lay there, not quite large enough for two persons. Dynamite said something and Amiable retorted. Suddenly Dynamite slapped her; Amiable hit back once and then stopped; Dynamite continued to slap her. Amiable sat there crying, even after the blows had stopped.

The girl who had been cleaning inside the house came out and headed for the fields; soon afterward, a group of workers including both *responsables*—China and Dora—arrived. Everyone gathered in the driveway.

"What happened?" China asked.

Her two words led to a half hour of shouting, laughing, and crying: not a chaos, this time, but a noisy ballet, with some of the company whirling around in the driveway while others shouted from more or less fixed positions on the sidelines. Not one sentence was distinguishable. Amiable, still crying, lurked red-eyed behind the water tank. Dynamite stood next to a palm tree, tall and disdainful. China said to the black girl, "Look, you realize we will have to report this. We cannot have any *compañera* hitting another. That is absolutely out." Dynamite shrugged, "I know." But a minute later, she looked to be on the verge of tears. Everybody was down on her.

Then a girl imitated the way Amiable was crying—"boo hoo-hoo"—and everybody laughed. She repeated the imitation. By now Dynamite had sat down amid the group and was laughing too. It looked as though the whole mess would blow over. But then someone revived the question of how the incident had started—who said what to whom—and they were off again, whirling into new positions amid a fury of voices rising and falling; I counted seven people all talking at once, until China threw up her hands in mock-real helplessness. Yet the climate had changed subtly. It seemed as though people were getting tired of Amiable's crying. No one could champion Dynamite but they had begun to view Amiable as a draggy little ragtail who almost enjoyed being a victim. She had never been particularly well liked, in any case.

The frenzy subsided; the ballet slowed. When Grandfather arrived and asked, "What's happened?" one or two girls answered quietly, "Oh, nothing." Five minutes later everyone was trailing back to the fields to work, and the rest of the afternoon rolled by smoothly. At the end of the day the trucks arrived, and the girls climbed aboard. The driver was ready. For some reason, a few workers were still wandering around on the grounds and in the house.

"I am missing a new brassiere—new and *pink*," a girl announced. Some of the girls on the truck opened their blouses to show that they were not wearing it. "Look at this rag I have on," one laughed sardonically, "new and *pink,* ha." Others jumped off to help look for it. "Didn't you leave it drying on the bush?" "Sure it isn't in the house?" The owner of the bra was upset, suspicious. China let this new drama run on for forty-five minutes and then packed everyone into the truck. "I am very troubled by the way people reacted to this," she murmured as the truck rolled along in the dusk. The quick assumption of theft, the sarcasms, the efforts to prove innocence rather than to help. "It was a bad day," I said. She shrugged and smiled, a faint smile this time.

It was after eight when the truck finally reached the camp. The sun had set. The sound of children shouting came from the nearby homes of workers and, from the old prison, the rhythmic clack of marching feet. In the courtyard, girls still stood in line waiting to shower. The palm trees on the mountains beyond lay in shadow. Above, the sky was empty except for one cloud in the west; soundless lightning struck behind it repeatedly, making the patch of gray look translucent and haunted.

On the front veranda, some workers were playing Ping Pong. Cusa was kneeling on the floor, painting a poster. It said, "Platoon #5—Oct. 21 Seal." I asked her how she knew her platoon would win the seal. "Because we will," she answered at once.

The old prison was almost silent now except for the birds in the *circulares,* which were chattering loudly enough to be heard over the camp's loudspeaker, the murmur of girls' voices, the Ping Pong game. The world of Escuadrón rested at peace, the bad day passed into night.

Friday, September 1

I woke up at four-thirty in the morning under the mosquito net, hearing the music of a popular song called *"Otro Amanecer"*—Another Dawn. It sounded like a radio, but why was it on so loud? There were no cries of *"De pie,"* yet everybody was up; I could hear and feel them rushing around. Baffled, I got up and walked toward the sound—out onto the balcony of the dormitory. The sky was still black and the moon high. The sound was definitely coming from down below. I looked and there, in front of the building, under a few powerful electric lights, stood a twenty-two-piece army band complete with music stands and conductor, swinging now through a mambo. Girls were hanging over the balcony, beating out the rhythm; more were down on the ground, watching the band. It was the Cuban answer to Alarm Clock Radios.

A thin, hip-looking black girl stepped out under the lights and made a brief speech between numbers. "Today, we start the drive for October twenty-first," she ended. "Let us work as hard as we can. We thank the *compañeros* for coming here to play for us. Thank you."

The music started again with a young man moaning a love song in the best nightclub style. I went back into the dormitory and looked around. Every bed was empty. It was only five A.M.; the reveille problem appeared to have been solved.

Saturday, September 2

The sun that day seemed hotter than ever before: a murderous eye that never strayed, burning down on the workers as they hoed and fertilized the long rows of orange plants. China was one of the few who never looked wilted, yet she wore more clothing than anyone else. Pants, a shirt, a long-sleeved cotton jacket, a large straw hat tied on with a scarf so that her face was half-hidden—it seemed too much and too hot, yet she never appeared uncomfortable. From the others rose the constant cry, "Dora, bring us water." People complained, sometimes listlessly and sometimes with animation. The heat. The work. The calluses on their hands. Their backaches.

Suddenly, China said to nobody in particular, "Did you hear—love is free now in Havana?"

Silence fell. Then someone asked, "What do you mean?"

"Oh," answered China with studied casualness, "the article about free love in *Juventud Rebelde*—didn't you see it?"

No one had. "What did it say?" someone asked.

China did not answer; she went on hoeing in her relaxed, efficient way. Someone else repeated the question. "What did it say?"

Then China straightened up to answer and a hush fell over the field. Each girl was leaning on her hoe, attentive, waiting for the word.

"Vaya," China began, "it was not exactly an article. They just took a poll of people's opinions. The question is whether you have to sign a paper in order to go to bed together. It seems that the majority was in favor of *el amor libre"*—free love. China tilted her head back and eyed her audience, smiling gleefully. "So now—love is free!"

There were whoops and shouts and declamations from her audience. A few approved, like China; some had doubts, many did not like the idea. "Everybody will just go from one person to another and never get married," was the familiar-sounding consensus. "No, no," said China, "you are confusing liberty with libertinism. It is not the same."

Finally Ramona said, "Well, I am against it because if you don't sign, when your man dies you won't get a pension!" She was wrong about the Cuban law, but everyone laughed at her realism. "That's a pretty capitalistic attitude, Ramona," I teased her. The girl smiled, chagrined.

At the camp that evening, free love continued to be discussed among the women in the dormitory. The same range of opinions was heard, and again China said, "They think liberty in love means libertinism." One of the workers—a roly-poly, enthusiastic young woman—announced that she had just received a four-page letter from her *novio* at another camp on the Isle. "It's all politics," she laughed, "all about Marxism-Leninism and economics. Listen . . ." And in fact it was, except for the beginning and the ending.

Walking to the showers, I asked China if she really did believe in free love. She answered promptly, "I have never thought —even before the talk about 'free love'—that a woman should be trapped at home. No man will ever prevent me from going somewhere I want to go, from working where I want to work. But a lot of men don't accept that. They want you to sit at home and be faithful. I won't do that."

She had no more to say on the subject, it seemed, and walked in silence for a moment. "What do you think of me?" she asked abruptly, with a keen expression in her eyes. The question was startling, as though independent-minded China suddenly needed approval. I thought about how I would like to say that she was an exceptional person, strong and intelligent and humanistic, but I just said, "I think you are right about things." China looked satisfied and walked on without speaking for a while. "Tomorrow is Pass Day, I want you to come with me and meet my *novio*. We will go swimming at the Hotel Colony, all right?" Then she did a little skipping step and stopped, her head tilted to one side, smiling her happiest smile. "Love—isn't it delicious? *Ay,* how nice it is!"

After dinner there was a special assembly in the courtyard. Cacha read a long list of new regulations for conduct, dress, discipline, pass rules, some of them already in effect and some of them not. "Girls are to dress properly inside the camp, not just when they go out on Sunday." "They are to bathe every day." "There will be no smoking in the dormitories unless ashtrays are improvised." "Girls can be expelled for prostitution, homosexuality, etcetera." She then read the requirements for the camp to win an October 21 seal, the same which Dora had announced at the platoon meeting. She also announced that there would be a contest between Escuadrón and Patria in various activities connected with the October 21 requirements.

At that moment there was a commotion inside the building; a few seconds later a contingent from Patria came marching smartly into the courtyard carrying a bright red, satin banner with the full name of their camp embroidered on it in gold. They were singing a song whose chorus says optimistically, *"Siempre se puede"* (from *"Siempre se puede más,"* a popular slogan of the day which means, "You can always do still more"). All of the girls at Escuadrón joined in the catchy tune. Then the Patria contingent, looking a little like proud, self-conscious children in a school pageant, marched into the building, about-faced, and stood at attention with their banner while Cacha resumed speaking.

She was talking about Cusa, who was to have been expelled but who had asked for another chance. Cusa had been doing much better, she said, and asked if the others thought that Cusa should definitely stay at the camp. From the assembly came a roar of *"Sí!"* and then the tongue-twisting camp cheer: ". . . Cusa, Cusa, rrah, rrah, rrah!" Everybody called for her but she could not be found; someone said she was taking a shower.

Cacha then swung into an energetic pep-talk. This camp was going to be the best on the island, she said. Everybody would work hard—"remember, *siempre se puede.*" Those words sounded like a signing-off and four girls dashed toward the laundry to get on with their washing. "We aren't finished!" Cacha shouted, and the girls ran back into the assembly. But Cacha had a point to make. She shouted for the four workers to go back to the laundry now so everyone could see exactly who had behaved so badly. None of them moved; the audience became tumultuous. *"Oye, oye—"* Cacha called for attention. Nobody seemed to hear her. "Put them back at the laundry— put them there," Cacha shouted. Two of the guilty ones went back voluntarily and the other two were led back.

Peace restored, Cacha concluded her exhortation. "This camp will be the best—you can do it. We will win," she said. "We will win the October twenty-first seal!" The courtyard rang with applause, loud and long; the enthusiasm of the audience was unmistakable. Suddenly Cusa appeared beside me. "Clap," she said, wagging her head impatiently. My hands were full of clothes to be washed, but somehow I managed. Cusa's brown eyes, illuminated by the light shining down from the second-floor dormitory, seemed to be aglow.

The loudspeaker crackled at that moment and a recording of "The International" began to play. The girls stood still and sang the words at first. Then, still singing, they spread out to form circles with hands entwined. There was a large circle and a smaller one; as the larger one turned, it gradually absorbed the smaller one. New girls kept arriving and also joining hands, until a single giant circle ringed the entire courtyard. Then, without any signal being given, the whole ring rushed toward its own center while the girls held their hands high and sang the chorus of the song. As swiftly, the cluster dissolved back into a large ring again, the girls holding their arms down now, new ones still joining in, everyone smiling at each other. Again the ring converged on its center, again the cluster flowed back into a ring. It was a dance, it was a Cecil B. DeMille spectacular, it was a Socialist Be-In, with no director except the energy of the moment and no choreographer except the Cuban love of music and movement. Everything just happened: the rhythm, the pattern, the dazzle, the communal high.

Finally, "The International" faded out and the July 26 anthem began. There went Rosa, running past the showers and out of the courtyard, pursued by whooping girls. Nobody knew why. Up in the sky, heat lightning filled the whole horizon. Flashing again and again, one hollow rumble after another, it sounded like the phony storm effects in a high school play. Cuban nature was exaggerating once again; the whole atmosphere was filled with unpredictability and a crazy sort of joyousness.

Inside the building, two contests between Escuadrón and Patria had begun. Fifteen chessboards were laid out on the dining tables; girls from each camp played one another, a little more slowly tonight than their usual checkers pace. The Ping Pong table had been moved into the entrance hall and a young man tried to referee seriously while girls darted behind and around the players. Cusa had just finished winning a game and was standing on the sidelines. She stopped me and asked eagerly, "Were you at the assembly when Cacha talked about me? Did you hear what they said?" "Yes, but where were you—were you in the shower?" "No," she grinned, "I was hiding in the darkness near there. I was crying. And laughing, and crying." She looked down at her feet and then up again quickly, to see if she was going to be teased.

The lounge was full of people. In one corner, the jukebox stood with its back open to the room and all its internal mechanisms showing. Wires led from it to different spots in the room; apparently, it had somehow been made to work at last. There was a sudden blast from an old Elvis Presley record and everybody began to twist. A big, African queen of a girl with the unlikely name of Isis—one of those Greek names that often turn up in Cuba—dominated the dance floor. Her movements and the sound were a final assault on the senses. The entire camp seemed to have burst free this night: not that all problems were solved forever, but that some kind of limitation had been transcended, a unity made visible, a balance struck. One could speak of "the collectivity" as hero in a new kind of non-Western drama, as a living being, a whole yet with its individual parts intact.

From the darkness outside, a straight-faced militiaman leaned through an open window of the lounge and observed the scene. His gun drooped over the sill casually. It was midnight.

Sunday, September 3

Instead of going to the Casa Americana that morning, I went with another platoon to pick grapefruit. The trip was long, through a different part of the island; and when the trucks arrived at the groves, no one could begin working because the boxes in which to pack the fruit had not yet come. The day before, over a thousand boxes had been filled; when they reached the packing plant, it was Saturday night and apparently no one had been around to empty them. So a lot of woman-hours were lost while trucks rushed back and forth bringing boxes from the plant to the groves. But few people seemed to feel like working hard anyway.

It was a lazy, dreamlike morning, a half day at that. The trees in the groves, some twenty years old, were heavy with the green-ish-yellow fruit. Their thick leaves cast a cool shadiness over the entire area and only an occasional patch of sun gleamed down into the long, quiet lanes between trees. To work cradled in this greenery was an entirely different sensation from standing vertical and alien on a bare field, the sun above burning blankly.

Cusa, who had been working here for several days, scrambled up her tree like a monkey. Perched on a slim branch at the top, she glanced down with a wicked smile and began throwing grapefruit—almost, but not quite, too fast for the helper to catch and pack. It is hard to explain in words why Cusa did not seem obnoxious with all her little tricks. She had some kind of basic seriousness, as well as a way of laughing at her own nonsense, which made her a lovable person rather than simply childlike. There was an incident that morning, in which she borrowed my pen and accidentally broke it. She sat on the ground for half an hour, taking the pen apart and trying to repair it. I told her not to worry, showing that I had another, but she still looked glum. Then she took the other pen for a moment and wrote in my notebook: "Cusa Montero, who broke your pen. But she will fix it."

At the other trees, some of the teams were working well and some sloppily. One girl, on the ground, was dropping grapefruit into the box instead of placing it there gently to avoid bruises. An older woman, probably a Party worker, told her politely that she was not using the right technique, and the girl began to sing *Guantanamera* mockingly in the woman's face. At other trees, fallen grapefruit was being packed when it should have been set aside. Everywhere, the girls seemed to be taking time out to eat almost as much as they picked. They were fed up: no pass last weekend, difficult living conditions at the camp, too much work, not enough crates today. "They know how to work correctly," said a *responsable,* "but they are rebelling by not doing things right."

At quitting time, the trucks arrived half an hour late to take the workers back to camp. After lunch, everyone was in the dorm dressing and making up. China curled her heavy black hair and pinned a large red bow on the back of her head. All over the camp, butterflies in skirts and eyeshadow were emerging from grimy pants and mud-caked boots. Buses took everyone into town who wanted to go; from there, China and I hitched a ride to the Colony Hotel.

The luxury of it seemed overwhelming: the lobby with its big armchairs, the air-conditioned dining room, softly lit bar stacked with gleaming bottles, the free-form swimming pool, cabanas—and the tile bathrooms which had no smell. China went off to swim with her *novio*, Orestes, who looked pleasant and innocuous; later we would all eat together.

In the early evening, I ran into some Havana acquaintances who were staying at the hotel; with them was a *vaquero* on pass. The young cowhand, very blond and blue-eyed, turned out to be a former minister.

His mother was half-French, he said, and he had been born in Oriente. He grew up next door to a Protestant minister and in due time became a seminarian. "In 1954, I read Fidel's *History Will Absolve Me*, after the Moncada attack," he recalled. "I was impressed but I didn't understand—I could not imagine how it would be possible to have a revolution in Cuba. Then it just happened." He quit the church and became regional director of education in the city of Trinidad, a post which included fighting counter-Revolutionaries with a gun in the Escambray mountains. "Then I came here and became a *vaquero*—perhaps because my life in the church had been so much the opposite, sweet-smelling and soft. Working with cattle is not! But what counts are things like milk.

"I am personally a materialist, in the philosophical sense—I reject the idea of a God who rules our lives through the church, the idea that we live for a future in heaven instead of man's well-being now. Oh, I went through being a pantheist, then an existentialist before getting to materialism." He smiled in passing at the recollection, then said simply but fiercely, "And my materialism is communism." His passionate manner seemed at odds with his paleness, his horn-rimmed glasses and diffident look.

"What, for you, does being a Communist mean?" I asked.

"Look, what has happened here is that we are reclaiming our land—reclaiming it with agricultural work and thus redeeming our nationhood. The land didn't belong to us before, it belonged to the Yankee landlords. Now it is ours. And the most important thing is that imperialism will never be allowed to dominate in Cuba again. Beyond that, we must create the new consciousness which you have heard about—of communism. That means, for example, that if I have cigarettes and you don't, then I don't go away now leaving you without any—"

"Look," I interrupted, "there is one thing I would like to understand better. At the camp, people frequently say that a person should not act in such and such a way because 'that's not being a good Communist.' But often they just seem to be talking about the Golden Rule, of Christianity. And you—isn't it possible that your communism has its roots in your former religious tendency?"

"No, no. Because I am not talking about an individual conscience, about doing good individually, but about a sense of collectivity. The idea is that what *I* do, how *I* live, is important not for myself, for the state of my soul, but for all people." He paused and smiled. "But your question is an interesting one . . ."

China was waiting in the bar with her *novio*, Orestes. Before we went in to eat, she made a formal little declaration which sounded almost like a farewell speech to me. Leaning forward on the table and pronouncing her words very carefully, she said, "I know that you and many others are struggling for a change in the United States. We want you and all the others to know that the Cuban people are with you. Please give them my greetings and tell them that there are many people like me." Her full, dark hair fell forward as she spoke; her whole being was intent yet without pretension. "Tell them that we are ready to lay down our lives for the black people in the United States and for the struggle there. We are with all those in the struggle. We would die for you if that would help—if that is necessary."

Then she turned to her *novio*. "Oh, in some ways the struggle there is more beautiful than here. There, the black people are actually fighting. Here, we are mostly struggling with ourselves."

"That is not *quite* true," he said, smiling. But he knew what she meant.

Tuesday, September 5

The next morning, at the Casa Americana, a truck arrived from Havana with a load of young mango trees. The driver complained about the long trip while the workers formed a chain to unload the heavy plants under the *jagüey* tree. Grandfather was nagging them, "Come on, come on, look at me, an old man, I work twice as fast as you." The job was finally finished and most of the girls headed out to the fields to hoe. Only China, Dora, and two other persons were left, when a girl I had never seen before arrived to tell China how, at a meeting of the camp executive committee the night before, this platoon had been described as one of the worst. Also, it was said that Dora, the second *responsable*, could not handle things. "I don't understand," the girl ended. "I always thought this was a good *pelotón.*"

Her news met first with protest. "We are always the first to form in the morning," China argued. "Of course the girls talk a lot and take time off from work, but we have almost none of the problems you find in other platoons. And often we don't get *merienda*"—the afternoon snack. "We have had it four times in fifteen days, and two of those times we had to go and get it ourselves."

Grandfather spoke up firmly. "This is a good group. I would be the first to complain if it was not. I *know*. And I don't like these criticisms without reason. Raúl is on the island now," he added, referring to Fidel Castro's brother, "and I am going to speak to him about this!"

The atmosphere became hushed and dead serious. There was no shouting, no prancing around this time. Except for Grandfather, people spoke in voices more hurt than angry and more baffled than indignant. Dora sat very still, crying quietly by herself. I remembered her telling me how she had left the art school where she was preparing to become an artisan in marble because she decided that agricultural work was more important to the Revolution, and had come to the Isle.

269

"Unfortunately," China began slowly, "I am not a *militante*," —a full member of the Communist Youth League. "Neither is Dora. We have to improve ourselves in many ways. But I don't understand some things. I do not understand how Anna can be a *militante*," she said, referring to a quiet, industrious girl in the platoon. "She is a fantastic worker—as a worker, you cannot criticize her in any way. But she just works, eats, sleeps, and that's it. She doesn't let herself get involved in anything. Me, I want to know the why of things—and I want to know why we have been criticized in this way."

"You must have a meeting with Cacha to find out the reason for this criticism," said the girl who had brought the news.

"And I'll come," Grandfather put in, "if that will help. I'll tell them how you are a good group."

Later, after lunch, China spoke to me alone. "I want to be a *militante,* you understand. I am not even an *aspirante* now. There are many defects in me. It is like that cigarette"—she pointed to the one she was smoking—"before it is a cigarette, you have to get rid of all the impurities in the tobacco. It must be cleaned out perfectly. I have many things to clean out of my character. I have much to improve.

"For example, when there is a problem they like it to be discussed in the small group of those in charge. I talk about it with *la masa*, the body, because I think people have to learn by being involved in the thing itself. But they think there are elements in *la masa* who lack the necessary education and understanding, and it is better for them to make decisions and discuss things among themselves." There was a faintly implied criticism in her shrug. "Look, I think Cacha is wonderful. I would go to the end of the world with that woman. But there are some . . ." She stopped. "I came to the island to work. I knew it would not be a game, a picnic. But I will have to change in many ways to become a *militante*."

Then she smiled and changed the subject. "Orestes has left the island for twelve days."

"Will he definitely be back?" I asked.

She shrugged and then smiled. "You know I don't believe in women being trapped."

270

"And what will you be doing—are you staying at Escuadrón?"

"No, I am going back to Patria tomorrow. Other places," she said in a lighthearted echo of Che Guevara's famous statement, "other places call for my modest efforts."

The next three days were a blur. Everything was changing, changing. China left, along with most of the others who had come from Patria, so that no meeting ever took place to discuss the criticism of her platoon. All the Party women were also leaving, to work as a unit wherever needed and to live together in a house where things would be more "calm."

One night I came home from work and the big dormitory looked almost empty. Eighty girls who worked at the packing plant had left to live in a camp on the plant's premises, and their beds had gone with them. By 1968, someone said, everybody would be moved out and the building taken over to house agriculture students from the new school in the Presidio. Things ran more smoothly at the camp. There were no more two-hour lines to get into dinner. The marching was sharper; Rosa did not have to give any more long lectures at dawn. Procedures and people were more orderly.

Cusa had become a *responsable* of her platoon and was very proud. Then she had to stop working because of infected mosquito bites on her face and feet. I went to see her in the infirmary on my last night. Her face was wildly dotted with Mercurochrome; she looked like a clown made up by a drunk. But there was nothing wrong with her spirit. She showed me a picture of an aging popular singer: "That's my *novio*." Then: "No, it's not. My boyfriend rides a motorcycle." After inducing me to con a glass of ice water out of the kitchen staff for her, she said, "I'm going to the hospital in Havana early tomorrow morning. I won't be back here." And again she winked.

On the final morning, Friday, I said goodbye to a hundred people and made the mistake of promising to write fifty of them. I gave away most of my clothes because people needed them and anyway that is the way it goes in Cuba. While I cleaned up around my bed, Miriam—the plump young girl who had once asked for *chicle* and cigarettes—came in with several others. We were talking but had to stop after a while because Miriam was singing so loudly. She went through four or five pop hits and then began reciting long sections of speeches by Fidel. The more people shushed her, the louder she declaimed. Finally she went back to singing and wound up with "Auld Lang Syne," in Spanish. Then she made me say her name five times so that I would not forget it—Miriam Lafitte, Miriam Lafitte, Miriam Lafitte, Miriam Lafitte, Miriam Lafitte—and reminded me to send the chewing gum and cigarettes. "That's not right," Ramona protested, "you can ask her for a photo of herself but not for material things. That's not Revolutionary." Miriam Lafitte grimaced.

The camp was strangely peaceful after everyone had gone off to work. The latrines had just been cleaned and smelled tolerable. Cacha, the last of the people borrowed from Patria, would be going back to her camp in an hour. She was at the kitchen now, talking with the workers there and still trying to improve the system. "At night, you must leave everything ready for the morning so that breakfast will be on time." She offered me a perfect, ripe mango and then we drank coffee together standing by the kitchen door.

Cacha was in high spirits. "I just received a letter from one of the girls who was expelled," she said. "Here, read it."

The letter, datelined Havana, said:

Dear Cacha,

I am very sorry for what I did. I know that I cannot come back to the island. But when I got here, my family would not let me stay in the house. I have nowhere to go. I am truly sorry for what I did. I cannot undo it but I am writing to ask if I could come back to work, without pay, on the island. I hold the deepest respect and affection for you, Cacha, and Rosa and the others.

"We are sending her money to come back," said Cacha. "*Now* go tell them what communism is like!" She tipped her head back with a broad smile, half serious and half joking.

Just before I left, I asked her what she thought the island would be like in a year or two. Cacha glowed. "We will make

Cuba the top citrus-producing country in the world," she said. "Right now, we have big technical problems. But we just will do it. And someday everything will be free for everybody—even the ice cream at the Coppelia! There is tremendous enthusiasm here on the Isle, even if you cannot always see it at this camp. The youth here have a fever—and the fever is *comunismo*.

"We expect a United States invasion and we are ready to fight. People ask, with what? Listen, we will fight with oranges if we must. And they will have to kill every last one of us. But our attitude is not, 'I'm ready to die and that's it.' Our attitude is, 'I am ready to die and I am going to live.' You must tell that to the revolutionaries in the United States."

The truck driver, the one who took the workers back and forth and also brought lunch to the fields, arrived then. It was time to go to the airport. On the way, he did not say a word except to ask if there were special dormitories for truck drivers in the United States like the one he lived in on the island. At the airport, the plane arrived on time from Havana: it loaded up immediately for the return flight with passengers and their odd luggage: cartons tied with rope, awkward wooden suitcases, a tricycle. On board, the universal stewardess, in blue uniform with white kerchief tied over her head, passed out hard candies.

It was a bumpy flight, through the first gray sky in several months. I thought a while about the camp, about the last night China had been at Escuadrón. Movies had been shown in the courtyard, with everyone sitting on the ground and a screen propped up against one wall of the building. A short, idiotic musical comedy from Italy had come on the screen first, then a newsreel of the July 26 anniversary celebration at Santiago. There was Fidel addressing the crowd, then the platform with all the dignitaries and foreign guests of honor, the Vanguard Youth at the front of the audience, the banners and the huge pictures of martyrs like Frank País and Abél Santamaría. All the pageantry of Revolutionary Cuba flashed across the screen and China watched every image intently. When it was over, she let out a sigh and smiled to herself. *"Ay,* Cuba," she murmured in a tone of forbearance, pride, and love all mixed together, *"Ay,* Cuba."

Some words
from Leroy Lucas

When Afro-American photographer Leroy Lucas went to Cuba, he wrote several letters to me and another friend, Howard Schulman. A few excerpts are presented here because they tell interesting things about his work in Cuba and because Leroy is a beautiful person whose words as well as pictures should be known.

I

One of the first things a person say when they don't write often is that they are sorry, well I am, I have been wanting to write you but I said to myself I will write when i get to Santiago. Well I havn't got to Santigo yet. I did manage to get very good photographs this other trip, but not exactly when I had in mind, everybody like to look into the camera, that not so good, cause one could easily have a book of pictures of everyone looking at you. It was sort of a drag. I kept saying "no ?eter in la camera, por favor" many times a day. Lately I h?ve been trying to capture drama instead of tractor, it's hard you know cause it so dam hot here people work hard but show little drama.

Lately also after returning to Havana I have a sense that some of that phoney art crowd have begun to get jealous of me because of the publicity of me and my work. Cuban artists are funny, more so than american artists. Some of them don't have any soul, and if any artist that was born in Cuba hasn't acquired any soul during the Cuban Revolucion, he should fly to the Moon, I mean get the fuck off this planet . . .

The minister of education said that they will fly me to santigo to photograph the alfabetization. From now on I will work only with the minister of this, the minister of that, and so on, you dig, cause it creates less problems and save time. I could have done this at first but I don't like to play Mr. Big Shit, but since I am Big Shit in a way here in Cuba, I might as well play the role. I should have brought with me 2 or 3 suits, few Knox Hats, about 4 pairs of shoes plus a walking cane. You know, America really sinned this island long time ago so I have to play Mr. Big Shit, from now on everybody including uncle sam must call me Mr. Big Shit of rebellious photography. I am now Mr. Big SHIT.

II

If I could speak the language I would stay in cuba for a longer period, at the present I'm very lonely here but somehow I have managed not to infect the loneliness in the photographs, which is good, cause the cuban people are very happy in this revolucion and if I infected the photographs they would be dam sure false. Of course I have encountered some unhappy cubans but very, very few. My loneliness is within self.

One can't say "baby I dig making with you, cause you get to my soul," you have to say more than just that here. Even when I am dancing with chicks some times I just stop and walk away, cause what's the use . . . When I walk down the street and all those Big Swinging Asses pass me by, I go sort of Loco, most of the time I just close my eyes. At least with the camera I am thinking of making photographs. Every time I photograph I think, does the photo say anything about the revolucion? Does it say anything to me? Most pictures I have seen of Cuba are not so good, feeling somehow missing from them.

III

Even if I was flying a fast jet plane, whereas I could dig all the great vastness of the surface of the earth, I still wouldn't learn or understand the most important thing: the human soul.

To dig the human soul, one have to get about on foot or horse, into the small places and holes, digging all there is to dig.

Perhaps I asking for the un-touchable. Man is a lonely creature most places, all-the-time, though in cooba man is beginning to feel fresh for the first time since the B.C.'s. To capture this spirit isn't easy for an outsider not born in the land and lacking the language. If only the world had one verbal language, the madness would disappear some. The cubans are wonderful and beautiful people, to live with them for a period has been more than glory; not able to converse, my love for them is solid. Their soul is all honest and just and their soul is something like a baby, newborn.

Cooba is heavenly lovely, to leave her makes me wonder of no place better. Cooba you're still in the cradle, you will rock a while longer, while you're rocking, larger rock will bump you, you will not decay, your foundation is solid.

        most of god's children got rhythm
        yes lord
        most of your children got rhythm
        yes lord
        now when the man says to your children to get on their knees
        will they get on their knees or will the rhythm move in their
            souls
        will that rhythm move in their souls, will it lord
        do you hear us calling on you, we know you long ways away
        my friend, miss holiday, ain't here to help call on you
            but i have her part of the rhythm to carry on to the battle
            we going to need rhythm in the soul to win the battle

ELIZABETH SUTHERLAND (Martinez) is a journalist and critic who writes mainly on subjects of political interest. She is the editor of *Letters from Mississippi*, which was published in 1965, and her magazine articles have appeared in the *New Republic*, *The Guardian*, *Mademoiselle* and elsewhere.

Miss Sutherland has worked as an editor in a New York publishing house and was Books and Arts Editor of *The Nation*. From 1965–67, she worked for SNCC—first in their communications department and then as director of their New York office. She now lives in New Mexico where she publishes a newspaper for the Mexican-American community, *El Grito del Nordo*.

LEROY LUCAS was born in St. Louis, Missouri, in 1937. His photos have appeared in *Negro Digest*, *Harper's Bazaar*, *Esquire*, *Downbeat* and many other magazines. He is best known for his photographic essays in *The Shoshoneans*, which was published in 1966, and his camerawork for the film *The Cool World*.

DATE DUE

NOV 3 '69			
MAR 19 '70			
MAY 7 '70			
DEC 5 '72			